Recipes for Success:
A Guide to
Advanced Cuisine

Roland Chaton
Walt Talmage

NOTICE TO THE READER

Cover photograph courtesy Four Seasons Hotels Limited

Delmar Staff

Administrative Editor: Karen Lavroff-Hawkins
Managing Editor: Barbara Christie
Production Editor: Ruth East
Publications Coordinator: Karen Seebald

For information, address Delmar Publishers Inc.
2 Computer Drive West, Box 15–015
Albany, New York 12212

Printed in the United States of America
Published simultaneously in Canada
by Nelson Canada,
a division of International Thomson Limited

10 9 8 7 6 5 4 3 2 1

Library of Congress Cataloging-in-Publication Data
    Chaton, Roland, 1919–
        Recipes for success.

        Includes index.
        1. Cookery, International.   2. Quantity cookery.
    3. Food service.   I. Talmage, Walter.   II. Title.
    TX725.AlC525   1988   641.5'7   87–22380
    ISBN 0-8273-3027-8
    ISBN 0-8273-3028-6 (instructor's guide)

Contents

Editor's Preface

Chefs do not have an easy job. At any given moment they may have to assume the role of a head cook, preparations cook, manager, steward, teacher, bookkeeper, sales person, artist, butcher, baker, or public relations person.

Great chefs, people who can do these things not only successfully but also famously, day after day, year after year, are as rare as diamonds on the ground. Rarer still are such chefs who are also educators. And, if it is possible, rarer even than that are such chef–educators who write textbooks.

We believe that this book, a distillation of over a half-century's experience in the best kitchens of the world, will play an important role in hospitality education for many years to come.

KAREN LAVROFF-HAWKINS

Preface: To the Teacher, Student, and Working Professional

This textbook is a complete course in Advanced International Cuisine. It covers materials that both authors have used for years in teaching such courses. All the methods and recipes, both classic and modern, are in use today in fine restaurants and hotels. In fact, nearly all the information contained in this book is derived from knowledge gained by working in restaurants both in America and abroad.

This book was written for advanced culinary students who aspire to become chefs, food and beverage managers, and restaurant owners. It can also be of great value for those cooks who seek to improve their craft and to obtain fresh idea and insight.

But the scope and usefulness of this book goes far beyond its title. It is valuable reading for anyone, whether at the junior college, university, or specialty school level, who is aiming at a management career in any part of the vast hospitality industry. No matter where you are positioned in the industry—front or back of the house, food, beverage, or hotel operations—it is still valuable reading.

You may well ask why, for example, students who aspire to be the manager of a large hotel needs to read this textbook. The answer is simple. They must be well informed. The harried operations manager of a famous hotel in New York once said, "This whole business is like the emergency room in a hospital; there are so many crises every day that crisis becomes a normal routine condition."

In a well-run operation, things may not be *that* bad. But emergencies do occur. Chefs and sous-chefs get sick just like anyone else. For whatever reasons they sometimes quit at the most inconvenient moments. Managers then have to take on that responsibility. Although they usually need not do the actual cooking, they must know enough to oversee the kitchen staff. Consequently, they must, at the very least, have a pretty good idea of what is going on in the kitchen.

And, even during routine daily operations, good managers should be able to determine whether their kitchens are running well. To do this they must have an accurate overview of what cuisine is all about. That, this textbook will provide.

Why Classic Cuisine?

The teachers and chefs using this book will discover that the chapters that cover such things as cooking methods and stock preparation contain techniques that are neither new nor likely to change. The poet Shelley's father-in-law* said on the subject of knowledge that "We stand on the shoulders of our forefathers and see farther." Many techniques have not changed in hundreds of years and will not change. There are many shortcuts, but shortcuts save time at the expense of the final result. In this book we describe the best way, which often (but not always) is the classic way. When the modern chefs taste the classic result they are then in a position to decide whether a shortcut is worth the time saved. But, if they have never made a sauce using classic demi-glace or a soup with real chicken stock, they cannot fairly make a judgment.

Readers will find that the technical material and the recipes are presented with an economy of verbiage. We assumed that the students and professionals reading this book have some background in cooking. Consequently, there is no need to warn the reader to be careful of hot pans or to explain what size strainer is required.

The Recipes

This book is a collection of international hors d'oeuvres, stocks, sauces, soups, salads, entrées, vegetables, and desserts. They are important recipes, of the caliber currently being used in world-class restaurants all over America. Some are classic, with their origins in antiquity. Some are original, developed by Chef Chaton.

What makes the recipes unique is that whatever their origin, they have been adapted to use ingredients readily available in America, reproducing as nearly as possible the classic taste or international flavor of the original dish.

Such adaptation may sound easy. It is not. Many French chefs, flushed with success in a restaurant in Paris, Rome, or London, have failed when attempting to expand into New York or Chicago. Why? The ingredients are different—so different that French chefs catering special parties in the United States often bring all their ingredients with them, including basics like cream or beef.

*William Godwin, a top political writer of the eighteenth century (the height of the era of Grande Cuisine).

The recipes in this book have been painstakingly adapted to widely available ingredients in the United States. In some cases, this took years of trial and error. It would take a similar length of time for a Spanish chef to produce perfect Southern Fried Chicken or New England Clam Chowder or Blackened Redfish!

All the recipes in this book are standardized for commercial restaurant use because the book is intended for working professionals and senior culinary students. All measurements are given in both U.S. and metric units, for the sake of convenience and so the recipe can readily be used with whatever type of measuring equipment is available.

All recipe yields are commercial quantities. They have been kitchen and customer tested in quantities that are most convenient for commercial use. In some cases, these quantities are the only feasible quantities in which to prepare a certain dish.

Note that a recipe, any recipe, is a guide for the cook and only a guide. Food products are not uniform. They vary according to the season, the geography, and the supplier. For example, the strength of herbs and spices varies according to the packer, their age, and the way they are stored. The strength of stocks varies with each batch. Some meats are tastier, and some brands of wine are stronger. In addition, cooking heats and times vary according to the attention of the cooks. These variables, as well as many others, influence the final taste of a soup or a sauce or an entrée. You may follow a recipe precisely and have perfect results. On the other hand, you may find you need more spice or more wine or more thickener or more color than the recipe indicated to make your product perfect. Learn to trust your own judgment. In this sense, we stress again that any recipe must be considered only a guide.

This also applies to cooking times, which will vary according to the type of pot and other equipment used. Do not overcook or undercook because of what a recipe says. Trust your own judgment. Chefs are paid to exercise their judgment.

Special Features

Because *Recipes for Success* was designed as a teaching tool, it contains many features that will help students learn.

☐ Format. The text and recipes are laid out to be used in an active kitchen/training lab setting.

☐ Student aids. Introductions, summaries, and reviews are included for each chapter. Important terms are defined in the body of the text and also appear in a comprehensive glossary at the end of the book.

☐ Illustrations. Presentation is important in haute cuisine. A full-color insert suggests presentations for many of the complex and perhaps unfamiliar dishes found in the text.

☐ Emphasis on the practical. We know that the haute cuisine restaurant is a *business*. Procuring ingredients, increasing sales, and including new items on the menu are all discussed where pertinent.

Acknowledgments

We thank the following educators whose own teaching and cooking expertise contributed greatly to the development of this project:

Randall Coleman, Sullivan County Community College, Loch Sheldrake, NY
Jim Douglas, Everett Community College, Everett, WA
Gary Kelm, 916 Vo-Tech, White Bear Lake, MN
Linda Hierholzer and Douglas A. Fisher, Spokane Community College, Spokane, WA

The Editorial, Manufacturing, and Sales Departments at Delmar Publishers helped to make the book readable, attractive, and successful! We also thank them for their efforts.

About the Authors

Chef *Roland Chaton* currently teaches Advanced International Cuisine at Pinellas Vocational Technical Institute in Clearwater, Florida. He is often named "Teacher of the Year."

What pleases him most is when his students succeed. His students (those that survive the rigors of his teaching techniques) have graduated to become chefs in fine restaurants and hotels all over the world. One of his former students is now employed by the White House. Another has just received the "Golden Spoon" award in New York.

At one three-star restaurant (La Chaumière, in Sarasota, Florida, which won the French Gastronomic Writers Haute Cuisine Award for being the best French restaurant outside of France), the entire staff consists of his former students.

Chef Chaton's course is nearly pure laboratory. He rarely lectures, uses films, tapes, or learning packets. His teaching laboratory is a luncheon restaurant specializing in haute cuisine and serving 100 or more customers per day.

Students are assigned different stations each week (for example, entrée, pastry, potwasher, waiter, and soup). Students arrive in the morning and complete whatever must be done to have all stations ready for lunch. Chef Chaton constantly moves from station to station, checking, correcting, explaining, and demonstrating. When lunch is over, the students clean up until all is in order for the next day. Chef Chaton's advanced curriculum is contained in this textbook.

Chef Chaton began his career in the kitchens of France at the age of 12; he worked the embassy circuit in Saudi Arabia, Africa, and the Middle East; and he worked for top-of-the-line restaurants in New York and Paris. In fact, he had nearly a half century in the kitchen before he taught his first class.

Chef Chaton says: "My students are the chefs of the future. They will play a role in the evolution of haute cuisine. They are my legacy to the world of fine food. . . ."

In his early days, *Walt Talmage* apprenticed with Chef Chaton in New York. He spent many years in the Far East and on his return to the United States taught advanced cuisine at Marchman Vocational Center and Pinellas Vocational Technical Institute. He is now a freelance writer and is employed by a major hotel chain that specializes in haute cuisine.

To my wonderful wife, Dominique, and my friend Walter, who both encouraged me to do this book.

R. C.

Chapter 1

✛ Introduction to the Book and Recipes

This book is a collection of international hors d'oeuvres, soups, sauces, entrées, salads, and desserts. They are important recipes, of the caliber found only in world-class restaurants around the globe. Some are classic, with their origins in antiquity. Others are original, available only in those fine restaurants staffed by Chef Chaton's former students.

What makes these recipes unique is that, whatever their origin, they have been adapted to use ingredients readily available in America, reproducing as nearly as possible the classic taste or international flavor of the original dish. We have tested these recipes by selling them to two generations of customers.

For those readers not yet trained in International or French Cuisine, we offer a word of advice: Do not pass over a recipe because you think, based on the list of ingredients, that you will not like the taste. Try everything. The tastes, when you are familiar with them, are pleasure beyond description.

We also have some advice for the working chef: Do not underestimate the tastes of your customers. Sneak a smashing classic soup into your menu as a "special." Add a classy entrée to your meat-and-potatoes bill of fare. Do not hesitate to try it. You will be amazed and delighted by your customers' reactions.

The Recipes

All the recipes in this book are standardized for commercial restaurant use because the book is intended for working professionals and senior culinary students.

Measurements
All measurements are given in both conventional and metric units, for the sake of convenience and so the recipes can readily be used with whatever type of measuring equipment is available. See Table 1-1.

Table 1-1. Metric Equivalents of U.S. Customary Units.*

Volume

1 tsp = 5 cc = 5 ml

1 tbsp = 20 cc = 20 ml

1 cup = 250 ml = ½ pint

1 oz = 30 cc = 30 ml

1 qt = .9463 liter = 4 cups = 2 pints

1 liter = 1 qt + 2 tbsp

Weight

1 oz = 28 g

1 lb = 453.6 g

2.2 lb = 1 kg = 1,000 g

*Most ingredients in our recipes have been quantified in conventional and metric units, except where to do so is inconvenient or impractical for kitchen use. Figures are rounded off for ease of measurement in instances where mathematical precision is unnecessary. For our purposes, a teaspoon = 5 ml of liquid; a tablespoon = 20 ml of liquid. For dry measure, the same sized spoons are used; however, the metric weights are not used because of the wide variations in the density of many foods. In any case, using a scale for such small amounts is not practical.

Yield

The yield, or number of portions, varies from recipe to recipe—although all are commercial quantities. There are a number of reasons for this.

First, any recipe is only a guide for the cook. Food products are not uniform like machine tools or pencils. They vary according to the season, the geography, and the supplier. The same foods ordered from the same supplier may vary from shipment to shipment.

Kitchen equipment is very different from kitchen to kitchen, depending on the manufacture or even the age of the equipment. A brand-new steamer will probably cook faster than an old one whose pipes are clogged with scale. An aluminum grill will cook meats faster than a cast-iron grill.

It is difficult to give precise instructions for some cooking operations. What is "slightly brown" to one chef may be "golden brown" to another. What is "tender" to one saucemaker may be "firm" to yet another.

Back to the yield of our recipes. We have written and kitchen and customer tested our recipes in quantities that are most convenient for commercial use. In some cases, these quantities are the only feasible quantities in which to prepare a certain dish. For example, our recipe for *Coq au Vin* has a yield of eighteen portions. To attempt to cook any more than this in one batch would court disaster. The chicken on the bottom of the brazier would overcook to the point of becoming a puree.

Our recipe for lemon cake is another example. Made one cake to a batch, the cake meets the highest standards. Made in huge batches of batter, it is only barely acceptable.

Our Stuffed Cabbage is another case in point. Our yield is forty portions. Made in that quantity, the subtle balance of ingredients has pleased the experienced palate of many sophisticated diners. We have tried larger batches, but then, no matter how we juggle ingredients, the delicate balance of tastes seems to blur. In any case, larger batches are impractical for most restaurant operations because this dish cannot be held—hot or cold—for more than a few hours.

Conversion Factor

What if you need 500 lemon cakes or just ten portions of Stuffed Cabbage? Of course, we can do it. But the technique is not as simple as it first appears. Read carefully!

The basic formula for converting recipe yield (increasing or decreasing ingredient quantities to change the number of portions) is:

1) Divide the desired yield by the recipe yield:

$$\frac{\text{new yield}}{\text{old yield}} = \text{conversion factor}$$

2) Multiply each ingredient quantity by the conversion factor:

$$\text{conversion factor} \times \text{old quantity} = \text{new quantity}$$

Remember that ingredients must be calculated in compatible units of measure. Pounds, when multiplied by the conversion factor, remain pounds. Pounds cannot become gallons or any other unit of measure.

If, for example, you have a recipe for Bordelaise Sauce that will make enough sauce for forty portions and you want to convert the recipe to make enough sauce for eighty portions, you will need to use the conversion formula:

$$\frac{\text{new yield}}{\text{old yield}} = \frac{80}{40} = 2$$

Now simply multiply all ingredients by the conversion factor, which, in this case, is 2. Since the original recipe required 1 gallon of demi-glace and 1 quart of red wine, you will now need 2 gallons of demi-glace and 2 quarts of wine. This formula works the same way, whether you are increasing or decreasing yields.

It sounds easy, and the basic formula is easy. The basic formula will hold true for most ingredients and for most recipes. But beware the heart-burn factors! Some ingredients refuse to play the game of simple mathematics:

Flavorings and extracts—lemon extract, vanilla extract, liquid smoke, wines, salt
Aromatic vegetables—carrots, celery, onions, scallions, shallots, garlic
Leavening agents—yeast, baking powder, baking soda

If you double a recipe for Beef Burgundy for fifty portions that requires 1 liter of wine, you will need only about 1 cup more of wine, certainly not double! If you increase the yield for a soup recipe from 25 to 500 and you apply the formula to the liquid smoke in the recipe, the soup will be fit only for the garbage can. Similar exceptions to the rule will apply to mire-poix. In baking, if you multiply the quantity of baking powder using this formula, your cake will explode.

Remember to be very cautious when you change recipe yield. Only trial and error and your own good judgment will enable you to convert yields to your own standardized, kitchen-tested recipe adapted to the needs of your operation.

Finally, keep in mind that some foods can be made only in small quantities. Try 500 gallons of scrambled eggs at one time and you get disaster.

Summary

This textbook is in itself a complete course in International Cuisine.

All of the recipes in this book have been carefully adapted to ingredients available in America. This is necessary because ingredients vary so much from country to country.

The basic formula for recipe conversion is:

$$\frac{\text{new yield}}{\text{old yield}} = \text{conversion factor}$$

The recipe quantities are then multiplied by the conversion factor.

The cook must always remember that a recipe can never be more than a guide. All the variables (such as the strength of the aromates, the heat and equipment used, the cooking times, and the quality of the herbs and spices—which vary from plant to plant) make the skill and judgment of the cook the determining factor in final taste.

Take care in converting yields. Some products cannot be made in large quantities. Others contain ingredients like wine or yeast that cannot be increased mathematically.

Discussion Questions*

1) You are a working chef. You develop a recipe for dinner rolls that are so popular with your customers that they constantly buy them to take home. Suddenly you are offered and accept a postion at a large hotel in Bangkok. Will you dinner roll recipe work as well there?
2) How will you instruct your newly hired sauté chef on the degree of doneness you want the veal for Veal Marsala?
3) Why do some professional recipes contain food quantity measurements in conventional and metric units?
4) You purchase a new broiler for your kitchen. Suddenly, the experienced broiler chef is sending out overcooked steaks. Why?
5) You have followed exactly a recipe for tomato sauce. Yet, when finished it is too thin. What should you do? How could this happen, assuming that the recipe is correct?

Test Questions

1) The recipe for Shrimp Sauce Chef Chaton (page 119) is for 24 portions. Convert it to yield 36 portions.
2) Why would it be inadvisable to cook 200 portions of *Coq au Vin* in a large steam kettle?
3) What is meant by the phrase, "a recipe is only a guide"?
4) List some ingredients that require special attention when increasing recipe yields.
5) The recipe for Allemande Sauce (page 76) is for 1 quart. Convert it to yield 1½ gallons.

*Some discussion questions require culinary deductive reasoning. They may not be answered *directly* in the text, but enough information is given to deduce the answer logically.

Chapter 2

⚜

Restaurant Procurement: Options and Alternatives

It is just before dawn at the *Marché Forville* in Cannes. The working day is just beginning for the chefs of this city. The narrow streets are mostly deserted. Now and again a motorbike carrying an early maid or breakfast cook to work putts toward a hotel. A few streaks of dawn are beginning to appear in the sky, and on the horizon it is almost possible to tell where the sky ends and the sea begins. The city itself is dark. The port near the market is quiet except for one fishing boat preparing to depart.

Although it is very early, the vendors have finished setting up for the day and the customers are beginning to arrive. Empty trucks pull away; full trucks unload.

The market is perhaps one city block in size. It has a roof but no walls. In the evenings it is used for a parking lot. It is quite near the port. The salt smell of the sea blends with the perfumes of the market: fresh produce and fruit, coffee, old and new fish, cheese, flowers, earth, smoke, and the blood of new cut beef.

Just across the street, in the Taverne Lucullus, the smells are mixed also but are easier to identify. Strong coffee, sweat, old and new beer, wine, tobacco, *pastis*, cognac, croissants, and bread still hot from the oven create an atmosphere that can almost be sliced.

The Taverne is small, designed to seat perhaps forty people. Now it is jammed past capacity. The voices of truck drivers, produce sellers, fishmongers, and chefs mingle with the clatter of crockery.

The chefs mostly sit together; they sip coffee or wine and gossip about the weather, prices, and business. One red-faced man is raging about the high price of red mullet, the little fish used in bouillabaisse. Another, who works in a small restaurant that is open late and attracts the cabaret crowd after dinner into the wee small hours, is discussing his new cashier. His companion snorts into his coffee.

In a little while, their coffee, wine, croissants, and *pastis* are finished. One by one the chefs rise, pay, and cross the narrow street to the market. They are not yet dressed in their work clothes—in the spotless whites that some will change three or four times a day. Some look like prosperous suburbanites headed out for a day of golf. Others seem dressed to rake leaves and work in the garden.

The chefs straggle into the market. They walk slowly past each stall. They may look like tourists, but they miss nothing. Their decisions this morning will make the difference between profit and loss for their restaurants today.

To the visitor the *Marché Forville* is a vast cornucopia of multicolored delight: beets, endive, red cabbage, white cabbage, cucumber, white dandelions, chicory, celery, romaine lettuce, tomatoes, eggplant, artichokes, asparagus, broccoli, celery root, carrots, brussel sprouts, sea kale (*choux de mer*), squash, zucchini, spinach, broad beans, hop sprouts (*jets de houblon*), haricot beans, haricot flageolets, red beans, French beans, chestnuts, turnips, onions, sorrel, sweet potatoes, fennel, peas, pimientos, potatoes, mushrooms, pears, apples, grapes, pineapples, bananas, apricots, peaches, figs, strawberries, raspberries. Even a seasoned New York chef is likely to have never seen such a huge variety of beautifully arranged fresh produce under one roof at one time. And unlike the commercial markets in New York, the market in Cannes at five in the morning is as neat as a general's desk.

The mushroom stall is full of fresh mushrooms in a dozen varieties—edible boletus, morel, orange agarid. They are stacked as if drawn by a drafter's pen! The colors at the fruit stalls are incredible. There is row on row of glistening reds, greens, whites, yellows, purples, and all the shades in between. The fresh spices cannot be overlooked. There is neat pile after neat pile of basil, tarragon, thyme, rosemary, chervil, basil, and oregano.

Individually, each with his own style, the chefs continue their stroll. They have just noticed the price differences this morning. Henri—over there—has marked down his peaches. The tourist season is over and besides they are too ripe to hold much longer since there is no refrigeration in the market. For some reason the potatoes are two francs cheaper here on the kilo. The chefs stop and nod, whisper, or yell at the vendors. As nods and whispers are exchanged, cases are marked.

The stroll continues past the fishmonger with the incredible variety of fish: turbot, whitebait, perch, octopus, haddock, eels, cod, smelts, brill, sardines, carp, oysters, skate, scallops, mussels, crabs, shrimp, red mullet, tuna, frog, lobsters, crayfish, trout, salmon, mackerel, herring, pike, whiting, char, sole, and mullet. All are very fresh and bright eyed (except the salt cod), and many are alive and jumping.

Here again the visitor, who is accustomed to the American wholesale markets, is awed by the neatness and cleanliness of the fishmonger. The fish are arrayed as if for a photographer.

The chefs inspect, place their orders, and walk on to the butcher. Here is beef, pork, lamb, chicken, turkey, rabbit, partridges, ham—raw, cooked, cut, uncut, in chops, in slices, roasts, legs, filets, etc. Everything is arranged with great precision and care in the butcher's spotless shop. It is the glutton's dream! And, unlike in the U.S. markets (where wholesale meat is Cryovac® packed), the meat can be touched, smelled, and tasted. Nothing is wrapped in plastic; it is all open to inspection. Again, there are nods, whispers, greetings, and smiles; deals are made, credit is used, and money is exchanged. With marketing done for the day, the chefs depart for their restaurants. Some grab a quick coffee at the Taverne while their trucks are being loaded. Others load cases into cars and depart. For still others the purchases will be delivered later today or tomorrow.

And today at lunch the reduced-price peaches, perhaps in a tart or a melba, may disappear down the bejeweled throat of a countess at the Hotel Carlton or be eaten by a shop girl with no francs left to her name, in some backstreet (but profitable) café.

Procurement

What we have just described is the best system of restaurant procurement yet devised. It is best for the chef and best for the customer, for reasons that are obvious. But this system, for most of us in the hospitality business, is only a model. A market like *Marché Forville* is not found everywhere, and, even if it were, such a buying system would not be practical for everyone.

No, we are forced by the realities of local availability and the cynicism of our accountants to do our buying in a way that is best suited to our location and operation. In America, chefs at top-line restaurants make frequent visits to local markets for selected items, but the majority of supplies are ordered by telephone and delivered by truck.

There is nothing wrong with this system provided that two conditions are met. First, chefs must know their suppliers and know that they are dependable. A good working relationship with the salespeople is also essential for they can save a chef an enormous amount of time and work. Second, chefs must inspect each and every delivery, not only for quantity but also for quality. This responsibility can be delegated to someone who is knowledgeable.

Delivery Inspection

At far too many restaurants, deliveries are accepted without inspection. Even a reputable vendor, knowing this, will be tempted to ship poor quality food. If meat, for example, is accepted and later found to be spoiled, a reputable vendor will replace it. But what of the time lost? What if the meat is needed immediately and cannot be used?

And there is a more subtle but much more serious risk. Imagine meat is needed for a prepaid expensive banquet. It arrives spoiled and, because of slack conditions in the kitchen, is accepted. When the condition of the meat is discovered, it is too late to replace it. Every basic culinary student knows the rule: "When in doubt, throw it out!" But what if the owner says to the chef: "Look, we could lose thousands here. Use that meat or find another job!" Now we are talking not only about the chef's reputation, but also the health risk to the customers.

Each and every food shipment must be inspected. There can be no exceptions.

Fresh meat, even the Cryovac®-packed type (the fresh meat that is sealed in airtight plastic), must be checked. If the Cryovac®-packed meat is to be used quickly, open the plastic, look at the meat and smell it. If it won't be used for some time, inspect it and then freeze it. If it is not up to standard, refuse to accept it. If your meat is discovered to be spoiled a week later, it is unlikely that any vendor will replace it.

Fresh fish must also be inspected. Spoiled fish is the easiest to detect. The odor leaves no doubt. But you should also watch for fish that is reaching the end of its shelf life. If it must be used immediately, it is too old for you to accept.

It is important too in the case of fresh meats, fish, and poultry to check the temperatures. They should be cold when they come off the truck. Internal temperatures of fresh meats, for example, should be no more than 50°F. Higher temperatures than this indicate either poor handling or defective or nonexistent refrigeration on the delivery truck.

Frozen foods must be inspected with equal care. They should arrive hardfrozen, not soft. Foods that are delivered partially thawed should be refused.

Even *hard-frozen foods* should be checked carefully. Open cases and inspect sample boxes and bags. Frozen fish filets that are curled in the box, for example, and have ice formed in one corner have probably been thawed and refrozen at some point during handling. The same would be true of a bag of frozen peas with a big lump of ice at the bottom. Such signs do not necessarily mean that these foods are dangerous to use. They do mean, however, that the foodstuffs are suspect. If food is routinely received in this condition, there are some serious deficiencies in the handling procedures of your supplier.

Canned goods should not be overlooked. Open cases when they are delivered and check a few sample cans. Extremely rusty cans, badly dented cans, and cans that bulge outwards should be returned. Leaking cans should, of course, never be used. A can that, when opened, discharges a large quantity of liquid under pressure should be discarded immediately. The liquid under pressure indicates that the can seal has leaked enough to allow bacteria to enter the can and multiply or that improper procedures were used during processing. The bacteria create gases that put the contents under pressure. A can in good condition is under negative pressure—it is vacuum packed (the air pressure inside the can is less than the atmospheric pressure outside.)

Dry groceries must also be checked. Refuse bags of flour or sugar, for example, that are leaking, have been resealed, or are wet or water stained. When foods like flour, rice, or cornmeal are delivered, check them for bugs, alive or dead. If they are contaminated or infested with insects, return them to the dealer for replacement. Items like flour and cornmeal should never be purchased too far in advance. Virtually all flour and cornmeal contain some insect larvae that will, in time, hatch and infest the meal. Many chefs add bay leaves to their flour storage bins to prevent this. There is no scientific evidence to support this practice, but it seems to work.

Even *paper goods* should be inspected to insure that they are clean, unstained, dust-free, and in good condition.

No matter how much you trust your suppliers and regardless of how long you have been dealing with them, it is still necessary to check each and every shipment. Routine blind receiving of foods will eventually cause problems and could be catastrophic.

Regardless of whether chefs shop daily in the market at Cannes or order provisions by phone and have them delivered, the food must be inspected.

We recently interviewed Chef Christian Madoux in his marvelous restaurant in the Hotel du Parc (two star) in Draguignan, near the French Riviera. He discussed his procurement procedures at some length.

Chef Madoux said: "My veal, for example, always comes from the same butcher and I have known him for years through my other restaurants. But still I always check everything. And still there are sometimes problems.

"The fish we buy off the boat. We know the captain and he saves what we need for the Parc. If a fish is alive, we are quite sure it is fresh, no?

"The produce we buy at the Draguignan market, a few meters away. We check every carrot, every potato. . . ."

Based on the quality of the foods he presents at the Hotel du Parc, we believe Chef Madoux. His *Foie Gras*, a house specialty, is enough to tempt the most determined dieter down the happy path of gluttony!

Centralized Purchasing and Receiving

In large hotel operations, such as at the Don Cesar Hotel in St. Petersburg Beach, Florida, centralized purchasing and receiving of foodstuffs and food-related suppplies is the most common procurement method. At the Don Cesar, there are three restaurants, room service, and a banquet department. Because of the vast quantities and the large amounts of different types of food used daily, the procurement system like the one we described at the *Marché Forville* would be impractical.

So a centralized system is used. With this system, all purchases are ordered, received, and stored by a special department set up for that purpose. The hotel executive chef, the subchefs for various restaurants, the chef-baker, the banquet chef, the room-service chef, the beverage managers, and the like, all requisition foods and supplies as needed on a daily basis.

The chefs are freed from the drudgery of constant ordering, which usually involves many hours on the telephone and endless inspections of foodstuffs on delivery. Such drudgery often ties up the most experienced personnel when their presence is most needed in the kitchens.

Another advantage of this system is that the bookkeepers and accountants can easily keep track of the purchases and costs from the requisition sheets and the vendor's invoices. The chefs can keep track of the foods issued and used from accounting reports.

There are two disadvantages to this system. One is that the chefs must depend upon receiving personnel to check the quality of foodstuffs as they arrive. The other disadvantage is that, if the receiving personnel do not promptly fill requisitions and deliver them to the kitchens, the timely rhythm of food preparation is disrupted.

The successful function of this system depends on a conscientious receiving staff. If they are careless or poorly trained, problems will soon appear on the customer's plates.

Economic Realities

We do not intend to cover here the bookkeeping side of the hospitality business—that is another course of study entirely. But there are some critical points that should be firmly and permanently fixed in the mind of every chef.

The most important is the relationship between food cost and menu price. As a rule, *menu price should be at least five times the food cost*. This formula, which applies in nearly all cases, takes into account the actual production cost of a food item, which is sometimes difficult to calculate.

Let's look at a simple menu item like Codfish Cakes. We have the cost of the cod, the potatoes, the flour, the seasonings, and any other foodstuff that is used. Then there is the cost of labor, utilities, uniforms, rent or mortgage, pilferage, spoilage, breakage, and so forth. Our formula will in most cases compensate for these hidden costs and cover them in the menu price.

This formula will *not* work in very high-volume fast-food operations.

Every chef and restaurant owner should calculate the daily *break-even number*. This figure is reached by adding all actual costs for a month (include food bills, uniforms, rent, salaries, supplies, utilities, and taxes) and dividing that number by 30 days. The quotient is the amount of money you must make to break even on a given day. Everything over this figure represents profit.

All good chefs, owners, and managers must keep close tabs on the fiscal side of their operation. It is not uncommon for a restaurant that appears to be doing well suddenly to file for bankruptcy.

Summary

The best procurement method remains the oldest one—chefs go to the market and select precisely what they need.

This is often not practical or even possible in many modern restaurant operations, but the concept remains a valuable model. The model serves to remind chefs to tailor their modern system to achieve the same results as the old individual-shopping system.

Chefs must be aware of the necessity of checking each and every shipment upon its arrival in the kitchen. Even in centralized hotel operations, someone in the purchasing-receiving department must be responsible for checking the quality and condition of shipments.

Such diligence is necessary to insure that the restaurant is getting exactly what is ordered, in the quantity required, and in good (fresh and unspoiled) condition. Fresh meat, poultry, fish, frozen foods, dry groceries, and even canned goods must be checked.

All this checking and inspecting must be done to prevent even the possibility of loss—monetary loss, loss of quality, and the catastrophic loss of customers that can occur if the highest standards of commercial food sanitation are not maintained.

The test of a good procurement system is simple: It is a good system if the chefs get exactly what they want, when they want it, and in the best possible condition.

Discussion Questions*

1) Why is so much space in this chapter devoted to the wholesale market in Cannes?
2) Cannes, like the rest of France, is every bit as modern as any city in the United States. Why would a chef in Cannes prefer to shop every morning in the old outdoor market instead of simply ordering by phone?
3) Fresh meat packed in airtight plastic has been heralded by the meat industry as an important breakthrough in the packing, preservation, and storage of fresh meat. Why do the authors dislike the practice?
4) How do most American restaurants order their food supplies? What are the advantages of such systems over the *Marché Forville* type of system? What are the disadvantages?
5) Why do good chefs keep abreast of the fiscal side of the operations? What are the possible consequences if they do not?
6) What are the factors that determine the type of procurement system to be used in a restaurant or hotel operation?
7) Why is it important to have a conscientious and knowledgeable salesperson as well as a dependable food supplier?

Test Questions

1) If you are inspecting a just-delivered shipment of frozen meat and you observe that it is thawed completely, what should you do?
2) Under what circumstances would it be appropriate to use spoiled or almost spoiled fish in cooking?
3) A case of 5-pound bags of pancake mix is delivered to your restaurant. The bags are leaking and are water stained. What should you do?
4) Why is it necessary to inspect even airtight, plastic-wrapped meat when it is delivered?
5) What are some of the advantages of a separate department for food purchasing and receiving, especially in large operations?

*Some discussion questions require culinary deductive reasoning. They may not be answered *directly* in the text, but enough information is given to deduce the answer logically.

6) Why might some chefs neglect to inspect food shipments? Why is this a dangerous practice?

7) Why is it necessary to inspect canned goods and dry groceries?

8) What are some signs that frozen food has been thawed and refrozen during shipping and handling?

9) What are two conditions that might cause you to refuse a shipment of bulk flour in 100-pound bags?

Chapter 3

Cooking Methods and Restaurant Kitchens

Before we can examine cooking methods, we must eliminate some of the misconceptions that are prevalent even among some very successful chefs. Much of this confusion is semantic.

The names and descriptions of different cooking methods describe *models*, rather than actual, absolute *things*. These models are used as a way of understanding and classifying the different cooking techniques. Thus, terms like "deep fry," "bake," or "steam" are only artificial distinctions that are used to clarify and describe cooking methods. These models are useful, but they are also limited. The thermotics of different methods of cooking overlap, because of the nature of food and the nature of heat. Deep frying has elements of steaming, baking has elements of frying, broiling has elements of baking, and so on.

You should understand precisely what is meant by each method of cooking. But to understand exactly what is happening to the food being cooked, you must also clearly grasp the limitations of the method's terminology (or model). You must realize precisely where the development of cooking techniques stands today.

Cooking Methods

Old Versus New Techniques

Modern chefs are often too hasty when they dismiss old techniques and methods of cooking. In fact, they often use the old tried-and-true techniques daily, while remaining convinced that they are using something new and modern.

A good case in point is the question of whether searing meat and vegetables seals in the juices, improves flavor, or serves any purpose at all. For centuries, the great chefs of the world believed that it did all of these things. Roasts were seared under high heat to seal the juices and preserve flavor and moisture before they were cooked to perfection under lower temperatures. Meats to be braised were browned first for the same reasons. Meats to be boiled were plunged into rapidly boiling water before the cooking temperatures were reduced for a long period of simmering. It was also widely believed that vegetables were best when added to a boiling pot of water—to seal the delicate flavors, juices, nutrients, and color—rather than starting with cold water. Many haute cuisine chefs continue these practices today, some without really being aware of it.

Today, some chefs believe that searing meat causes too much shrinkage (it does not) and serves no good purpose (it continues, in fact, to serve the same good purposes it has for centuries). Many meats today (such as prime rib and other roasts) are cooked at a lower temperature (250–275°F) to reduce shrinkage. When meats are cooked in this way in modern convection ovens, the constant stream of blowing heated air sears the meat all around before the actual interior cooking begins. Thus, many chefs who claim they do not sear their meats are actually doing it every day.

Slow-cook ovens that cannot be set above 200°F are becoming popular for roasting meats because shrinkage is virtually eliminated. They can produce prime rib that is medium rare throughout in about 6 hours. It is interesting to note that one problem with meats cooked in this fashion is that when finished, although medium rare, they appear to be raw on the outside. To make these meats customer acceptable (especially when served bone-in or carved in front of the customer), they must be seared in a very hot oven prior to use. Customer perceptions demand the very dark, seared appearance on the outside of the roast. And so the old searing technique survives, albeit at the end of cooking.

Despite whether chefs and cooks using the technique are completely aware of it, searing meats is a technique that is alive and well. With a few exceptions, it is not usually done as a separate cooking step. One exception is banquet service of steak. Here steaks are marked on a grill or in a broiler just enough to produce the cross-hatch marks expected by the customer. The process also seals in the juices. Then, just before service, the cooking is finished in sheet pans in a very hot oven. Another exception is in the preparation of Beef Wellington. Here the fillet must be seared as well as cooled and dried before enclosing it in puff pastry. This step not only prevents bleeding into the pastry before and during cooking; but it also colors the meat in a customer-acceptable fashion.

Meats cooked with the broiler or on the griddle or in the sauté pan are seared as part of the cooking process. In many cases, the cook is unaware that the process is taking place. Because it is difficult to cook meat without searing it, to argue pro or con for searing is rather a moot point.

Today, especially in banquet work, fresh vegetables are often immersed in rapidly boiling water to obtain the best color. It avoids brown or off-colors that sometimes result when vegetables are steamed and then held warm.

Many of the old techniques survive for good reason. Smart chefs will try everything and use what works best.

Boiling

Boiling includes all techniques of cooking in which the food is immersed in a flavored or unflavored or seasoned liquid. The temperature of the water determines the name of the method or its variation.

Boiling, cooking in rapidly bubbling and agitated water or other liquid, is normally used only for such foods as pasta. Water, which boils rapidly at 212°F, will break up foods that are cooked at this temperature and has a tendency to make them tough and rubbery. Beans, for example, will break up into small pieces. Beef has a tendency first to become tough and then to fall apart.

Simmering, cooking in a slowly bubbling liquid at about 205°F, is the technique of choice. Cooking at this temperature avoids the breaking up of the food and the destructive effects of cooking at the higher temperatures. Sauces cook well but do not scorch at the bottom of the brazier. Beef does not become tough and rubbery. Fish does not fall apart. And, in a busy kitchen, it is not necessary to "babysit" the sauce or the stock quite as much. Evaporation is slowed, and it is not necessary to add water as often. Cooking time, because the temperature variation is minor, is not significantly affected.

The only exception to this general preference for simmering is when rapid boiling is required to produce a quick reduction in volume of liquid, as when stock is reduced for glazes or for a concentrated *jus* or gravy.

Poaching, cooking in a hot liquid that is just barely bubbling, is the technique of choice in cooking very delicate foods such as eggs and fish. The temperature of a poaching liquid ranges from 160 to 180°F.

Blanching is a technique used when foods are cooked for very brief periods of time, usually not completely. Blanching is done in either boiling water or hot oil. For example, meat is blanched in hot water to remove blood. Vegetables are blanched in hot water to set the colors, destroy enzymes, and loosen skins. Potatoes are blanched in hot fat to remove excess water.

Braising usually refers to a technique of cooking meat in a small amount of liquid, most often in a covered pan. It can be done either in the oven or on top of the stove. Properly done, braising is an excellent technique.

Meats should always be seared, then partially covered with a liquid, usually stock. Additional liquid is added from time to time until the meat is completely cooked. After cooking, fats are removed from the resultant liquid, which is used as a natural sauce or gravy or with other ingredients to make the desired sauce.

Steaming

Steaming food means that steam, rather than water, contacts the food. There are three methods of steaming food.

1) *Indirect steaming:* Here the food is cooked inside a pot or other vessel that is heated by steam. In this case, the food is cooked in its juices or in another liquid that is added to the vessel. Double boilers and steam kettles are good examples.
2) *Direct steaming:* Here the food is held above the boiling water and is cooked by direct contact with the steam. An example is the oriental steamer.
3) *Low-pressure steaming:* This is accomplished by using a commercial device that produces steam in its own boiler and then releases it directly into contact with food in a closed, sealed chamber. A pressure cooker is a good example.

For commercial applications, the most common uses of steam in cooking are the familiar double boiler and the now increasingly common low-pressure steaming equipment.

The great advantage of the commercial steaming units is their speed. Free steam is the same temperature as boiling water (212°F). As steam is pressurized, the temperature increases and the time required for cooking decreases. For example, steam at 5 psi (pounds per square inch) is 227°F; at 10 psi, 240°F; at 15 psi, 250°F. Yet despite these high temperatures that rapidly decrease cooking times, there is no danger of burning the food (although it can be overcooked). In addition, there is little deterioration in color or nutritive value.

Stewing or Cooking à l'Étuvée

Stewing or *cooking à l'étuvée* is not to be confused with boiling or braising or steaming. Rather it is a combination of all three methods.

Here, the food, usually a tough cut of meat such as beef shin, is cooked inside a closed pot with a small amount of liquid. The food is cooked by the simmering liquid, by the steam created by the liquid and its own internal juices, and by the constant dripping of hot condensed water from the lid, which also serves to baste the food continuously as it cooks. The electric "crockpots" that were so fashionable a few years ago used this technique of cooking.

Baking and Roasting

Baking and roasting are the same; *baking* usually refers to breads and cakes, and *roasting*, to meats. The product is cooked by heated air that surrounds it in the oven. In a conventional oven, the small degree of air circulation is due to the hotter air at the bottom near the gas flame or heating element moving to the top of the oven. In the modern convection oven, hot air is constantly circulated around the product. This hastens the cooking time.

In roasting meats in an oven, remember two things. First, cook the meat uncovered. Covering the meat results in its being steamed rather than roasted. If meat is correctly roasted, it is very important at the beginning of cooking to sear the outside of the meat to obtain the crust that seals in the juices. After an initial crust is obtained, the meat is then finished, often at a much lower temperature. At the very end of cooking, if the meat appears to be becoming too brown, it is correct to cover the meat with foil to prevent burning on the outside. Second, always roast the meat so that air circulates freely around all parts of the meat. The best way to do this is to use a roasting pan with a wire rack at the bottom to prevent the meat from sitting in its own fat. If a wire rack is not available, make a raft of carrots, celery, and onions split in half. The roast then rests on this raft in the same way it would with the wire rack. In addition, of course, the aromatic vegetables enhance the flavor of the meat.

Many cooks have great difficulty in determining when a roast is done. The experienced cook can easily tell by the time elapsed and by the color of the fluid produced when the roast is pricked with a fork. Some old hands can tell by the temperature of the same fork placed against their wrists. It is not necessary to guess or to calculate. Simply use a meat thermometer. There are printed tables of temperature for all manner of roasted products. (See Table 3–1.) With prime rib, for example, if the temperature on the inside of the thickest part is 110°F, you know without any doubt whatsoever that after the rib has rested outside the oven for 30 minutes the inside of the rib will be rare.

Another method of roasting is *spit roasting*. This was originally used in medieval kitchens, with a piece of meat roasting over an open fire. The technique was later used with charcoal in the great kitchens of France. Today it is rarely used commercially, except in specialty restaurants where, I suspect, the technique is more useful in attracting customers than in im-

Table 3–1. Roasting Meats: Thermometer Temperature Guide.*

Veal	170°F
Ham	170°F
Fresh pork	185°F
Turkey	190°F
Chicken	†
Beef	rare: 110°F
	medium rare: 120°F
	medium: 130°F
	well: 140°F+

*When using a meat thermometer, insert it into the thickest part of the meat and move the thermometer up and down. Use the lowest reading obtained. The temperatures here take into consideration that cooking continues even after the meat is removed from the oven. They assume some holding time, as they are intended for commercial cooks. Thus, the temperatures for beef are somewhat lower than ones quoted by the Department of Agriculture and the National Beef Board.

†Using a thermometer for small chickens is not reliable. For a 2-pound chicken, about 1 hour at 325°F (convection oven) is average.

parting flavor to the meat. Used correctly, with the right equipment, it is a simple and perfect technique for roasting.

Broiling

Probably due to the different usage in Britain and the United States, there is some confusion as to the meaning of the verbs "broil," "grill," and "griddle." In both countries, the vocabulary used in the kitchen usually depends on the training of the chef and the traditions of the kitchen.

In actual fact, broiling and grilling are the same. They mean to cook a food product with radiant heat from either above or below. In common American usage, *broiling* usually refers to cooking in a broiler where the heat comes from above. Usually *grilling* refers to an appliance where the heat comes from below. In any case, the method and the end result are the same. The taste difference, for example, between a steak cooked in a pan and a steak broiled or grilled, is due to the slight difference in taste caused by the smoke created by burning fat.

Griddle means to fry on a flat heated metal surface, the temperature of which is usually controlled by a thermostat. Griddlecakes or pancakes are a good example.

Sautéing

Sautéing means to cook quickly in a small amount of fat. It is important that the pan is very hot before the food is added and that the pan is not overloaded. The food must be cooked quickly and finished quickly, otherwise it will begin to fry, braise, or steam (depending on the product) and will fail to produce the desired result.

Meats and fish to be cooked in this fashion are often dusted with flour to prevent sticking and to achieve uniform browning. Especially with fish, this always helps in the formation of a hard crust on the outside that prevents the flesh from falling apart.

Deglazing is the use of wine, stock, or water to remove the browned bits of food and glazed-on matter from a sauté pan. The resulting liquid is used to make the sauce for the sautéed product.

Pan frying is similar to sautéing except that it usually involves larger pieces of food and more fat. The cooking time is also much longer.

Deep frying almost always uses a commercial fryer in which the product is completely submerged in hot fat and the temperature of the fat is regulated by a thermostat. In many ways, it is similar to sautéing and pan frying, but there is an important difference; the temperature of the fat is always controlled.

Since the temperature is controlled, the product results are more standardized and dependable. Deep frying is a very versatile and useful technique that can produce extremely desirable and high-quality foods that have a crisp surface with very little fat absorption. Properly cooked, foods produced in this way will be tender and juicy and will contain all their own natural flavors.

The key word is "properly." Good-quality fat must be used. The baskets must not be overloaded. Proper temperatures must be used. Strongly flavored foods (such as fish) should not be cooked in the same fat as mildly flavored foods (such as potatoes).

Above all, the fat must be replaced at the first hint of an off-flavor or odor. Straining and filtering help, but they only postpone the inevitable. Worn-out, over-used fat produces overly brown and bad tasting fried food, in addition to being very unhealthy. The fryer must be completely cleaned each time the fat is changed.

Pressure frying is very similar to deep frying. The food is cooked in a special vessel similar to a pressure cooker, except that the liquid is fat instead of water. As with the pressure cooker and steamer, food is cooked more quickly and at lower temperatures. It is interesting to note that even though the temperature of the fat may be, say 375°F, the internal temperature of the food will never go above 212°F, which is the boiling point of water.

Kitchen Equipment

Having discussed the basic cooking methods and techniques, it seems appropriate to look briefly at kitchen equipment. It is easy to be impressed by the technological advances in cooking equipment. And today's equipment, certainly in terms of reduced labor and drudgery, is vastly improved over that used in the past. But the technological advances are not as overwhelming as they might first appear.

New Equipment
The really significant advances in modern cooking came before World War II, with the development of modern fuels and refrigeration. These two areas of development produced a revolution in the cooking industry and made haute cuisine a reality for anyone who wished to attempt it. Prior to the development of modern gas and electric cooking systems and refrigeration, great cuisine was possible only for the very wealthy.

The Microwave
Despite enormous amounts of advertising money invested by the microwave industry to tout its product, the microwave has not assumed any significant role in the commercial haute cuisine kitchen. It is useful for thawing and emergency reheating of cold food, but, beyond that, it remains a "nice to have" but low-priority equipment item in most commercial kitchens.

Some operations, because of their nature (such as all-night room service in a large hotel or quick snack stands) depend upon the microwave. It is much cheaper to reheat cooked foods to order than to pay the salary of a cook during low-demand hours.

Perhaps at some time in the future the microwave will become a critical equipment item in the commercial kitchen, but for now it is most useful in the place it can be found most often—in the home kitchen.

In this age of convection ovens, microwaves, instant this, and freeze-dried that, nothing really has changed throughout the centuries in cooking.

European ovens differ from those in the United States. And, of course, the metric and customary settings on ovens vary. See Table 3–2.

Table 3-2. Oven Temperature Conversions.

Degrees F	Degrees C	Gas Mark (European ovens)
225	110	¼
250	130	½
275	140	1
300	150	2
325	170	3
350	180	4
375	190	5
400	200	6
425	220	7
450	230	8
475	240	9

Minimum Requirements

No two kitchens are alike because no two kitchens are devoted to the same kinds or quantity of cooking. Thus, a banquet kitchen has different requirements from a kitchen producing individual orders, and an airline catering operation has different requirements than a cafeteria kitchen.

To familiarize students with the large amounts of equipment required in a large commercial kitchen, the minimum equipment requirements for a kitchen designed to prepare 2,000 meals per day are listed on the next page.

4 gas or electric ranges, with conventional ovens
4 compartment steamers
2 large (200+ gallon) tilting steam kettles
1 griddle
1 overhead broiler
1 gas grill
4 reach-in refrigerators
4 two-compartment, three-rack convection ovens
2 work tables with sinks
1 floor model electric mixer with slicing, grinding, and chopping attachments
2 salad preparation tables

1 salad refrigerator
1 fish refrigerator
2-quart electric mixer
1 mobile flour bin
1 mobile sugar bin
1 walk-in refrigerator for meat
1 walk-in refrigerator for vegetables and dairy products
1 walk-in freezer
1 refrigerator for baked goods
1 pass-through refrigerator for waiters, opening near serving line
5 small steam kettles for soups and sauces
1 steam table
1 cold table

In addition to these basic items of cooking equipment, other items must be added to the list. These include such things as ice-makers, coffee makers, milk and cream dispensers, and juicers. Such sanitation equipment as dishwashing and drying machines, pot-washing sinks, and garbage disposers must be included. We have not even attempted to list the vast variety of pots, pans, baking pans, sauté pans, strainers, colanders, whips, and so on. Nor have we mentioned cutting boards, plastic storage containers, and the like. The list of required kitchen equipment is extensive and quite expensive.

Personal Kitchen Tools

New cooks learn early in their careers that they must have their own tools. Professional cooks may start with only a French knife wrapped in a kitchen towel, but in time they will acquire enough tools to fill a large tool box.

Even in the rare kitchen that provides knives and small cooking utensils for its staff, wise aspiring chefs will invest in their own. There are many reasons for this. A cook cannot function without good-quality sharp knives of many different types designed for different purposes. In the fast pace of a commercial kitchen, it takes too much time to search for the right knife, only to find that it must be sharpened before it can be used. Many kitchens do not provide knives, and many cooks hesitate to lend their personal knives to anyone. It is much more efficient to reach into your personal tool box to find exactly the knife you need, razor sharp and ready for use.

Most professional cooks will keep the following items in their tool boxes:

3 or 4 French knives	meat thermometer
boning knives	poultry shears
butcher knives	sandwich knife
paring knives	egg slicer
slicing knives	cheese knife
bread knife	apple corer
oyster knife	potato peeler
spatula	apple sectioner
pastry bag and tips	rubber spatulas
whip	steel spatulas
pliers	

Good-quality personal tools, well maintained and cared for, will last many years. They are an important investment that will save time and improve the quality of a cook's daily work.

Required Herbs and Spices for Your Restaurant Kitchen

Allspice Known also as Jamaican pepper, it is the only major spice cultivated exclusively in the Western Hemisphere. The pea-sized berries are picked green from tall trees. It is used with meats, stews, soups, and pastry.

Anise This spice is the fruit of a small plant in the parsley family. The taste is similar to licorice. It is used in pastries, breads, liqueurs, and some medicines.

Sweet Basil This is a member of the mint family, which is native to India and Iran. Leaves and stems are used in soups, sauces, stews, salad dressings, and with vegetables.

Bay Leaves Native to the Mediterranean countries, this spice is used in soups, sauces, stews, and meats like corned beef or tongue and with vegetables, tomato dishes, and even seafood aspics.

Caraway Seed Another member of the parsley family, this plant is native to Russia, Poland, Africa, and Holland. It is used in rye bread, rolls, and cakes as well as with some vegetables, soups, cheese dips, and stews.

Cardamom Seed A native of India, this plant is a member of the ginger family. It is an ingredient in pickling spice, curry powder, and sausage spice. It is used to flavor coffee, with some roasts, and in soups, custards, puddings, fruit dishes, some breads, and Danish pastry.

Celery Seed Grown widely in Southern France, it comes from a plant similar to American celery. An excellent substitute when celery is unavailable to flavor anything normally using celery, it is used in sauces, soups, and salads.

Chervil An aromatic sweet herb similar to parsley, it is widely used in European dishes, especially for sauces and soups.

Cinnamon Ceylon and Cassia cinnamon are the two main types of this important baking spice. It can be used with almost any baked or cooked sweet dish containing fruit. It is also used to flavor beverages (such as coffee) and in some soups.

Cloves Imported mostly from trees in Madagascar and Zanzibar, it is used in baked and boiled meats, stews, and roasts, with vegetables, and to make pickled fruits, mincemeat, plum pudding, and pie fillings. The oil is sometimes used in dentistry as a non-narcotic temporary pain killer.

Coriander This spice was known to be used in cooking as far back as 5000 B.C. It is one of the bitter herbs prescribed for Passover. It is the dried fruit of a member of the parsley family now grown primarily in Morocco and Argentina. It is used in many processed meats (especially frankfurters). It is also used in Spanish and Mexican cooking and in rice dishes and pastry.

Cumin This herb predates Biblical times and is used in most Oriental meat cookery. It is now cultivated primarily in Morocco, Cyprus, and Malta. It is an important ingredient of processed meats, pickles, cheeses, sausages, curry powder, chili powder, and chutney. It is often used on canapés, bread, rice, eggs, and sauces. It is also excellent with some vegetables (such as sautéed carrots).

Dill This aromatic seed is used in processed meats (especially liverwurst, frankfurters, and bologna), pickles, and rye and pumpernickel bread. It is used with lamb and with other meat, fish and vegetable dishes.

Fennel Native to Europe, this seed today is supplied primarily from India and North Africa. The taste is similar to anise. It is used in breads, pastry, soups, sauces, and fish. The plant itself is used in salad.

Ginger This spice is imported mostly from Jamaica, Sierra Leone, Africa, and India. It is one of the few whose roots are used, mostly in ground form. It is used heavily in pastries and puddings, with some vegetables, and in beverages.

Mace Derived from the lacy covering around the nutmeg seed, this spice has an aroma similar to nutmeg but its flavor is different. It is used in fish sauces, pastry, puddings, cream and egg dishes, vegetables, and forcemeat stuffings.

Marjoram Grown in southern France, North Africa, Germany, and Chile, it is used in sauces and with meat, fish, chicken, eggs, and vegetables. It is great with peas, lima beans, and spinach.

Mustard Most of the world production of this seed comes from North America, expecially California and Montana. It is part of the watercress family, and even the most novice cook is aware of the long list of its uses. It is important to have the American, Dijon, and dry varieties on hand.

Nutmeg Nutmeg is the seed of a tropical evergreen tree. This spice is cultivated in the West Indies and Indonesia. It is used in pastry, puddings, vegetables, and beverages. It is also a valuable addition to vegetables and fruits and is important for quiche batter.

Oregano With a flavor similar to marjoram, this herb is a member of the mint family. It is imported from Greece, Italy, and Mexico. It is critical for Italian and Mexican dishes and is a must for most tomato-based foods. It is also good for salads and beef, seafood, and egg dishes.

Paprika This mild, bright-red spice is used to process meat and to prepare ketchup and chili sauce. It is imported from Spain and South America and is grown in California. It consists of the pods of a kind of red pepper. It is used as a flavoring for poultry and meats and is a popular garnish for light-colored foods. Hungarian dishes, of course, are the most well known for the use of paprika.

Black Pepper Said to have changed the history of the world, this spice, once so expensive it was known as "black gold," is probably the oldest spice in the world. According to some historians, a large quantity of pepper was required by Alaric the Goth as part of the ransom of Rome in 408 A.D. The world today consumes more pepper than any other spice, and it is used in almost all foods, both for taste and as a preservative.

Cayenne Pepper This is derived from capsicum hot peppers, the most fiery of all spices. Yet used with care, as in Hollandaise Sauce, it is an important item in the gourmet spice repertoire. It is, of course, used in the hotter Mexican and Spanish foods and frequently in sausage.

Red Pepper This spice is similar to cayenne but not as hot.

White Pepper This spice is essentially the same berry as black pepper, but it has been allowed to ripen longer and has been washed and bleached in the sun. Less biting, this spice is preferred, for obvious reasons, in white or light-colored foods. In the peppercorn form, variations such as green and pink peppercorns are used whole in haute cuisine and are usually sold canned in brine.

Poppy Seed Imported primarily from Europe, this seed is so small that it takes almost a million seeds to make a pound. It is used primarily for pastry and bread products.

Rosemary This herb is the dried leaf of an evergreen shrub native to the Mediterranean countries. It is used in cooking vegetables, eggs, and fish. In the fresh form, it is fantastic to put on the tops of beef roasts during cooking.

Saffron It is currently the world's most expensive spice because it takes the stigmas of 75,000 blossoms to make a pound! It is used with some meats and in tea, pastry, and rice. Because of the price, it is fortunate that a little goes a long way.

Sage A popular herb in America and Europe, the best quality of sage comes from Yugoslavia. It is an important seasoning for pork and poultry and is a critical ingredient for old-fashioned turkey stuffing.

Sesame Seed A native of Asia, this aromatic seed is primarily used in baked goods and candy. Some chefs like it in soups, especially bean and pea, and it is good sprinkled over tomatoes and asparagus.

Tarragon Used in meats, sauces, eggs, and tomato dishes, this herb is the critical one in the preparation of Béarnaise Sauce. It is used especially with lamb and poultry and in vinegars and flavored butters.

Thyme This is the most important herb in haute cuisine. Primarily imported from France, it is used in nearly everything—soups, sauces, beef, veal, poultry, fish, lamb, cheese, and salads. Deprived of everything else, a knowledgeable cook can manage with salt, pepper, thyme, parsley, garlic, and wine.

Turmeric Known in the kitchen as "the poor cook's saffron," it is often used as a substitute for saffron and an ingredient in curry powder. It is used in pickle and relish formulas, mustard, and chutney.

In addition to these herbs and spices, it is also wise to keep the following blended spices available: Apple Pie Spice, Crab Boil, Chili Powder, Curry Powder, Pickling Spice, Poultry Seasoning, Pumpkin Pie Spice, and Mint Flakes.

Lastly, we mention garlic and parsley, which must always be available in the kitchen in fresh form. They are as important to serious cooking as salt and pepper. MSG should never be used. Some customers are allergic to it, and, in isolated cases, it could be fatal.

Summary

The basic cooking methods are: boiling, simmering, poaching, blanching, braising, steaming, stewing, baking, roasting, broiling, sautéing, pan frying, deep frying, and pressure frying. All cooking methods either are included in these categories or are some variation or combination of these categories.

High-volume commercial kitchens require a large quantity of equipment for cooking, cooling, food preparation, and sanitation. In addition to the electrical and mechanical equipment, an astounding number of small kitchen tools such as strainers, tongs, forks, spoons, and spatulas are also needed. In addition, professional chefs have their own knives, of many kinds and sizes.

Well-equipped kitchens also stock a variety of dry and fresh herbs, spices, extracts, and flavorings.

Discussion Questions*

1) There are new commercial cooking appliances constantly appearing on the market. Usually they are marketed as equipment that uses a *new* cooking technique. Are these claims likely to be true?
2) Would a modern three-star chef be likely to sear the meat before braising?
3) In the early Elizabethan period, spits for roasting meat were turned by clockwork (wound up like a clock and driven by springs). A giant spit was invented that could take 130 different roasts. It also played 24 musical tunes. The chef could tell which roast was done by listening to which tune was being played. Do you think that then, in the seventeenth century, this was considered a *new* technique of cooking?
4) What would motivate a restaurant owner to use deep-fryer fat long past the point where it both tastes and smells bad?
5) In deglazing a sauté pan, is the fat normally used in the sauce made from the deglazing liquid?

Test Questions

1) Define sauté.
2) What is a griddle?
3) What is the boiling temperature of water?
4) What is *direct* steaming?
5) What is poaching?
6) What is the difference between baking and roasting?
7) What is blanching?
8) What is the purpose of blanching?
9) Why is meat often seared at the beginning of the cooking process?
10) Explain the differences between broil, grill, and griddle.

*Some discussion questions require culinary deductive reasoning. They may not be answered *directly* in the text, but enough information is given to deduce the answer logically.

Chapter 4

⚜

Hors d'Oeuvres

Duxelles Champignons
Stuffed Mushrooms
Roquefort Mousse
Chicken Liver Mousse
Mushrooms Stuffed with Crab

Puff Pastry
Barquette of Lobster à
   l'Américaine
Snails
Clams Riviera

B y definition, hors d'oeuvres are served in addition to the meal. Cold appetizers are usually served before lunch, while hot appetizers or a combination of hot and cold appetizers are served before dinner. There are some exceptions to this practice. For example, in American banquet service, both hot and cold appetizers are usually served with cocktails prior to either lunch or dinner. In individual restaurant service, they may be served with cocktails before dinner or in a variation of the Russian style, now very popular in France, after the soup, a sort of mini-course.

Importance of Hors d'Oeuvres

In America, the importance of the appetizer is often forgotten. The hors d'oeuvre should stimulate the appetite. A beautiful tray of a variety of appetizers should also clear the guests' minds of their problems and predinner thoughts and put them in the mood to enjoy the rest of their dinners.

Appetizers, both hot and cold, are made from a nearly limitless variety of ingredients. These include eggs, fish, shellfish, liver, beef, poultry, game, vegetables, and cheese. Needless to say, they are not limited to potato chips and cheese dip or tinned sausages and processed cheese wrapped in dough.

There are few American restaurants that feature excellent hors d'oeuvres. Even some very successful caterers have a limited repertoire of hors d'oeuvres. However, customers are impressed with those that do. In fact, there is one restaurant in New York whose customers come primarily for the hors d'oeuvres.

Preparation and Service of Hors d'Oeuvres

Following a few simple rules when preparing hors d'oeuvres not only will help guests savor these appetizers but also will enhance their meals. Hors d'oeuvres must be beautiful. They must be easily eaten. And they must taste good.

Chefs should serve a wide variety of appetizers to their guests until they learn which are the most popular. They should then insure that their kitchen staff is well trained in the preparation of these items and prepares them daily. In fact, it would be wise to include them as part of the dinner price.

In this chapter we have included only a few of our favorite hors d'oeuvres. They are most popular with American guests. Mixed with the standard items that can be found in any cookbook, these recipes should suffice for almost any situation.

Duxelles Champignons (a Chef Chaton speciality)

Yield: 10 portions   Prep time: 20 min
                                       Cook time: 6 min

Equipment
French knife, cutting board, sauté pan, mixing bowl, kitchen spoon

Ingredients
mushrooms, fresh, chopped fine; 1½ cup (200 g)
shallots, chopped fine, about 12; 1 cup
butter; 5 oz (140 g)
flour; 1 tbsp
sherry or port; 9 tbsp (1.8 dl)
heavy cream; 7 tbsp (1.4 dl)
bread crumbs; 5 tbsp

Method
1) Sauté the mushrooms and shallots in butter, adding flour. Cook about 4
   minutes.
2) Remove mushrooms and shallots after cooking with butter and flour.
3) Deglaze pan with sherry or port.
4) Add heavy cream and bread crumbs.
5) Combine all the ingredients well.

Uses
Serve with hearts of artichoke or use for stuffed mushrooms. Also use as
garnish for red meats and vegetables.

Stuffed Mushrooms

Yield: 18 portions   Prep time: 20 min
                                      Cook time: 7 min

Equipment
snail dishes, sauté pan, sheet pan, spatula

Ingredients
mushrooms, large, fresh; 18
*garlic butter; as needed
snails, canned; 3 doz
oysters, smoked, canned; 3 doz
Swiss cheese, grated; 2 tbsp
paprika; as needed
lemon wedges; as needed

Method
1) Wash mushrooms and reserve stems for another use.
2) Moisten the bottoms and sides of the mushroom caps with a generous
   amount of garlic butter.
3) Place the caps in snail dishes.
4) Fill the caps with alternating layers of snails and oysters until they are
   slightly overfilled, to compensate for shrinkage.
5) Sprinkle cheese on top and bake in preheated 350°F oven for 7 to 8 minutes.

Service
1) Sprinkle lightly with paprika.
2) Garnish with lemon wedges.
3) Serve hot.

*Prepare garlic butter by briefly sautéing a combination of finely diced garlic, chopped
parsley, and butter. Add a touch of Pernod™ at the end.

Roquefort Mousse

Yield: 6 portions

Prep time: 20 min
Chill time: 4 hr

Equipment
potato masher or heavy whip, French knife, saucepan, mixing bowl, cutting board, small cake mixer or blender, 6 molds, grater, scale, saucepan

Ingredients
unflavored gelatin; 1 envelope (10 g)
lemon juice; ¼ cup (60 ml)
water, boiling; 1 cup (¼ liter)
Roquefort cheese; ¼ lb (125 g)
cucumber, grated, drained; 1 cup
parsley, minced; 4 tbsp
pimiento, minced; 2 tbsp

capers, minced; 1 tbsp
onion, grated; 1 tsp
salt; 1 tsp
pepper, fresh ground; to taste
heavy cream, whipped; 1 cup (250 ml)
capers; as needed

Method
1) Soften gelatin in lemon juice.
2) Add water and stir until gelatin is dissolved.
3) Mash cheese and add to the liquid gelatin along with the cucumber, parsley, pimiento, capers, onion, salt, and pepper. Mix very well.
4) Chill for 20 minutes or until mixture is slightly thickened.
5) Fold in whipped cream. Pour into mold and chill for at least 4 hours or until firm.

Service
1) Demold by dipping molds momentarily into hot water to loosen mousse. Invert onto service plate.
2) Garnish with capers. Serve crackers on the side.

Chicken Liver Mousse

Yield: 20 portions

Prep time: 20 min
Cook time: 10 min
Chill time: 4 hr

Equipment
sauté pan, spatula, French knife, cutting board, grinder or food mill, kitchen spoon, medium bowl, 20 small casseroles

Ingredients
chicken livers, fresh; 3 lb, 12 oz (1.7 kg)
butter; 1 lb, 3 oz (500 g)
shallots, chopped very fine; 10
cognac or armagnac; ¼ cup (60 ml)
salt; to taste
black pepper; to taste

raisins; 1 tbsp (optional)
cognac; ¼ cup (60 ml) (optional)
heavy cream; 1½ cup (625 ml)
onions, thin slices; as needed
pimiento; as needed
parsley; as needed

Method
1) Sauté chicken liver with butter about 4 minutes.
2) Add shallots and cook about 2 minutes.
3) Grind chicken liver and shallots very fine. Depending on grinder available, it is usually best to grind twice.
4) Add melted butter, cognac or armagnac, salt, and pepper. (If desired, macerate raisins with additional cognac for 3 to 4 hours. Add this to the mousse when the butter is added.)
5) Blend heavy cream until firm (almost but not quite to the point of whipped cream) and then add chicken liver puree.
6) Pour into small casseroles and cool at least 4 hours.

Service
1) Serve cold.
2) Garnish with very thin (usually machine sliced) slices of onion, cut pieces of pimento, and parsley.
3) May be served with small crackers.

Mushrooms Stuffed with Crab

Yield: 6 portions

Prep time: 10 min
Cook time: 15 min

Equipment
French knife, cutting board, sheet pan, broiler pan, electric mixer, spoon, medium bowl

Ingredients
mushrooms, large, white; 24
Alaskan king crab meat, drained, rinsed; 4 oz (115 g)
lemon juice; 1 tbsp (20 ml)
Parmesan cheese; 4 tbsp
cream cheese; 8 oz (230 g)
olive oil; 3 tbsp (60 ml)
parsley, fresh, chopped; 2 tbsp
bread crumbs; 2 tbsp
lemon juice; of ½ lemon

shallots, minced; 1½ tsp
cognac; 1½ tsp (8 ml)
Dijon mustard; 1 tsp (5 ml)
salt; 1 tsp
ground pepper; ½ tsp or to taste
butter, melted with minced garlic; as needed
parsley, fresh; as needed
lemon wedges; as needed

Method
1) Preheat oven to 425°F. Lightly butter large sheet pan. Remove stems from mushrooms.
2) Refresh crab with lemon juice.
3) Combine 2 tablespoons Parmesan cheese with cream cheese, crab, olive oil, parsley, bread crumbs, lemon juice, shallots, cognac, mustard, salt, and pepper. Beat about 5 minutes.
4) Fill the mushroom caps, forming a ½-inch dome on top of each.
5) Arrange on baking sheet and bake 10 minutes. Remove from oven and sprinkle with remaining Parmesan cheese.
6) Place mushrooms under a preheated broiler set on medium heat until Parmesan cheese melts and is golden brown.

Service
1) Garnish with garlic butter, parsley, and lemon wedges.
2) Serve hot.

Puff Pastry

Yield: 2.2 lb (I kg)   Prep time: 3 hr

Equipment
rolling pin, floured board, parchment paper

Ingredients
bread flour; I lb, 3 oz (540 g)
salt; I ½ tsp
ice water; I cup (¼ liter)
butter; as needed (½ détrempe weight)

Method
1) Pile flour on a pastry board, making a well in the center.
2) Dissolve salt in water.
3) Add water to well, little by little, kneading together with flour until the two ingredients are smooth and elastic. Form dough into ball and let stand covered with a damp cloth for one hour. (You may not need all the water, depending upon the flour used.)
4) This dough is called the *détrempe*. Weigh it and divide the weight in half to determine the amount of butter needed. The weight of butter used must be half the weight of the dough.
5) Roll dough into a sheet about 8 inches (20 cm) square.
6) Insure that butter is the same temperature as the dough. Put butter between two sheets of parchment paper and roll into a sheet about ½-inch thick, slightly smaller than the dough. Remove paper. Place on dough.
7) Folding the four edges of the square piece of dough into the center, completely enclose the butter. Let stand for 20 minutes.
8) *Tourage* is the first step in rolling. Remember that the dough must be rotated one-third to the left, before each rolling, to insure even distribution of butter and dough. Thus each operation is called a "turn." A turn involves turning, rolling, folding, turning, and rolling and folding again.
    a. Roll dough on a floured board or table into a rectangle about 25 × 8 inches (63 × 20 cm) and about ½ inch (12 mm) thick. The first roll must be done carefully to avoid forcing butter through the dough. Be sure to brush off excess flour with pastry brush when required.
    b. Fold the rectangle of dough, top edge to center and bottom edge to top, creating three layers.

9) Rotate the dough one-third turn to the left. Roll out again into a rectangle as above. Mark with the imprint of two fingers (to keep track of the number of times the dough is folded and rolled). Rest ½ hour.

10) Repeat the above operation two more times. Allow 20 minutes of rest for the dough between each rolling. When finished, the dough will have been turned, rolled, and marked six times.

11) Puff pastry is now ready for use.

The most practical way to make puff pastry is to do everything on a work table inside a walk-in cooler. It is difficult to make it in a kitchen, because normal room temperature will cause the butter to melt and run through the dough. If it must be made outside the cooler, then the dough must be refrigerated after each step, making the process much more time consuming and complicated.

There are shortcuts available that do work, but the results are not nearly as good. They reduce the number of layers of pastry, and the layers of pastry are what makes the pastry tender and flaky.

Puff pastry can be made cheaper by using other types of fat, but butter is by far the best choice. Butter contains a great deal of water. When heat changes this water to steam, the pastry rises. Other types of fat contain less water and will not cause the pastry to rise as nicely. Puff pastry produced with butter is also not nearly as greasy as it is when it is made with other fats.

Commercial frozen puff pastry is difficult to find in the same quality as the product made from scratch. The sheets are too thin, and it is usually made with fewer layers. Also, a cheaper shortening is often used.

Puff pastry can be made in large quantities and stored almost indefinitely in the freezer if you wrap it as you would wrap meat.

Barquette of Lobster *à l'Américaine*

Yield: 12 portions   Prep time: 20 min
                                      Cook time: 20 min

Equipment
French knife, cutting board, spoon, brazier

Ingredients

2-lb (1-kg) lobster; 1
olive oil; 8 tbsp (160 ml)
onion, diced fine; 4 tbsp
shallots, diced fine; 2
tomatoes, diced, canned, drained; 2
  cup (½ liter)
garlic cloves, chopped fine; 2
parsley, chopped; 1 tbsp
tarragon, chopped; 1 tbsp
dry white wine; ⅔ cup (165 ml)

*Fish Stock; ½ cup (125 ml)
cognac; ⅓ cup (85 ml)
cayenne pepper; to taste
salt; to taste
butter, melted; ½ cup (⅛ liter)
lemon juice; to taste
heavy cream; 3 tbsp (60 ml)
†barquette shells, baked; 12

Method
1) Cut tail of lobster into 1-inch (25-cm) slices along joints.
2) Split carcass lengthwise.
3) Crack shell of claws.
4) Remove gritty substance near head and retain coral for sauce.
5) In sauté pan, brown pieces of lobster quickly in olive oil. Remove from pan.
6) Add onion. Cook slowly until transparent.
7) Add shallots, tomato, garlic, parsley, and tarragon.
8) Put lobster back into pan with wine, stock, cognac, pepper, and salt.
9) Simmer for about 20 minutes.
10) Remove lobster pieces and separate flesh from shells. Set aside meat.
11) Reduce pan juices by half.
12) Pound coral fine and add to pan juices.
13) Using whip constantly, stir over medium flame, adding melted butter along
    with a touch of lemon juice and cayenne. Finish with heavy cream.

  *Commercial fish, shrimp, or lobster base may be used to make stock; in this case, exercise
  caution with salt.
  †Any unsweetened pastry may be used. For volume production, commercial frozen pie dough
  (factory-packed in tiny aluminum foil pans) can be used.

14) Adjust taste with salt and pepper as required.
15) Fill hot barquette shells with lobster pieces and cover with sauce.

Service
1) Fill hot shells to order; do not hold filled.
2) Garnish with lemon slices.
3) Serve very hot.

Snails (*Escargots*)

Yield: 5 doz   Prep time: 25 min
                               Cook time: 8 min

Equipment
sauté pan, spatula, kitchen spoon, mixing bowl, sheet pan, French knife, cutting board, special snail dishes and forks if available

Ingredients
snails, tinned, drained; 5 dozen
Chablis; 1 cup (250 ml)
shallots, diced fine; as needed
garlic, diced fine; as needed
stuffing
    butter, melted; 1 lb (450 g)
    garlic cloves, diced fine; 10

shallots, diced fine; 10
parsley, chopped fine; 1 bunch
salt; to taste
black pepper; to taste
nutmeg; to taste
cognac; 1½ oz (45 ml)
snail shells, clean; 5 dozen

Method
1) Drain the juice from the snails and then briefly sweat in Chablis. (Being canned, the snails are, of course, already cooked.)
2) Mix snails and equal parts of shallots and garlic with wine. Marinate about 1 hour.
3) To make stuffing, combine well butter, garlic, shallots, parsley, salt, pepper, and nutmeg. Add cognac last. Consistency should be like wet poultry stuffing. If stuffing is too thin, add butter.
4) Put a dab of stuffing into each shell. Insert the snails, "tongue" on the outside. Add more stuffing and pat firm.
5) At this point, snails can be held overnight in refrigerator or frozen.
6) Bake in 350°F oven for 8 minutes.

Service
Serve at once.

(See color plate 4)

Clams Riviera

Yield: 25 portions

Prep time: 20 min
Cook time: 15 min

Equipment
French knife, cutting board, small brazier, kitchen spoon

Ingredients
bacon, chopped very fine; 2 lb (900 g)
green peppers, chopped very fine; 10
onions, medium size, chopped fine; 5
pimiento, canned, chopped fine, drained; 1 lb (453 g)
clams, chopped fine; 4 lb (1.8 kg)
eggs, whole, beaten slightly; 5
tabasco; 1 tsp (5 ml)
clam juice; 2 cup (½ liter)
bread crumbs; as needed

Method
1) Sauté bacon until brown, but not crisp.
2) Add green peppers and onions and sauté about 5 minutes.
3) Add pimientos and clams and sweat about 5 minutes.
4) Remove from heat and add eggs, tabasco, clam juice, and bread crumbs for consistency.
5) Stuff clam shells and bake in 400°F oven 5 or 6 minutes or until golden.

Service
Serve very hot, four shells per order.

Summary

In most American restaurants, the selection of hors d'oeuvres is rather limited, or there is one house specialty. As a rule American appetizers are rather lackluster affairs.

The purpose of the hors d'oeuvre is to stimulate the appetite. And there is an almost unlimited number of possibilities. They can be hot or cold and made from eggs, fish, shellfish, liver, beef, poultry, game, vegetables, or cheese. The sky is the limit.

Chefs must make hors d'oeuvres beautiful, easy to eat, and good tasting! They should also serve a wide variety of appetizers until they find which sell the best.

Discussion Questions*

1) On page 36, the mushrooms stuffed with snails, oysters, and cheese are listed as an appetizer. Could they also be used as an entrée?
2) What are the advantages and disadvantages of making Puff Pastry from scratch, as opposed to buying it frozen in sheets?
3) What causes Puff Pastry to puff up during the baking process?
4) What would happen to the final product if Puff Pastry was made from scratch in a hot kitchen?
5) If both live snails and the canned variety are available, which type is more convenient for the chef to use?

Test Questions

1) In preparing Clams Riviera, what, precisely, is the function of the bread crumbs?
2) At what point in the preparation of snails can the product be frozen?
3) In serving Barquette of Lobster à l'Américaine, why is it a poor idea to hold filled, hot shells in a warmer while waiting for orders?
4) In the preparation of Puff Pastry, what is the *tourage*?
5) In preparing Mushrooms Stuffed with Crab, what must be done to the mushrooms before filling?
6) How is Chicken Liver Mousse usually served?
7) What is the first step in the preparation of Roquefort Mousse?

---

*Some discussion questions require culinary deductive reasoning. They may not be answered *directly* in the text, but enough information is given to deduce logically the answer.

8) List the ingredients for *Duxelles Champignons*.
9) What does the two-finger imprint in the dough indicate when preparing
   Puff Pastry?
10) In making Puff Pastry, what is the best choice of fat?

Chapter 5

✠

The Stocks
(Les Fonds)

White Stock
Clear Brown Stock
Brown Veal Stock

Fish Stock
Vegetable Stock

I f sauces are the soul of cuisine, then stocks are the heart. Not only are stocks the basic ingredient of nearly all sauces, they are also the one indispensable ingredient of soups, stews, aspics, and glazes. In addition, they are used for braising meats.

Many aspiring young chefs believe that, because most restaurants today—even the good ones—do not use stocks to the same extent that they were used in the days of the grande cuisine of France, they are no longer important. This is a grave mistake. Although the bases and concentrates available today are an adequate substitute for stocks made from scratch, they are just that, a *substitute*.

Admittedly, it is more difficult to make good, consistent stocks in the average restaurant today than it used to be. There are many reasons for this. First of all, the regional centralization of slaughterhouses and the increasing tendency to portion-control meats have created a problem in obtaining a good quality supply of bones and very cheap cuts of meat. Another reason is the very high cost of kitchen help. A third reason is the critical shortage of skilled help. In the average good restaurant today, probably only the chef and the sous-chef have any idea of how to make good stocks. If they have no time to do it themselves and no time to train anyone else, their only choice is to use bases and concentrates.

These problems are not insurmountable. They can be solved, and they must be solved if a restaurant is determined to produce good cuisine and a consistent profit. Chefs should remember that they need not be operating French restaurants in the grand manner to require good stocks.

Nearly all cuisine in every Western country is in some way derived from or influenced by the French. Good stocks *must* be available if good food is to be produced. For anyone who doubts this conclusion, note that the best-selling American (bottled) barbeque sauce contains as a basic ingredient beef stock produced in the classic way.

Types of Stocks

Depending, of course, on the menu, most restaurants require that the four basic stocks listed below be available constantly. Fresh, they will keep about a week if properly chilled after initial cooking and properly refrigerated. They will keep longer if brought to a boil every other day and re-chilled. Frozen, they have a shelf life of about a year at −20°F.

White Stock is a broth that, by definition, has no color. It is made from white meat, bones, and aromatic vegetables. White Stock is used in the preparation of white sauces and stews.

Brown Stock is made from beef, veal, or poultry and the usual aromatic vegetables. The beef and bones are browned before simmering. Brown Stock is used in the preparation of brown sauces and stews.

Fish Stock is prepared from the bones and trimmings of fish. Sole, flounder, and other flat fish are the fish of choice because they retain their flavor. The others are relatively tasteless when cooked into stock. The liquid used is generally dry white wine and water. The aromatics are onions, parsley, thyme, bay leaf, and lemon juice. Stalks and parings of mushrooms are often used. Fish Stock is used to prepare fish sauces and to poach fish.

Vegetable Stock is obtained from carrots, onions, celery, parsley, thyme, bay leaf, and garlic. It is used in the preparation of vegetable dishes.

Glazes are produced by reducing the stocks to the desired consistency. Beef Stock simmered until the volume is reduced by half is called *demi-glace*. It is a strong stock. *Glace* is demi-glace reduced even further, almost completely, until it attains a jellylike consistency. This glace is usually called glaze (to avoid confusion with "glace," which refers to the coating on fruits, confections, and frozen deserts). Glaze is used to make aspic and to glaze meats. It can be diluted with water to make stock or demi-glace.

Making Stocks

There is a restaurant in Paris that claims its stockpot has been simmering without interruption since before the American Revolution. If this is indeed true, I would hate to be the potwasher in that establishment when they finally wash the pot.

In reality, beef stocks are rarely cooked for more than 6 to 8 hours. After that the taste begins to deteriorate and a subtle, bitter, unpleasant taste develops. The rule of thumb for most stocks follows: cook beef for 6 hours, chicken for 3 hours, and fish for 1½ hours.

There are some practical things to remember in the production of stocks. Even though some of these suggestions are obvious, remember that they will make the difference between a mediocre stock and a good one.

First of all, your stock pot must be surgically clean. Traces of detergent or old grease will doom your stock before it begins.

It is also important to prepare the ingredients for the stock properly. Beginning with cold water, blanch (heat to the boiling point) all bones for white stock. For brown stock, brown all bones and meat. All bones should be sawed or broken up so that the full flavor of the marrow is obtained. All vegetables should be carefully washed.

A stock pot is not a garbage can. No good chefs will put spoiled meat or filthy vegetable scraps into the stock pot.

Take care to prevent spoilage of the finished stock. Finished stocks are an ideal growth medium for bacteria. Strain stocks as soon as the cooking process is complete and discard all vegetables, bones, and meats. Stocks should be chilled either in a bath of ice water or in a running cold water bath to bring the liquid to room temperature. This should be done as quickly as possible after cooking. Above all, do not refrigerate stocks when they are still hot. If a stock at boiling temperature is placed in a refrigerator, it may not chill to a safe temperature for as long as 24 hours. A stock can easily sour overnight. Improperly handled, a stock can become dangerous to consume after only a few hours.

Finally, probably the step most frequently neglected or done sloppily is skimming off the fat (*dépouiller*). Even though this step takes time, all fat must be skimmed from the top of a finished stock. It is easiest to do when the stock is cold and the fat has hardened and can be picked off like pieces of ice. It is possible to skim the fat with a spoon or ladle, if you need the stock right away. Do not neglect this most important step. It is essential if you want to create fine sauces.

The Recipes

Our recipes for stocks are designed to firmly guide the chef in successfully preparing beautiful stocks. The techniques and ingredients used evolved over centuries of experimentation.

The production of good-quality stocks is a nearly scientific process that leaves little margin for error. To obtain a fine standard of taste, standard methods must be used. A chef may create a new sauce or a new cake, but never a new stock. The ingredients and cooking times cannot be varied substantially without adversely affecting the results.

Novices who have never worked with stocks made from scratch must learn both the ingredients and the methods. Above all, they must learn the taste of such products. Only through experience can new cooks acquire the judgment needed to make fine sauces, soups, and stews. Without this acquired judgment, they cannot even hope to make a close substitute, when forced by industrial requirements to use commercial bases, if they do not know what real stock tastes like.

White Stock (*Fond Blanc Ordinaire*)

Yield: 2 gal (8 liter)

Prep time: 30 min
Cook time: 4 hr

Equipment
meat saw, large stock pot, French knife, cutting board, skimmer, kitchen spoon, china cap

Ingredients
*veal bones; 13 lb (5.5 kg)
water; 3 gal (12 liter)
onion, chopped rough; 18 oz (500 g)
carrots, chopped rough (optional); 9 oz (250 g)
celery, chopped; 9 oz (250 g)

bouquet garni
  thyme; 1 tsp
  parsley; 1 tsp
  bay leaves; 3
cloves, whole; 1 tsp
peppercorns, crushed; 1 tsp
salt; to taste
black pepper; to taste

Method
1) Cut bones and wash in cold water.
2) Place bones in stock pot and cover with cold water. Blanch bones.
3) Discard water and wash bones again.
4) Cover bones with water. Add onions, carrots, celery, bouquet garni, cloves, and peppercorns.
5) Simmer for 4 hours. Remove scum as it accumulates.
6) Remove from heat and strain. Discard strained foodstuffs.
7) Skim off fat if stock is to be used immediately; otherwise, refrigerate and remove fat when cool.
8) Adjust taste with salt and pepper as required.

Uses
This stock is used in soups, meat dishes, white sauces, veloutés, and white stews (such as blanquettes). It is also used to poach poultry.

---

*This recipe may be converted to chicken stock by adding 3 pounds of chicken or 2 pounds of chicken carcass and giblets.

❋

Clear Brown Stock (*Brun Clair*)

Yield: 1 gal (4 liter)   Prep time: ½ hr
                                          Cook time: 8 hr

Equipment
French knife, cutting board, meat saw, large stock pot, china cap, cheese-cloth

Ingredients

veal and beef bones; 2 lb (.9 kg)

salt pork, blanched, diced large; 1 lb (.45 kg)

beef, fat trimmed, diced large; 5 lb (2.27 kg)

veal knuckle, approximately 6 lb (2.7 kg), diced large; 1

ham hock, blanched, diced large; ½ lb (.27 kg)

carrots, chopped rough; ½ lb (.27 kg)

onions, chopped rough; ¾ lb (.33 kg)

bouquet garni
    parsley; 6 tsp
    thyme; 3 tsp
    bay leaves; 3
garlic cloves, crushed; 2
water; 1 gal (4 liter)
salt; to taste
black pepper; to taste

Method
1) Crack or saw veal and beef bones into 2-inch pieces.
2) Sauté salt port until it just begins to brown.
3) Sauté veal and beef bones, beef, veal, ham, carrots, onions, bouquet garni, and garlic in the pork fat until lightly browned.
4) Add water and simmer for 8 hours.*
5) Remove from heat and strain through china cap. Discard strained foodstuffs.
6) When stock has cooled, skim all fat from the top and strain again through cheesecloth.
7) Adjust taste with salt and pepper as needed.
8) Chill in ice bath and refrigerate.

Uses
This stock is used to braise meat and make brown sauces and brown stews.

---

*Tomato puree may also be added, if desired.

Brown Veal Stock (*Fond Brun de Veau*)

Yield: 1 gal (4 liter)

Prep time: 10 min
Cook time: 6 hr

Equipment
French knife, cutting board, meat saw, sauté pan, brazier, skimmer, spoon, china cap, cheesecloth

Ingredients
veal shoulder; 6 lb (2.7 kg)
veal knuckle; 2 lb (.9 kg)
vegetable oil; ½ cup (125 ml)
veal bones; 2 lb (.9 kg)
carrots, chopped rough; ½ lb (225 g)
onions, chopped rough; ½ lb (225 g)

bouquet garni
  parsley; 6 tsp
  thyme; 3 tsp
  bay leaves; 3
White Stock; 7 qt (7 liter)
salt; to taste
black pepper; to taste

Method
1) Tie meat with string and brown in oil on all sides.
2) Saw bones into 3-inch pieces.
3) Place bones, browned meat, carrots, onions, and bouquet garni in a brazier. Cover and sweat for 15 minutes.
4) Add 2 quarts of white stock and simmer for 1 hour, covered.
5) Skim and add the remainder of the stock.
6) Simmer for 5 hours more.
7) Remove from heat and strain through china cap. Discard strained foodstuffs.
8) Adjust taste with salt and pepper as required.
9) Cool. Skim off fat and strain through cheesecloth.

Uses
This stock is used for making brown sauces and consommé and for braising meats and soups.

Fish Stock (*Fond de Poisson*)

Yield: 2½ gal (10 liter)

Prep time: 10 min
Cook time: 45 min

Equipment
French knife, cutting board, stock pot, skimmer, kitchen spoon, china cap, cheesecloth

Ingredients
*fish bones; 13 lb (6 kg)
onions, chopped; 6 oz (170 g)
celery, chopped; 3 oz (80 g)
butter; ½ cup (120 g)
garlic; 3 cloves
mushroom trimmings; 6 oz (170 g)
bay leaves; 3

cloves; 4
water; 2½ gal (10 liter)
white wine; 1 pt (½ liter)
parsley; almost 1 oz (28 g)
orange peel; of ½ orange
salt; almost 1 oz (28 g)
black pepper; to taste

Method
1) Chop and wash bones.
2) Sauté onion and celery in butter.
3) Add fish bones, onions, celery, mushrooms, garlic, bay leaves, cloves, and cold water.
4) Heat to the boiling point. Remove scum as it accumulates.
5) Add wine, parsley, orange peel, and salt and simmer for 45 minutes.
6) Using a china cap lined with cheesecloth, strain twice.
7) Adjust taste with salt and pepper as required.
8) Chill in ice bath and refrigerate.

Uses
This stock is used for poaching and braising fish and in making fish stews and sauces.

---

*Best results are obtained with flat fish such as flounder and sole.

Vegetable Stock (*Fond de Légumes*)

Yield: 2½ gal (10 liter)

Prep time: 20 min
Cook time: 2 hr

Equipment
French knife, cutting board, stock pot, skimmer, spoon, china cap, cheese-cloth

Ingredients
fat; almost 6 oz (170 g)
onions, chopped; 11 oz (310 g)
leeks, sliced; 11 oz (310 g)
celery, diced; 6 oz (170 g)
cabbage, shredded; 6 oz (170 g)
tomatoes, chopped rough; 4 oz (110 g)

fennel; 4 oz (110 g)
garlic gloves; 2
bay leaves; 2
cloves, whole; 3
salt; 1 tbsp
water; 3 gal (12 liter)
black pepper; to taste

Method
1) Sauté the onions and leeks for a few minutes in the fat.
2) Add celery, cabbage, tomatoes, and fennel and sauté until transparent but not brown.
3) Add garlic, bay leaves, cloves, salt, and water and simmer for 2 hours.
4) Remove fat, if any. Using a china cap lined with cheesecloth, strain.
5) Adjust taste with salt and pepper as required.
6) Chill in ice bath and refrigerate.

Uses
This stock is used primarily for vegetarian and some fish items.

Summary

Stocks are the primary ingredient of nearly all sauces and soups in the repertoire of Western cuisine. In addition they are used for cooking and glazing and in the preparation of aspics.

For many reasons, modern restaurants increasingly use commercial bases and concentrates to make the stocks they need. Although they are often adequate, stocks obtained in this manner are always a less than perfect substitute for the real thing.

The basic stocks are: White Stock, Brown Stock, Fish Stock, and Vegetable Stock.

Finished stocks are an ideal growth medium for bacteria. Great care must be taken in the handling of finished stocks to prevent spoilage.

The final, and in some ways the most important, step in the preparation of stocks is skimming off the fat.

Stocks of good quality are an absolute requirement in the production of haute cuisine.

Discussion Questions*

1) Why is it more difficult to make stocks today than in the past?
2) What are the primary uses of stocks?
3) Why must stocks be handled with extreme care after they have been prepared?
4) What are the cooking times for the basic stocks?
5) What is likely to happen if the cooking times are exceeded?

Test Questions

1) Are good stocks required only in the kitchens of haute-cuisine-type restaurants?
2) What type of bones are normally used in the production of White Stock (*Fond Blanc Ordinaire*)?
3) What vegetable ingredients are common to almost all types of stocks?
4) In the preparation of Fish Stock (*Fond de Poisson*), what are the fish of preference?
5) What meats are used in the preparation of Clear Brown Stock (*Brun Clair*)?

*Some discussion questions require culinary deductive reasoning. They may not be answered *directly* in the text, but enough information is given to deduce the answer logically.

6) How are glazes produced?
7) Describe how stocks should be handled from the point when they are finished until they are refrigerated.
8) List the ingredients of Vegetable Stock (*Fond de Légumes*).
9) Describe two applications of the use of stocks in cooking.
10) Why must all fat be skimmed from the top of a finished stock?

Chapter 6

✣

Aspics and Court Bouillon

Meat Aspic   Court Bouillon #1
Fish Aspic   Court Bouillon #2
Clarification of Aspics and Stocks Court Bouillon #3

B oth aspics and court bouillon use stock to achieve special effects. Aspics, with their subtle tastes, enhance the appearance of food. Court bouillon is used to cook fish, vegetables, and some meats.

Aspics

Aspic, in its most simple form, is strained and clarified stock that has been reduced and chilled.

We are all familiar with gelatin—the odorless, tasteless (when mixed with water and chilled), jellylike substance obtained by boiling animal bones and tissues and vegetable fibers. Aspic is made in the same way, but it retains the taste and odor of the stock from which it is derived. It is often colored and flavored to make it suitable for the final product it is intended to enhance. Thus, beef aspic is made from beef stock; fish aspic, from fish stock; etc.

There are many variations of aspic, each tailored for a specific use. It is used to coat all manner of meat, fish, and fowl. It is used for eggs. It is often chopped and used as a plate liner for a dish, much as one would use lettuce or parsley. It can be used in one form or another, in almost every course of the dinner. Sometimes it is molded into various shapes and used to decorate products such as ham or fish, which have already been coated with a colorful sauce.

Whether using aspic on appetizers or entrées, the technique is the same. The chilled food is brushed with aspic and chilled again. The item is then brushed again with aspic and chilled yet again. The process is repeated until the aspic coating is the desired thickness. In the case of large items like chickens or ducks, the aspic is ladled on and chilled, for a smoother appearance.

Aspic is being used more and more frequently today. One Florida hotel, for example, recently hosted a party that featured 10,000 canapés in aspic and forty entrées in aspic. Fortunately for harried cooks, instant aspic is available in neutral and flavored versions that is equal in appearance to made-from-scratch aspic. It is as easy to use as instant coffee and is ideal for those establishments that use aspic only rarely or if there is a sudden demand for large quantities. In fact, gelatin is sometimes added to stock to make quick aspic when nothing else is available. Of course, for perfect flavor, the classic aspics are superior.

The stock used for the aspic should be of the same general type as the product to be coated; a poultry aspic for poultry, a fish aspic for fish, a beef aspic for beef. Also, care should be taken not to overseason the aspic. The aspic should enhance the dish and make it more appetizing; it should never overwhelm. With this in mind, we provide the basic aspic recipes.

If you have not worked much with aspic, experiment with it and then try using it with some very basic menu items. You will be surprised at the results.

Court Bouillon

Court bouillon is an aromatic liquor, a sort of very specialized stock, that is used to cook fish, various vegetables, and certain types of meats. It is made from water, vegetables, herbs, and wine or wine vinegar. It is always prepared in advance and may be used several times. Large fish, for example, are started in cold court bouillon, while small fish and fish pieces are added to the simmering liquid. Shellfish are added to lightly boiling liquid and boil during the entire cooking period.

There are about twenty standard variations of court bouillon in classic French cookery and uncounted variations of these. Here we mention only three, which are the most commonly used.

Meat Aspic (*Gelée de Viande*)

Yield: 5 qt (5 liter)

Prep time: 30 min
Cook time: 4 hr

Equipment
meat saw, large brazier, French knife, cutting board, kitchen spoon, skimmer, china cap, cheesecloth

Ingredients
veal and beef bones; 3¼ lb (1.5 kg)
beef shin; 4½ lb (2 kg)
veal knuckle; 3¼ lb (1.5 kg)
butter; 1 lb (.45 kg)
bacon; ½ lb (.22 kg)
carrots, large, chopped rough; 3
onions, medium, chopped rough; 2
leeks, well cleaned, chopped rough; 3

celery stalks, chopped rough; 3
calves' feet; 3 lb (1.35 kg)
water; 1½ gal (6 liter)
bouquet garni
   parsley; 6 tsp
   thyme; 3 tsp
   bay leaves; 3
   peppercorns; 12
   celery leaves; 1 cup

Method
1) Cut bones in 1-inch (2.5 cm) pieces.
2) Tie the beef with string. Brown beef, veal, and bones in butter.
3) After the meat is slightly brown, add bacon, carrots, onions, leeks, and celery and continue the browning process.
4) Add calves' feet and water and bring to a fast boil.
5) After a few minutes, skim well and reduce to a simmer.
6) Add bouquet garni with peppercorns and celery leaves and simmer for about 4 hours.
7) Skim and add additional water as needed.
8) Remove from heat and strain through china cap lined with cheesecloth. Discard strained foodstuffs.
9) Cool and remove all fat.
10) Clarify as described on page 65.

Fish Aspic (*Gelée Maigre de Poisson*)

Yield: 1 gal (4 liter)   Prep time: 20 min
                                          Cook time: ½ hr

Equipment
French knife, cutting board, brazier or stock pot, china cap, cheesecloth

Ingredients
white fish; 2 lb (.9 kg)   onions, diced; ½ lb (.22 kg)
fish bones; 2 lb (.9 kg)   leek, green part, diced; 2
bouquet garni   peppercorns; 5
  parsley; 6 tsp   cloves; 4
  thyme; 3 tsp   water; 1 gal (4 liter)
  bay leaf; 2   dry Chablis; 1 pt (½ liter) (optional)
shallots, chopped; 5

Method
1) Bring all ingredients to a boil.
2) Immediately reduce heat and simmer for ½ hour.
3) Remove from heat and skim.
4) Strain through china cap lined with cheesecloth. Discard strained foodstuffs.
5) Clarify as described on page 65, but do not use the chopped beef.

Clarification of Aspics and Stocks

Yield: 1 gal (4 liter)　　　　　Prep time: 10 min
　　　　　　　　　　　　　　　Cook time: 1 ½ hr

Equipment
French knife, cutting board, bowl, stock pot

Ingredients
beef, lean, chopped; 1 lb (.45 kg)
*leeks, green part, sliced; 2
*parsley; 2 tbsp
aspic or stock, cold; 1 gal (4 liter)
egg whites, beaten slightly; 4

Method
1) Insure that all traces of fat have been removed from the stock, pot, and equipment.
2) Mix beef, leeks, and parsley and place in stock pot.
3) Add the cold aspic or stock.
4) Bring to a boil, stirring gently.
5) Add egg whites and reduce heat to simmer. Simmer 20 minutes.
6) Impurities will rise to the top and form a raft. After cooking is finished, skim the raft off the top.
7) Strain the stock three times through cheesecloth, which has been rinsed in cold water.
8) The resulting stock should be quite clear.

---

*The parsley and leek do not contribute to clarification; they do bring the aspic one step further toward the final adjustment of taste.

Other Aspics

Chicken Aspic
Add one very finely chopped chicken, including the skeleton, to the ingredients in Meat Aspic.

Clear Aspic
The recipe is the same as for Meat Aspic except that the meats are not browned.

Madeira or Port Aspic
Add 1 pint of wine to 1 gallon of cold clarified meat aspic while it is still liquid.

Tarragon Aspic
Add ½ teaspoon of tarragon (or more according to taste and the strength of the spice) to 1 gallon of the chicken or fish aspic during clarification.

Court Bouillon #1

Yield: 1 gal (4 liter)   Prep time: 10 min
                                    Cook time: 45 min

Equipment
French knife, cutting board, medium stock pot, china cap, cheesecloth

Ingredients
carrots, chopped rough; 1 lb (450 g)
thyme; 1 tsp
celery leaves; 2 cup
bay leaves; 3
parsley, chopped; 3 oz (60 g)
wine vinegar; 1 cup (¼ liter)
salt; 1 tsp
dry white wine, 1 pt (½ liter)
water; 1 gal (4 liter)
peppercorns, crushed; 14

Method
1) Bring carrots, thyme, celery leaves, bay leaves, parsley, wine vinegar, salt, white wine, and water to slow boil.
2) Simmer for 35 minutes.
3) Add peppercorns and cook 10 minutes more.
4) Remove from heat and strain through china cap lined with cheesecloth. Discard strained foodstuffs.

Uses
This bouillon is used for salmon, lobster, and crayfish.

Court Bouillon #2

Yield: 1 gal (4 liter)

Prep time: 10 min
Cook time: 30 min

Equipment
French knife, cutting board, medium stock pot, china cap, cheesecloth, kitchen spoon

Ingredients
dry white wine; 2 qt (2 liter)
water; 2 qt (2 liter)
shallots, diced; 6
carrots, diced; ¾ lb (340 g)
celery leaves; 3 cup
onions, diced; ¾ lb (340 g)
parsley, stems only; ½ bunch
thyme; ½ tsp
bay leaves; 3
salt; 2 tsp
peppercorns, crushed; 14

Method
1) Bring wine, water, shallots, carrots, celery leaves, onions, parsley, thyme, bay leaves, and salt to slow boil.
2) Simmer for 20 minutes.
3) Add peppercorns and cook 10 minutes more.
4) Remove from heat and strain through china cap lined with cheesecloth. Discard strained foodstuffs.

Uses
This bouillon is used for trout, fish soups, and carp.

Court Bouillon #3

Yield: 1 gal (4 liter)

Prep time: 10 min
Cook time: 30 min

Equipment
French knife, cutting board, fine sieve, stock pot, kitchen spoon

Ingredients
water; 4½ qt (4½ liter)
bread flour; 1 cup
salt; 2 tsp
lemon juice; of 2 lemons
butter; ¼ lb (120 g)
carrots, diced rough; 4
onions, studded with 4 cloves each; 2

Method
1) Make a paste of the flour and water.
2) Add water and strain through sieve.
3) Pour into stock pot and add salt, lemon juice, butter, carrots, and cloved onions.
4) Boil slowly about 30 minutes.
5) Strain and use.

Uses
This bouillon is used for variety meats such as tongue, feet, and kidneys. By deleting the carrots and onions, it may be used for vegetables, especially those that have a tendency to turn dark, such as artichoke hearts.

Summary

Aspic is primarily reduced stock that has been chilled. It is used mainly as a decorative and tasty coating and as a plate liner. Sometimes it is molded into various shapes and used to decorate products such as ham or fish, which have already been coated with a colorful sauce.

The three basic aspics are meat, fish, and poultry.

Aspics and stocks are clarified using chopped beef and egg whites. Clarification removes the tiny particles that remain in the stock after straining. The liquid becomes limpid, without a trace of cloudiness.

Court bouillon is an aromatic stock used to cook fish, vegetables, and meats. There are about twenty standard variations of court bouillon in classic French cookery.

Discussion Questions*

1) Why do few restaurants today use aspic on a daily basis?
2) Chopped lean beef is an ingredient used in the clarification of stocks. Would this also be used in the clarification of Chicken Stock?
3) What will happen to aspic in a very hot dining room?
4) Why would court bouillon be used to poach salmon instead of plain water?
5) Why would court bouillon be used to cook vegetables and certain meats (like tongue) instead of plain water or plain stock?
6) Why is gelatin sometimes added to aspic?

Test Questions

1) What is aspic?
2) How is aspic made?
3) List five different types of aspic.
4) List three uses for aspic.
5) List the ingredients of Fish Aspic.
6) What is meant by the term "clarification of stocks"?
7) Describe how Beef Stock is clarified.
8) What is court bouillon?
9) List three uses for court bouillon.
10) List the ingredients of the court bouillon that can be used to poach salmon or crayfish.

*Some discussion questions require culinary deductive reasoning. They may not be answered *directly* in the text, but enough information is given to deduce the answer logically.

Chapter 7
The Sauces

African Sauce
Allemande Sauce
American Sauce
American-Style Lobster Sauce
Barbeque Sauce for Shrimp
Béarnaise Sauce
Béchamel Sauce
Bercy Sauce for Beef
Bercy Sauce for Fish
Beurre Blanc Sauce
Bigarade Sauce
Bonne Femme Sauce
Bordelaise Sauce
Brown Sauce
Champagne Sauce
Chef Chaton's Special Sauce for Fish
Cherry Sauce
Cider Sauce
Creole Sauce
Cumberland Sauce
Curry Sauce
Dugléré Sauce
Godard Sauce
Grande Bonne Femme Sauce
Hollandaise Sauce
Horseradish Sauce
Italian Mint Sauce

Lobster Thermidor Sauce
Marchand de Vin Butter
Marinara Sauce
Mornay Sauce
Mushroom Sauce
Nantua Sauce
Périgueux Sauce
Port Wine Sauce
Portugaise Sauce
Poulette Sauce
Princess Sauce
Provençale Sauce #1 (Hot)
Provençale Sauce #2 (Cold)
Rémoulade Sauce (Cold)
Robert Sauce
Rouille Sauce
Shrimp Sauce Chef Chaton
Smitane Sauce
Soubise Sauce
Stroganoff Sauce
Supreme Sauce
Tortue Sauce
Velouté Sauce
Victoria Sauce
Watercress Sauce
White Wine Sauce
Yorkshire Sauce

S| auces are the soul of cuisine, of all cooking—no matter who does it or where they do it. From the fragrant juices dipped from a pot of simple boiled chicken and vegetables to the most complex French sauce made with rare and expensive ingredients, sauces are magic and a delight. They are magic because they defy science and logic; they are more than the sum of their parts. The combination of ingredients becomes something totally different from the ingredients. They are a delight because a good sauce is like music—it can please the most difficult guest.

Sauces have made the French the acknowledged leaders in world cuisine from as early as the fourteenth century. But what we sometimes do not think about is the *influence* of the French in cuisine. They made the rules, and that authority has affected techniques and styles of cooking in every Western country for centuries. Frequently, the developments the media food experts and advertising people tout as "new" and "original" are in fact outgrowths of some standard technique or ingredient that would have caused only yawns if mentioned to a French kitchen crew a century ago.

Fundamentals

First, we must review the rules before plunging into the magic world of sauces.

The function of a sauce is to add to the appearance, flavor, and texture of food. It should improve the taste of the food, as a spotlight directs your attention to an actor or clothes enhance a person. But it should never overwhelm or distract. Thus, sauces should be rich, smooth, glossy, and flavorful; they should never be greasy.

Freshness

In top-of-the-line restaurant and hotel kitchens, sauces are prepared, as much as possible, fresh every morning. They are rarely kept more than a day or two; if they are not used, they are discarded. Basic stocks and *mother sauces* (such as Brown Sauce and Marinara Sauce) are always on hand; they are as familiar and available as salt or garlic. These basic stocks and mother sauces are essential ingredients of almost all sauces. Even if you are experienced, you may want to review the basic sauce recipes to jog your memory, especially if you have not worked with the more complex sauces for a while.

Glace and demi-glace are important basics, too, although they are not, strictly speaking, sauces. *Demi-glace* is finished and strained Beef Stock simmered until the total volume is reduced by half. *Glace* is the same stock reduced by boiling until nearly all the original liquid is gone; the result is almost the consistency of jelly.

Consistency

Another important aspect of saucemaking is attaining the desired consistency. A sauce will not accomplish its purpose, no matter how good the taste, if it is too watery. Also a horror to be avoided is the disgustingly thick sauce that sticks to food like wallpaper paste.

Historically, *roux* has been used to thicken sauces. This is made by cooking flour and fat together in a pan. We prefer *beurre manié*. This is a cold roux made by combining sixteen parts of butter or margarine with eighteen parts of flour (for example, 1 pound or 16 ounces of butter would require 18 ounces of flour).

Beurre manié has one major advantage over the cooked roux. At the very end of the cooking process, just before serving, the saucemaker has more control over the final thickness. At that time, the sauce is heated to boiling and beurre manié is added little by little until the sauce reaches the desired consistency.

Other agents used to thicken sauces are cornstarch, blood, egg yolks, cream, arrowroot (which is a ground starch made from the manioc plant and which gives a special shine to the sauce as well as thickening it), and gelatin for cold sauces. Of course, sauces are thickened also by simple reduction—allowing the water to evaporate by boiling.

To avoid curdling or breaking the sauce, some of these ingredients require standard techniques. When cream is used, it must be put in a small bowl so that the hot sauce can be added to it in small quantities, while being stirred constantly, until the cream and sauce mixture is about the same temperature as the hot sauce. Then add the mixture to the rest of the sauce. This applies to regular cream as well as sour cream.

When eggs or yolks are used, a little water should be beaten into them first, and then the same technique employed as with the cream. When eggs or cream are used, the sauce can be reheated, but it should never be allowed to come to a full boil.

Storage

All the basic sauces can be made in quantity in advance, frozen in small containers, and thawed and used as required. Finished sauces, however, should be made fresh and stored only for short periods of time. Cream sauces should be finished just before service. The fresher, the better is the rule with all sauces.

Stocks, too, are best fresh but can be frozen in advance and thawed when needed. If fresh stocks are not available, use bases and extracts, but experiment until you find the best quality product available. Good commercial bases can be used as a very reliable substitute for fresh stocks and can also be used to boost weak stocks.

We offer one caution here. Do not use salt in a sauce that is made with a commercial base. They are all very salty since the salt is used as a preservative. Also be very careful with reductions made with sauces using commercial bases. As the volume of water is reduced, the concentration of salt increases.

The Recipes

We have included in our selection of sauces kitchen-tested and adaptable recipes that have been developed over half a century in restaurant kitchens around the world. Some are classic recipes adapted for modern commercial use by Chef Chaton. Others are his exclusive creations. All have been well received by customers for many years, and all are suitable for many, many uses, some of which we will suggest. The rest we will leave to you—to discover, to create, to develop for your own kitchen and your own guests.

For those readers who are not totally familiar with them, we have included the following mother sauces: Béchamel, Brown, Hollandaise, Marinara, and Velouté.

Good chefs or saucemakers know these basic sauces as well as they know how to tie their shoes.

Remember that as important as these basic sauces are, we will rarely use them alone. They are not really finished sauces; they are the material from which finished sauces are made. Know them well. No canned or powdered substitute will ever produce the same results or the same revenue from pleased guests.

African Sauce

Yield: 1 qt (1 liter)

Prep time: 20 min
Cook time: 30 min

Equipment
French knife, cutting board, brazier, kitchen spoon, strainer

Ingredients

olive oil; ½ cup (250 ml)
onions, diced; 14 oz (400 g)
tomatoes, whole, canned, peeled,
  drained, chopped; 9
green peppers, diced; 8
garlic cloves, crushed; 8
bouquet garni
  bay leaf; 2

thyme; ½ tsp
parsley, chopped; ½ bunch
basil, fresh; 1 tbsp
white wine; 2 cup (½ liter)
*Veal or Beef Stock; 1 qt (1 liter)
salt; to taste
black pepper; to taste
beurre manié; as needed

Method
1) Sauté onions in oil until transparent.
2) Add tomatoes, green peppers, garlic, and bouquet garni with basil and simmer 10 minutes.
3) Add wine and cook 5 minutes more.
4) Add stock and cook 15 minutes more.
5) Adjust taste with salt and pepper as required.
6) Add beurre manié to obtain a consistency just a little thicker than pancake syrup.
7) Remove from heat and strain.

Uses
This sauce is used for pot roasted, braised, or boiled chicken or for small cuts of meat.

*If Veal or Beef Stock is not available, make from a commercial beef base.

Allemande Sauce

Yield: 1 gal (4 liter)   Prep time: 25 min
                                          Cook time: 15 min

Equipment
small brazier, whip, kitchen spoon, French knife, cutting board, strainer

Ingredients
egg yolks; 5
white pepper; ¼ tsp
nutmeg; ¼ tsp
lemon juice; 2 tbsp
*Chicken Stock; ½ cup + 2 tbsp
†Velouté Sauce; 1 qt (1 liter)
mushrooms, fresh, chopped; ½ cup (about 7 mushrooms)
salt; to taste
black pepper; to taste
beurre manié; as needed
butter; 6 tbsp (90 g)

Method
1) Beat egg yolks, pepper, nutmeg, lemon juice, and stock together until well mixed.
2) Add Velouté Sauce and mushrooms and simmer about 10 minutes.
3) Adjust taste with salt and pepper as required.
4) Remove from heat and strain. Thicken with beurre manié if necessary.
5) Stir in the butter a little at a time.

Uses:
This sauce is used for poached chicken, vegetables, eggs, and a variety of meats.

*If Chicken Stock is not available, use a commercial chicken base.
†See page 125.

American Sauce

Yield: 1½ gal (6 liter)   Prep time: 10 min
                                           Cook time: 45 min

Equipment
French knife, cutting board, brazier, whip, strainer, cheesecloth

Ingredients

olive oil; as needed   tomato puree; 12 oz (340 g)
mirepoix   tarragon; 1 tbsp
   carrots, diced fine; 2   bay leaf; 2
   onions, diced fine; 2   salt; to taste
   celery stalks, diced fine; 4   black pepper; to taste
cognac; 2 oz (75 ml)   cayenne pepper; to taste
*Fish Stock; 1½ gal (6 liter)   beurre manié; as needed
tomatoes, peeled, seeded, diced; 6   heavy cream; 2 cup (½ liter)

Method
1) Sauté mirepoix in oil.
2) When soft, but not brown, add cognac and ignite with lighted match.†
3) Add stock and simmer for 30 minutes.
4) Add tomatoes, tomato puree, and spices. Simmer for 10 minutes more.
5) Bring to boil and thicken with beurre manié until desired consistency is obtained. It should be thick enough to coat the back of a spoon, like pancake syrup.
6) Remove from heat and strain. Finish with cream.‡

Uses
This sauce is a very important and famous sauce for fish.

*If Fish Stock is not available, make from commercial lobster base or shrimp base.
†This is a critical step if the correct desired taste is to be obtained. The taste is from burned cognac and the aromatic vegetables.
‡See page 73 for technique to avoid "breaking" or curdling sauce.

American-Style Lobster Sauce

Yield: I gal (4 liter)   Prep time: I5 min
                                          Cook time: 20 min

Equipment
French knife, cutting board, sauté pan, small brazier, whip, kitchen spoon

Ingredients
shallots, chopped; 3
butter; 2 tbsp (30 g)
dry sherry; I cup (¼ liter)
*Lobster Velouté; I gal (4 liter)
salt; to taste
pepper; to taste
heavy cream; I cup (¼ liter)

Method
1) Sauté shallots in butter until tender.
2) Add shallots and sherry to the velouté and simmer for I0 minutes.
3) Adjust seasoning with salt and pepper as required.
4) Remove from heat and strain.
5) Finish with cream.†

Uses
This sauce is used for lobster or crayfish.

*See page 125.
†See page 73 for technique to avoid "breaking" or curdling sauce.

Barbeque Sauce for Shrimp

Yield: 1 qt (1 liter)

Prep time: 20 min
Cook time: 30 min

Equipment
French knife, cutting board, saucepan, large bowl, whip, kitchen spoon, china cap or strainer, cheesecloth

Ingredients
onions, quartered; 2
white vinegar; 3 cup (¾ liter)
ketchup; 2 cup (½ liter)
apple juice; ½ cup (125 ml)
dark brown sugar; ½ cup
vegetable oil; ½ cup (125 ml)
garlic cloves, chopped; 6
sweet gherkins, medium, chopped; 2
sweet gherkin juice; 4 tbsp (80 ml)

Dijon mustard; 4 tbsp (80 ml)
ground celery seed; 3 tbsp (60 ml)
Worcestershire sauce; 3 tbsp (60 ml)
tabasco; 2 tbsp (40 ml)
cayenne pepper; to taste (about ½ tbsp)
tumeric; 1 tsp
salt; to taste
black pepper; to taste

Method
1) Blend all ingredients well.
2) Simmer in saucepan for 30 minutes, stirring frequently.
3) Adjust taste with salt and pepper as required.
4) Remove from heat and strain through cheesecloth.

Uses
This specialty sauce is designed for shrimp, but it can be used for crayfish.

Béarnaise Sauce

Yield: 1 qt (1 liter)   Prep time: 20 min
                                         Cook time: 20 min

Equipment
French knife, cutting board, mixing bowl, whip, sauté pan, kitchen spoon, strainer

Ingredients
shallots, chopped; 8
peppercorns; 15–20
dry tarragon; 1½ tbsp
white vinegar; 1 cup (¼ liter)
white wine; 1 cup (¼ liter)
chervil or parsley, chopped; 1½ tbsp
*Hollandaise Sauce; 1 qt (1 liter)
salt; to taste
black pepper; to taste

Method
1) Combine shallots, peppercorns, tarragon, vinegar, wine, and chervil or parsley.
2) Over low heat, reduce until the consistency of wet sawdust.
3) Add reduction to Hollandaise Sauce and mix very well.
4) Adjust taste with salt and pepper as required.
5) Remove from heat and strain.
6) Finish with an additional pinch or two of tarragon and parsley or chervil.

Uses
This sauce is used for filet mignon, châteaubriand, fish, and Veal Oscar.

*See page 99.

Béchamel Sauce

Yield: 1 gal (4 liter)   Prep time: 5 min
Cook time: 40 min

Equipment
French knife, cutting board, saucepan, whip, kitchen spoon, strainer

Ingredients
milk; 1 gal (4 liter)
onion, studded with 4 cloves; 1
salt; to taste
black pepper; to taste
beurre manié; as needed

Method
1) Heat milk to rolling boil, stirring constantly.
2) Add onion studded with cloves and cook 20 minutes.
3) Adjust taste with salt and pepper as required.
4) Thicken with beurre manié to desired consistency.
5) Remove from heat and strain. Discard onion.

Uses
This sauce is used for vegetables, eggs, meat, and fish and is a basic ingredient for other sauces.

Bercy Sauce for Beef

Yield: ½ gal (2 liter)   Prep time: 10 min
                                       Cook time: 25 min

Equipment
French knife, cutting board, small brazier, whip, kitchen spoon, bowl, strainer

Ingredients
shallots, chopped; 15–18
butter; 3 oz (75 g)
dry white wine (preferably Chablis); 1½ cup (3.5 dl)
black peppercorns, crushed; 20
*beef demi-glace; 1½ qt (1½ liter)
salt; to taste
black pepper; to taste
beurre manié; as needed
parsley, fresh, chopped; ½ bunch

Method
1) Sauté shallots in butter until they are tender or colorless. Do not brown.
2) Deglaze with wine and add peppercorns. Reduce 5 minutes.
3) Add demi-glace and simmer 15 minutes more.
4) Adjust taste with salt and pepper as required.
5) Remove from heat and strain. Thicken with beurre manié until medium consistency is attained. It should be like brown gravy or pancake syrup.
6) Finish with parsley.

Uses
Serve this sauce with beef, especially tournedos and small filets.

---

*If demi-glace is not available, make from commercial beef base and use beurre manié to thicken. Do not reduce, or sauce will be too salty.

Bercy Sauce for Fish

Yield: I gal (4 liter)   Prep time: I0 min
                                Cook time: 30 min

Equipment
saucepan, kitchen spoon, whip, French knife, sauté pan, strainer, cheesecloth

Ingredients
shallots, diced fine; I cup (about I5 shallots)
butter; 8 oz (225 g)
dry white wine; 2 cup (½ liter)
*Fish Stock; 2 cup (½ liter)
parsley, chopped fine; I cup (about I bunch)
†Fish Velouté; I gal (4 liter)
salt; to taste
black pepper; to taste

Method
1) Sauté shallots in half of butter.
2) When shallots are nearly soft, add wine, stock, and half of parsley and simmer over low heat until volume of liquid is reduced by half.
3) Add reduction and a bit more parsley to the velouté and simmer I0 minutes.
4) Adjust taste with salt and pepper as required.
5) Remove from heat and strain.
6) Finish by whipping remaining butter and parsley into the sauce.

Uses
This is a classic sauce for fish.

Marinière Sauce
This variation is made by adding cooked mussel juice, thickening with egg yolks and using the mussels as a garnish. Use for fish.

*If Fish Stock is not available, make from commercial clam or shrimp base.
†See page 125.

Beurre Blanc Sauce

Yield: 3 cup (¾ liter)   Prep time: 10 min
                                          Cook time: 20 min

Equipment
French knife, cutting board, small brazier, kitchen spoon, whip

Ingredients
dry white wine; 1 cup (250 ml)
shallots, diced fine; 4 tbsp
butter, cut into 32 slices; 1 lb (450 g)
whipping cream; 1 cup (¼ liter)
Dijon mustard; 2 tbsp (60 ml)
salt; ½ tsp
white pepper; ¼ tsp

Method
1) Combine wine and shallots. Cook over medium heat until wine is reduced to about 4 tablespoons.
2) Remove from heat and whisk in butter, one piece at a time. Melt and combine each piece completely before adding another piece. If pan becomes too cool to melt butter, return to low heat. Sauce should be the consistency of light mayonnaise.
3) Whip in cream, mustard, salt, and pepper. Insure that all ingredients are well mixed.

Uses
This is an excellent sauce for fish.

Bigarade Sauce

Yield: ½ gal (2 liter)   Prep time: 20 min
                                 Cook time: 15 min

Equipment
saucepan, whip, kitchen spoon

Ingredients
orange juice; 1 qt (1 liter)
*beef demi-glace; 1 qt (1 liter)
brown sugar; ¼ cup or to taste
orange marmalade; ½ cup (125 ml)
currant jelly; 1 cup (250 ml)
salt; to taste
black pepper; to taste
beurre manié; as needed
orange liqueur; ¼ cup (60 ml) or to taste

Method
1) Mix orange juice, demi-glace, brown sugar, marmalade, and jelly.
2) Adjust taste with salt and pepper as required.
3) Bring to rolling boil and thicken with beurre manié until consistency is slightly thicker than pancake syrup.
4) Finish with orange liqueur.

Uses
This is an excellent sauce for duck.

---

*If demi-glace is not available, make from commercial beef base and use beurre manié to thicken. Do not reduce, or sauce will be too salty.

Bonne Femme Sauce

Yield: 2 qt (2 liter)   Prep time: 20 min
                                         Cook time: 20 min

Equipment
French knife, cutting board, whip, kitchen spoon, small brazier, strainer

Ingredients
shallots, chopped fine; 8
wine vinegar; 1 cup (¼ liter)
white wine; 1 cup (¼ liter)
*Fish Velouté; 1 qt (1 liter)
salt; to taste
black pepper; to taste
†Hollandaise Sauce; 2 cup (½ liter)
dry vermouth; ½ cup (⅛ liter) or to taste (optional)
whipped cream; 1 cup (¼ liter)

Method
1) Reduce shallots, vinegar, and wine over low heat until the consistency of wet sawdust.
2) Add velouté to reduction and simmer 10 minutes.
3) Adjust taste with salt and pepper as required.
4) Remove from heat and strain. Cool slightly.
5) Add Hollandaise Sauce (and vermouth, if used). Fold lightly to attain marbled effect.
6) Add whipped cream before serving.‡

Uses
This sauce is used for fish and some shellfish.

---

*See page 125.
†See page 99.
‡To dramatize the appearance of the entrée at presentation, sauce food and then brown
under the broiler on a heatproof serving plate. Add vegetables and garnish after browning.

Bordelaise Sauce

Yield: 1 gal (4 liter)

Prep time: 15 min
Cook time: 30 min

Equipment
French knife, cutting board, small brazier, whip, kitchen spoon, strainer, cheesecloth

Ingredients
red wine; 1 qt (1 liter)
shallots, diced fine; ¾ lb (340 g)
  (about 20 shallots)
peppercorns; 20
bay leaves; 3
thyme; ½ tsp
parsley, chopped fine; ½ bunch

tomato paste; ½ cup (125 ml)
*demi-glace; 1 gal (4 liters)
salt; to taste
black pepper; to taste
beurre manié; as needed
lemon juice; 1½ oz (50 ml)

Method
1) Reduce wine, shallots, peppercorns, bay leaves, thyme, and parsley until almost dry.
2) Add tomato paste and demi-glace and simmer 15 minutes.
3) Adjust taste with salt and pepper as required.
4) Remove from heat and strain through cheesecloth. Thicken with beurre manié until desired consistency is obtained.
5) Add a few drops of lemon juice; adjust seasoning.

Uses
This sauce is used for beef and grilled meats.

*If demi-glace is not available, use a commercial base. Do not reduce, or sauce will be too salty.

Brown Sauce (Espagnole Sauce)

Yield: 1 gal (4 liter)   Prep time: 15 min
                                          Cook time: 2 hr

Equipment
French knife, cutting board, brazier, skimmer, kitchen spoon, whip, china cap, cheesecloth

Ingredients
mirepoix
   onions, medium, diced; 18 oz
     (500 g)
   carrots, medium, diced; 9 oz
     (250 g)
   celery, medium, diced; 9 oz
     (250 g)
*butter; ½ lb (225 g)
†Brown Stock; 1½ gal (6 liter)

tomato puree; 8 oz (225 g)
bouquet garni
   bay leaves; 2
   thyme; ½ tsp
   parsley, chopped; ½ bunch
Chablis; 1 cup (¼ liter)
salt; to taste
black pepper; to taste
buerre manié; as needed

Method
1) Sauté mirepoix in butter until all vegetables are soft and slightly browned.
2) Add stock and bring to boil. After a few minutes, reduce to simmer and skim, if required.
3) Add tomato puree, bouquet garni, and Chablis and simmer about 2 hours. Stir from time to time and skim as often as required to keep surface clear of scum and fat.
4) Adjust taste with salt and pepper as required.
5) Remove from heat and strain through a china cap lined with cheesecloth.
6) Thicken with buerre manié.

Uses
This sauce may be used as is for beef. However, the primary use of this sauce in haute cuisine is as an ingredient in other sauces. It is one of the most important mother sauces.

*If desired, bacon fat can be substituted for butter.
†If Brown Stock is not available, use a commercial base.

Champagne Sauce

Yield: 2 qt (2 liter)   Prep time: 10 min
                                         Cook time: 1 hr

Equipment
saucepan, whip, kitchen spoon, strainer

Ingredients
*demi-glace; 1½ qt (1½ liter)
maple syrup; 8 oz (225 g)
champagne; 1 bottle (750 ml)
cloves; 5
peppercorns; 15–18
bay leaves; 3
salt; to taste
black pepper; to taste
buerre manié; as required

Method
1) Mix all ingredients together.
2) Heat to simmer and reduce volume of liquid by a third.
3) Adjust taste with salt and pepper as required.
4) Thicken with beurre manié if required.
5) Remove from heat and strain.

Uses
This sauce is primarily used for chicken and other poultry.

---

*If demi-glace is not available, use a commercial base. Do not reduce, or sauce will be too
  salty.

Chef Chaton's Special Sauce for Fish

Yield: 1 qt (1 liter)

Prep time: 30 min
Cook time: 20 min

Equipment
French knife, cutting board, saucepan, kitchen spoon, whip, strainer, cheese-cloth

Ingredients
*Fish Stock; 4 cup (1 liter)
†White Wine Sauce; 2 cup (½ liter)
shallots, diced fine; 2 tbsp
mushrooms, chopped; 5 oz (140 g)
bay leaf; 1
thyme; ¼ tsp
heavy cream; 2 cup (½ liter)
‡Béarnaise Sauce; ¼ cup (60 ml)
Pernod™; ¼ tsp (3 ml)
lemon juice; 1 tsp

Method
1) Combine stock, White Wine Sauce, shallots, mushrooms, bay leaf, and thyme and reduce volume of liquid by half.
2) Replace the evaporated liquid with cream and simmer for 5 minutes.
3) Remove from heat and strain through cheesecloth.
4) Just before serving, add the Béarnaise Sauce flavored with Pernod™.
5) Correct the flavoring with lemon juice.

Uses
This is a fantastic sauce for all types of finny fish.

---

*If Fish Stock is not available, an excellent substitute can be made from commercial bases.
†See page 128.
‡See page 80.

Cherry Sauce (*Montmorency*)

Yield: 1 qt (1 liter)   Prep time: 20 min
                               Cook time: 20 min

Equipment
grater, whip, mixing bowl, saucepan, kitchen spoon

Ingredients
cherries, dark, sweet, canned; 24 oz
  (680 g)
orange juice; ½ cup (125 ml)
brown sugar; 6 tbsp
lemon juice; 6 tbsp (120 ml)
vinegar; 1 tbsp (20 ml)
soy sauce; 2 tbsp (40 ml)
Worcestershire sauce; ½ tbsp
  (10 ml)

orange peel, grated; ½ tbsp
*Beef Stock; 1 qt (1 liter)
salt; to taste
black pepper; to taste
cornstarch; as needed
water; ½ cup
sherry or kirsch; ¼ cup (60 ml) or to
  taste (optional)

Method
1) Drain cherries and save the juice.
2) Using a whip, combine orange juice, brown sugar, lemon juice, vinegar, soy
   sauce, Worcestershire sauce, orange peel, cherry juice and stock. Bring to a
   slow boil.
3) Adjust taste with salt and pepper as required.
4) Make about ½ cup of thin paste by combining cornstarch and water.
5) Add cornstarch paste to sauce, a little bit at a time, until desired thickness
   is attained. Sauce should be slightly thicker than pancake syrup.
6) Add cherries just before serving. Sherry or kirsch may be added at this
   time.

Uses
This is a very popular sauce for duck.

*Beef Stock can be made from commercial base with excellent results.

Cider Sauce

Yield: 1 qt (1 liter)   Prep time: 15 min
                                         Cook time: 30 min

Equipment
French knife, cutting board, small brazier, whip, kitchen spoon, cheesecloth,
china cap

Ingredients
apple cider; 1 qt (1 liter)
*Brown Sauce; 1 qt (1 liter)
shallots, chopped fine; 8
cloves; 7
bay leaves; 3
salt; to taste
black pepper; to taste
cornstarch; as required

Method
1) Bring cider to boil. Add Brown Sauce, shallots, cloves, and bay leaves.
2) Reduce heat and simmer slowly until volume of liquid is reduced by half.
   Whisk from time to time to prevent scorching.
3) When reduction is complete, remove from heat and strain through cheesecloth.
4) Adjust taste with salt and pepper.
5) Thicken with cornstarch as required.

Uses
This sauce is excellent for ham or pork.

*See page 88.

Creole Sauce

Yield: 1 gal (4 liter)   Prep time: 30 min
                                    Cook time: 45 min

Equipment
French knife, cutting board, brazier, kitchen spoon

Ingredients
olive oil; 1 cup (250 ml)

celery, small julienne; 3 lb (1.35 kg)

onions, small julienne; 3 lb (1.35 kg)

green peppers, small julienne; 2 lb
 (900 g)

mushrooms, small julienne; 1½ lb
 (675 g)

parsley, chopped fine; ½ bunch

okra, fresh; 1 lb (450 g)

flour; as needed

garlic cloves, diced fine; 4

*demi-glace; ½ gal (2 liter)

tomato puree; 4 tbsp (80 ml)

salt; to taste

black pepper; to taste

bay leaves; 3

hot pepper, fresh, diced; 1

tomatoes, fresh, chopped, seeded,
 diced; 6

lemon zest, fine julienne; 2

orange zest, fine julienne; 2

orange, sliced; 1

Method
1) Heat oil in brazier.
2) Add celery, onions, green peppers, mushrooms, parsley, okra, and garlic.
   Sauté slowly but do not brown.
3) Add flour and stir. Allow to cook for a few minutes until roux† emits a
   nutlike odor and is slightly brown.
4) Add demi-glace, tomato puree, salt, pepper, bay leaves, and hot pepper and
   cook until all vegetables are well done.
5) Add julienne of lemon and orange and orange slices and cook 5 minutes.
6) Adjust taste with salt and pepper as required.

Uses
This sauce is used for shrimp, lobster, and crayfish.

*If demi-glace is not available, make from commercial beef base and use beurre manié to
 thicken. Do not reduce, or sauce will be too salty.

†Failure to cook to this point will result in an unpleasant taste of uncooked flour.

Cumberland Sauce

Yield: 1 pint (½ liter)   Prep time: 25 min

Equipment
French knife, cutting board, mixing bowl, saucepan, kitchen spoon, loaf pan

Ingredients
shallots, chopped fine, blanched,
  drained; 2 tbsp
orange zest, fine julienne, blanched;
  2 tbsp
lemon zest, fine julienne, blanched; 2
  tbsp
port wine; 12 oz (3.5 dl)
currant jelly, melted; 1 cup (250 ml)

orange juice; 4 tbsp (80 ml)
Dijon mustard; 2 tsp (40 ml)
cayenne pepper; ½ tsp
ginger; ½ tsp
salt; to taste
black pepper; to taste
gelatin; 1 envelope (10 g) (optional)

Method
1) Combine shallots, orange and lemon zest, port, jelly, orange juice, mustard,
   cayenne, and ginger.
2) Adjust taste with salt and pepper as required.
3) Chill before serving.
4) If desired, add gelatin and chill in small loaf pan. Slice like tinned cranberry
   sauce.

Uses
This sauce is used for turkey, venison, poultry, *pâté*, and *Pâté en Croûte*.

Curry Sauce

Yield: 1 gal (4 liter)

Prep time: 20 min
Cook time: 15 min

Equipment
French knife, cutting board, saucepan, kitchen spoon, china cap, cheesecloth

Ingredients
butter; as needed
apples, peeled, sliced; 2 lb (900 g)
onions, diced fine; 2 lb (900 g)
curry powder; 1 tbsp (15 g) or to taste
*coconut milk; 12 oz (350 ml)
†Chicken Velouté; 1 gal (4 liter)
salt; to taste
black pepper; to taste
beurre manié; as needed
heavy cream; 1 pt (½ liter)

Method
1) Sauté apples and onions in butter until soft. Do not allow to brown.
2) Add curry and coconut milk and simmer about 10 minutes.
3) Adjust taste with salt and pepper as required.
4) Adjust consistency using velouté and beurre manié if required.
5) Remove from heat and strain.
6) Finish with cream.

Uses
This sauce is used for poultry, eggs, and lamb.

---

*Coconut milk is available in tins. It can also be made by mixing 8 cups of finely grated coconut with 1 pint of warm milk. Allow to rest 15 minutes and then squeeze through cheesecloth.

†See page 125.

Dugléré Sauce

Yield: 1 gal (4 liter)   Prep time: 20 min
                                      Cook time: 30 min

Equipment
sauté pan, brazier, French knife, cutting board, whip, kitchen spoon, food
mill or blender

Ingredients
butter; as needed
shallots, minced; ¾ cup (7–8 shallots)
Chablis or other dry white wine; 1 cup (¼ liter)
peppercorns; 15
mushrooms, fresh, sliced; ½ cup (6–8 mushrooms)
tomatoes, canned, drained, diced; 1½ qt (1½ liter)
tarragon; 2 tsp
*Fish Velouté; 1 gal (4 liter)
salt; to taste
pepper; to taste
bourbon or vermouth; ½ cup (125 ml)

Method
1) Sauté shallots in butter until tender but not brown.
2) Add wine and peppercorns and reduce until almost all the liquid is gone.
3) Sauté mushrooms.
4) Add mushrooms, tomatoes, tarragon, and velouté to the reduction and simmer for 20 minutes.
5) Puree.
6) Adjust taste with salt and pepper.
7) Finish with bourbon or vermouth.

Uses
This sauce is fantastic for fish.

*See page 125.

Godard Sauce

Yield: I qt (I liter)　　　　　　　Prep time: 25 min
　　　　　　　　　　　　　　　　Cook time: 30 min

Equipment
French knife, cutting board, sauté pan, brazier, china cap, cheesecloth

Ingredients

mirepoix
　carrot, medium, diced fine; I
　celery stalks, diced fine; 2
　onion, diced fine; I
white wine; 2 cup (½ liter)
ham, fine julienne; 10 oz (300 g)

*demi-glace; I qt (I liter)
mushroom base; I tbsp
mushrooms, fresh, diced; 6
beurre manié; as needed
salt; to taste
black pepper; to taste

Method
1) Mix mirepoix, wine, and ham in brazier. Reduce until nearly all liquid is evaporated. Use care not to scorch.
2) Add demi-glace, mushroom base, and mushrooms and simmer 10 minutes.
3) Add beurre manié until the sauce is about the consistency of pancake syrup.
4) Adjust taste with salt and pepper as required.
5) Remove from heat and strain.

Uses
This sauce is great for all types of poultry.

---

*If demi-glace is not available, use a commercial base. Thicken with beurre manié. Do not reduce, or sauce will be too salty.

Grande Bonne Femme Sauce

Yield: 1¼ gal (5 liter)   Prep time: 15 min
                                           Cook time: 30 min

Equipment
French knife, cutting board, brazier, strainer, cheesecloth

Ingredients
onions, chopped fine; 3
butter; 6½ oz (185 g)
dry white wine; 2 cup (½ liter)
peppercorns; 20
tomatoes, canned, drained, diced; 4
 cup (1 liter)
tomato puree; 5 tbsp (100 ml)
cognac or bourbon; 3 oz (1 dl)

garlic cloves, crushed; 10
*Chicken Velouté, very rich; 1 gal
 (4 liter)
salt; as needed
black pepper; as needed
heavy cream; 1 pt (½ liter)
parsley, fresh, chopped; as needed,
 about 1 cup (1 bunch)

Method
1) Sauté onions in butter until golden brown.
2) Add wine and peppercorns and reduce the liquid by two-thirds.
3) Add tomatoes, tomato puree, cognac, and garlic and simmer for 15 minutes.
4) Strain through cheesecloth.
5) Add Chicken Velouté. Thicken with beurre manié if required.
6) Adjust taste with salt and pepper if required.
7) Finish with cream and parsley.†

Uses
This sauce is used for quenelles (veal or chicken), capon, or veal.

---

*See page 125.
†See page 73 for technique required to avoid "breaking" or curdling sauce when adding cold
 cream to hot sauce.

Hollandaise Sauce

Yield: 1 qt (1 liter)   Cook time: 10 min

Equipment
double boiler, whip, kitchen spoon, small saucepan

Ingredients
egg yolks; 12
water, cold; 2 oz (50 ml)
butter, clarified, warm; 1 lb (450 g)
lemon juice, fresh; of 1 lemon
cayenne pepper; to taste
salt; to taste

Method
1) Whip egg yolks and water together in top of double boiler.
2) Insure that water in bottom of double boiler is simmering well but that water is shallow enough that it does not touch the top pot.
3) Stirring with the whip, down from the edges and up from the bottom of the bowl, whip lightly until egg yolks are cooked to a soft peak. It should be the consistency of a thin pudding.
4) Remove from heat and drizzle butter slowly into yolks, whipping constantly.
5) Add lemon juice, cayenne and salt.

Uses
This sauce is used for meat, fish, eggs, and vegetables. It is, of course, the basic ingredient in Béarnaise Sauce (see page 80).

Hollandaise Notes

Sanitation

Hollandaise is a very difficult sauce to hold for any length of time. The egg yolks make it an excellent medium for the growth of bacteria. Held warm, it can spoil in a few hours. When chilled, the butter hardens and makes the sauce solid. Even though the sauce can be revived after chilling by briskly whipping a little hot water into it, it is bad practice. It is also a bad idea to mix leftover sauce with fresh. For these reasons, make it fresh and use it within a few hours.

Before making this sauce in quantity, sterilize all tools and equipment that will be used by dipping them into boiling water. This may seem a bit extreme, but it is an important precaution. In a restaurant kitchen, sauces must sometimes be held under conditions that are ideal for bacterial growth. This step of sterilization precludes contamination at the very beginning!

Popular Hollandaise Variations

Grimod: Hollandaise + saffron
Mousseline: Hollandaise + whipped cream
Mikado: Hollandaise + tangarine juice and zest
Maltaise: Hollandaise + orange juice and zest
Divine: Hollandaise + sherry + sauterne + whipped cream
Maximillian: Hollandaise + anchovy extract
Figaro: Hollandaise + tomato puree
Double: Hollandaise made with double the normal number of yolks
Mock: Half Hollandiase + half velouté
Sabayon or Diet Style: Hollandaise made in the normal way, but without butter

Horseradish Sauce

Yield: 1 gal (4 liter)

Prep time: 10 min
Cook time: 20 min

Equipment
brazier, mixing bowl, whip, kitchen spoon, French knife, cutting board

Ingredients
*demi-glace; 1 gal (4 liter)
buerre manié; as needed
prepared horseradish, fresh; 2½ cup (625 ml) or to taste
sour cream or heavy cream; 1½ cup (375 ml)
salt; as needed
black pepper; as needed
parsley, chopped fine; ½ cup (½ bunch)

Method
1) Heat demi-glace to boiling. Thicken with beurre manié until it is a bit thicker than pancake syrup.
2) Remove from heat and add horseradish, cream, salt, pepper, and parsley.†

Uses
This sauce is excellent on all cuts of boiled and braised beef (such as short ribs).

*If demi-glace is not available, make from commercial beef base and use beurre manié to thicken. Do not reduce, or sauce will be too salty.
†Do not heat to boiling again after cream is added. See page 73 for cream-addition technique.

Italian Mint Sauce

Yield: 2½ cup (625 ml)   Prep time: 10 min

Equipment
saucepan, mixing bowl, kitchen spoon

Ingredients:
vinegar, boiling hot; 2 cup (½ liter)
mint leaves, fresh, chopped fine; 8 tbsp
sugar; 4 tbsp
salt; to taste
black pepper; to taste
water, boiled; 8 tbsp (160 ml)

Method
1) Pour vinegar over mint leaves in mixing bowl.
2) Add sugar, salt, pepper, and water.*

Uses
This sauce is used on mutton or lamb.

*If not used immediately, bottle and keep in cool place.

Lobster Thermidor Sauce

Yield: 1 gal (4 liter)   Prep time: 25 min
                                          Cook time: 1½ hr

Equipment
French knife, cutting board, whip, brazier, strainer, kitchen spoon

Ingredients
*Brown Sauce; ½ cup (125 ml)   black pepper; to taste
white wine; 1 pt (½ liter)   beurre manié; as needed
shallots, diced fine; 10   heavy cream; 1 pint (½ liter)
tarragon; 2 tbsp   vermouth; 2 oz (75 ml)
marjoram; 2 tbsp   egg yolks; 8
chervil or parsley; 2 tbsp   English mustard or dry mustard,
†Fish Stock; 2 gal (8 liter)   made into paste with water; 2 tbsp
salt; to taste

Method
1) Add Brown Sauce, wine, shallots, tarragon, marjoram, and chervil to stock and boil about 30 minutes or until volume of liquid is reduced by half.
2) Adjust taste with salt and pepper as required.
3) Reduce heat to rapid simmer and add beurre manié until sauce is fairly thick.
4) Remove from heat and add cream‡ and vermouth. Finish with egg yolks and mustard.

Uses
This sauce is used on lobster, crayfish, and other shellfish.

---

*See page 88.
†If Fish Stock is not available, make from a commercial base. Insure that a weak stock is used, so it will not be too salty after reduction.
‡See page 73 for technique to avoid curdling.

Marchand de Vin Butter

Yield: 1¾ lb (850 g)   Prep time: 30 min

Equipment
sauté pan, French knife, kitchen spoon, mixing bowl

Ingredients
red wine; 1 cup (250 ml)
shallots, chopped fine; 8 to 10
demi-glace; 3 tbsp (60 ml) *or* Brand's A.1.® steak sauce; 1 tsp (5 ml)
*butter; 1½ lb (800 g)
parsley, chopped fine; ½ bunch
lemon juice; 1 tsp (5 ml)
salt; to taste
black pepper; to taste

Method
1) Using low heat, reduce wine and shallots for about 20 minutes or until the consistency of wet sawdust.
2) Add the demi-glace or A.1.
3) Mixing very well, add butter, parsley, lemon juice, salt, and pepper.
4) When served, this butter should be the consistency of petroleum jelly. If it is too hard, warm slightly; if it is too soft, chill slightly.

Uses
This compound butter is memorable when used on steak or filet of beef.

---

*Use a good quality lightly salted butter. This is one recipe where margarine *should not* be used as a substitute.

Marinara Sauce

Yield: 1½ qt (1½ liter)

Prep time: 15 min
Cook time: 20 min

Equipment
French knife, cutting board, kitchen spoon, brazier, whip

Ingredients
olive oil; 4 tbsp (80 ml)
garlic cloves, diced fine; 6
*tomato puree, canned; 56 oz (1550 g)
sugar; 2 tbsp
parsley, chopped fine; 2 tbsp
oregano; 2 tsp
basil; 2 tsp
salt; 2 tsp
pepper; ½ tsp

Method
1) Heat oil and sauté garlic until golden brown.
2) Add tomato puree, sugar, parsley, oregano, basil, salt, and pepper and simmer 15 minutes.

Uses
This sauce is used on pasta and vegetable dishes.

*If fresh tomatoes are used, insure that tomatoes are very ripe and increase cooking time. For production cooking, the canned produce is more practical.

Mornay Sauce

Yield: 1 gal (4 liter)   Prep time: 20 min
                                          Cook time: 20 min

Equipment
French knife, cutting board, grater, small brazier, whip, kitchen spoon

Ingredients
*velouté, thick; 1 gal (4 liter)
onion, whole, peeled, studded with 6 whole cloves; 1
Swiss cheese, grated; 1 cup (150 g)
Parmesan cheese, grated; 1 cup (150 g)
nutmeg; 1 pinch
egg yolks; 3
salt; to taste
black pepper; to taste
†vermouth or Madeira wine; ½ cup (125 ml)

Method
1) Cook cloved onion in velouté until onion is soft. Discard onion.
2) Add both cheeses, a little at a time, whipping constantly.
3) Add nutmeg and cook a few minutes. Remove from heat.
4) Add egg yolks and mix very well.
5) Adjust taste with salt and pepper as required.

Uses
This sauce is used on fish, eggs, chicken, and vegetables.

---

*See page 125. Fish Velouté is used if sauce is intended for fish. Chicken Velouté is used if sauce is intended for eggs, chicken, or vegetables. If stock is not available, use commercial base.
†Vermouth is added if fish base is used; Madeira is added if chicken base is used.

Mushroom Sauce

Yield: 1 pt (½ liter)

Prep time: 15 min
Cook time: 20 min

Equipment
bowl, saucepan, kitchen spoon, French knife, cutting board, whip

Ingredients
*Chicken Stock; 3 cup (750 ml)
flour; 4 tbsp
butter; 4 tbsp
green onion, white part only, chopped fine; 3 tbsp
mushrooms, fresh, sliced thin; 6 cup (600 g)
whipping cream; 1 pt (½ liter)
salt; to taste
black pepper; to taste
nutmeg; to taste
red pepper; to taste

Method
1) Combine stock and flour and stir until flour is dissolved.
2) Melt butter over medium high heat. Add onion and sauté until tender, about 1 minute or until onion is transparent.
3) Reduce heat to medium. Add mushrooms and sauté about 3 minutes.
4) Add stock, stirring constantly. Cook until slightly thickened. Reduce heat and simmer 10 more minutes.
5) Blend in cream.†
6) Working by taste, season with salt, pepper, nutmeg, and red pepper.

Uses
This is a quick and tasty sauce for chicken.

---

*If Chicken Stock is not available, make from commercial base.
†See page 73 for technique required to avoid curdling.

Nantua Sauce

Yield: 2½ qt (2½ liter)   Prep time: 15 min
                                        Cook time: 25 min

Equipment
French knife, cutting board, brazier, whip, kitchen spoon, china cap, cheese-cloth

Ingredients
mirepoix   tomatoes, peeled, seeded, diced; 12
  carrots, small, diced fine; 2   (about 3½ cup)
  celery stalks, small dice; 4   tomato paste; 3 tbsp (60 g)
  onion, large, diced; 1   salt; to taste
butter; 6 oz (175 g)   cayenne pepper; to taste
cognac; ½ cup (125 ml)   beurre manié; as needed
dry white wine; 2 cup (½ liter)   heavy cream; 3 tbsp (60 ml)
*Fish Stock; 2 qt (2 liter)

Method
1) Sauté mirepoix in butter until tender.
2) Ignite cognac and mirepoix.
3) Add wine and stock and simmer for 15 minutes.
4) Add tomatoes, tomato paste, salt, and cayenne and simmer for 18 minutes.
5) Remove from heat and strain through cheesecloth.
6) Return to heat and add beurre manié until sauce is the consistency of pancake syrup.
7) Adjust taste with salt and cayenne as required.
8) Finish with cream.†

Uses
This sauce is used on fish, shellfish, and eggs.

*If Fish Stock is not available, make from commercial base.
†See page 73 for technique required to avoid curdling.

Périgueux Sauce

Yield: 1 gal (4 liter)

Prep time: 20 min
Cook time: 25 min

Equipment
French knife, cutting board, sauté pan, saucepan, strainer, skimmer, kitchen spoon

Ingredients
ham, boiled, chopped very fine; 1 lb (450 g)
shallots, chopped very fine; 25
ham fat; as needed
*demi-glace; 1 gal (4 liter)
bouquet garni
   bay leaves; 2
   thyme; ½ tsp
   parsley; ½ bunch

mushroom base; 1 tsp (if available)
tomato paste; 1 tbsp (20 ml)
mushrooms, fresh, diced; 10
salt; to taste
black pepper; to taste
Madeira wine; 1½ cup (3 dl)
beurre manié; as needed

Method
1) Sauté shallots and ham together in ham fat until tender, not brown.
2) Add to demi-glace and simmer 10 minutes.
3) Add bouquet garni, mushroom base, and tomato paste and simmer 10 minutes more.
4) Sauté mushrooms.
5) Adjust taste with salt and pepper as required.
6) Bring sauce to boil and thicken with beurre manié until sauce is the consistency of pancake syrup.
7) Remove from heat and strain.
8) Add mushrooms and wine in the last 5 minutes of cooking.

Uses
This sauce is excellent with beef.

---

*If demi-glace is not available, make from commercial beef base and use beurre manié to thicken. Do not reduce, or sauce will be too salty.

Port Wine Sauce

Yield: 1 qt (1 liter)   Prep time: 10 min
                                          Cook time: 25 min

Equipment
French knife, cutting board, sauté pan, saucepan, kitchen spoon, strainer

Ingredients
shallots, chopped fine; ½ cup (about 8 shallots)
peppercorns; 20
thyme; ½ tsp or to taste
orange juice; of 1 orange
orange zest, fine julienne; of 1 orange
lemon juice; of 1 lemon
port wine; 1 pt (½ liter)
*Brown Sauce; 1 qt (1 liter)
parsley, chopped fine; ½ cup (about ½ bunch)

Method
1) Reduce shallots, peppercorns, thyme, orange juice, orange zest, lemon juice, and wine until almost dry. Insure that the zest is poached in wine before making the reduction.
2) Add to Brown Sauce.
3) Add parsley and simmer 15 minutes.
4) Remove from heat and strain. Thicken with beurre manié if necessary.
5) Remove the poached zest from the strainings and add again to the sauce.

Uses
This sauce is excellent for *pâté*, venison, and chicken.

*See page 88.

Portugaise Sauce

Yield: I gal (4 liter)

Prep time: 20 min
Cook time: 25 min

Equipment
French knife, cutting board, brazier, kitchen spoon, strainer

Ingredients
onions, diced fine; 4
garlic cloves, diced fine; 6
olive oil, ½ cup (125 ml)
tomatoes, whole, canned, diced, drained; 3 cup (650 g)
cognac; ½ cup (I dl)
*demi-glace; I gal (4 liter)
tomato sauce; I cup (250 ml)
parsley, chopped; I cup (about I bunch)
salt; to taste
black pepper; to taste
beurre manié; as needed

Method
1) Sauté onions and garlic in oil. Do not brown.
2) Add tomatoes, cognac, and demi-glace and simmer 15 minutes.
3) Add tomato sauce and simmer 5 minutes more.
4) Add chopped parsley.
5) Adjust taste with salt and pepper as required.
6) Remove from heat and strain.
7) Thicken with beurre manié if required. Sauce should be thin.

Uses
This sauce is used on eggs, fish, meat, poultry, and veal.

*If demi-glace is not available, make from commercial base and thicken with beurre manié. Do not reduce, or sauce will be too salty.

Poulette Sauce

Yield: 1 gal (4 liter)   Prep time: 10 min
                                          Cook time: 10 min

Equipment
French knife, cutting board, saucepan, whip, kitchen spoon

Ingredients
*Mushroom Stock, very strong; 1 cup (250 ml)
†Allemande Sauce; 1 gal (4 liter)
salt; to taste
black pepper; to taste
lemon juice; to taste
parsley, chopped; 1 cup (1 bunch)

Method
1) Add stock to the Allemande Sauce and simmer about 5 minutes.
2) Adjust taste with salt and pepper as required.
3) Finish with lemon juice and parsley.

Uses
This sauce is used for vegetables, variety meats, frog legs, and mussels.

*If Mushroom Stock is not available, use a commercial mushroom base.
†See page 76.

Princess Sauce*

Yield: 1 qt (1 liter)

Prep time: 10 min
Cook time: 15 min

Equipment
French knife, cutting board, whip, brazier

Ingredients
†Shrimp Velouté; as needed
pimiento, chopped very fine; 1 cup
saffron; 2 pinches (commercial pack is 0.24 oz)
raisins, chopped very fine; 1 cup
vermouth, very dry; 2 oz (75 ml)
salt; to taste
black pepper; to taste
heavy cream; 1 cup (250 ml)

Method
1) Add pimiento, saffron, and raisins to velouté and simmer for about 10 minutes.
2) Add vermouth and cook 5 minutes more.
3) Adjust taste with salt and pepper as required.
4) Allow to rest 1½ hours before service.
5) Strain and reheat prior to use.
6) Finish with cream.†

Uses
This sauce is used on all types of fish, especially the delicate, nonoily fish.

---

*Created by Chef Chaton, in his teaching kitchen, in 1982.
†See page 125.
‡See page 73 for technique to avoid curdling.

Provençale Sauce #1 (Hot)

Yield: 2 cup (½ liter)   Prep time: 15 min
                                          Cook time: 25 min

Equipment
French knife, cutting board, sauté pan, saucepan, kitchen spoon

Ingredients
olive oil; ¼ cup (60 ml)
onions, diced fine; 2 oz (50 g)
tomatoes, peeled, seeded, chopped; 4
garlic cloves, chopped fine; 4
white wine; 1½ cup (375 ml)
*Veal Stock; 2 cup (½ liter)
parsley, chopped; ½ bunch
salt; to taste
black pepper; to taste

Method
1) Sauté onions in oil until transparent.
2) Add tomatoes and garlic and sauté 3 minutes more.
3) Add wine and simmer 7 minutes.
4) Add Veal Stock and simmer 15 minutes.
5) Finish with parsley.
6) Adjust taste with salt and pepper.

Uses
This sauce is used on eggs, fish, small cuts of meat, frog legs, poultry, and
vegetables.

---

*If Veal Stock is not available, a light stock made with commercial chicken base (depending
on the intended use) may be substituted. If base is used, omit salt.

Provençale Sauce #2 (Cold)

Yield: 2 cup (½ liter) Prep time: 10 min

Equipment
French knife, cutting board, mixing bowl, kitchen spoon

Ingredients
olive oil; 1 cup (¼ liter)
vinegar; ⅓ cup (1 dl)
capers; 2 tbsp
pickle, chopped; 1 tbsp
parsley, chopped; ½ bunch
garlic cloves, chopped; 5
tomatoes, peeled, seeded, drained, chopped; 4
eggs, hard cooked, chopped; 3
salt; to taste
black pepper; to taste

Method
1) Combine well all ingredients.
2) Adjust taste with salt and pepper as required.

Uses
This sauce is used on cold poultry and cold variety meats.

Rémoulade Sauce

Yield: I qt (I liter)   Prep time: 15 min

Equipment
French knife, cutting board, mixing bowl, whip, kitchen spoon

Ingredients
mayonnaise; I qt (I liter)
dry mustard; I ½ tbsp
gherkins, chopped fine; 3 ½ oz (100 g)
capers, chopped fine; 2 oz (60 g)
tarragon; I tsp
chervil or parsley, chopped fine; I tsp
anchovy, chopped fine; ½ tbsp
parsley, chopped fine; I tsp
salt; to taste
black pepper; to taste

Method
1) Combine all ingredients and mix well.
2) Adjust taste with salt and pepper as required.

Uses
This sauce is excellent for lobster, poultry, and variety meats.

Robert Sauce

Yield: 1 qt (1 liter)

Prep time: 10 min
Cook time: 20 min

Equipment
French knife, cutting board, sauté pan, saucepan, strainer, whip, kitchen spoon

Ingredients
onions, chopped fine; 2
butter; 4–5 oz (125 g)
dry white wine; 1 cup (¼ liter)
wine vinegar; ⅓ cup (1 dl)
peppercorns, crushed; 1 tsp
*demi-glace; 1 pt (½ liter)
salt; to taste
black pepper; to taste
beurre manié; as needed
Dijon mustard; 1½ tbsp (30 ml)

Method
1) Sauté onions in butter until lightly brown.
2) Drain onions and put in saucepan.
3) Add wine, vinegar, peppercorns, and demi-glace and simmer 15 minutes.
4) Adjust taste with salt and pepper as required.
5) Bring to slow boil. Add beurre manié until sauce is slightly thicker than pancake syrup.
6) Remove from heat and strain.
7) Add mustard. (Do not boil after adding mustard.)

Uses
This sauce is used for grilled meats, especially pork.

*If demi-glace is not available, make from commercial base.

Rouille Sauce

Yield: 1 cup (250 ml)   Prep time: 5 min

Equipment
mortar and pestle or garlic press, small bowl, spoon

Ingredients
mayonnaise; 1 cup (250 ml)
garlic cloves, crushed; 4
salt; to taste, about ¼ tsp
*Harissa Sauce; 1 tsp (5 ml)
saffron; ½ tsp
salt; to taste
black pepper; to taste
potatoes, mashed; as needed (substitute powdered instant mashed potatoes)
 (optional)

Method
1) Combine well mayonnaise, garlic, salt, Harissa Sauce, and saffron.
2) Adjust taste with salt and pepper as required.
3) Use potato if desired for consistency. The finished product should be a
   paste, like thin peanut butter.

Uses
This sauce is used to garnish Bouillabaisse and other fish soups. Spread it on
toasted croutons (made from stale French bread cut slightly smaller than the
bowl or cup used for service).

---

*Harissa Sauce is a seasoning paste that is made from red hot peppers, oriental spices, cumin,
salt, and olive oil. It is available at most wholesale grocers and retail gourmet shops.

Shrimp Sauce Chef Chaton

Yield: ½ gal (2 liter)

Prep time: 20 min
Cook time: I hr

Equipment
French knife, cutting board, saucepan, whip, kitchen spoon, strainer

Ingredients

mirepoix
    carrots, small, diced small; 2
    onions, medium, diced small; 3
    celery stalks, diced small; 3
olive oil; ⅔ cup (2 dl)
*cognac; 2 oz (50 ml)
†Shrimp Stock; ½ gal (2 liter)
tomatoes, fresh, peeled, seeded,
    diced; 6

tomato puree; 12 oz (300 g)
curry powder; 3 tbsp
bay leaves; 3
tarragon, dry; I tsp
cayenne pepper; ½ tsp
beurre manié; as needed
heavy cream; 2 cup (½ liter)
salt; to taste
white pepper; to taste

Method
1) Sauté mirepoix in oil until tender, about 8 minutes.
2) Ignite cognac and mirepoix.
3) When flame is exhausted, add stock and bring to boil. Reduce heat and simmer 10 minutes.
4) Add tomatoes, tomato puree, curry, bay leaves, tarragon, and cayenne and simmer 10 more minutes.
5) Remove from heat and strain. Adjust consistency with beurre manié until the sauce has the consistency of heavy syrup.
6) Finish with cream and adjust taste with salt and pepper.‡

Uses
This sauce is used primarily for shrimp, but it may be used for crayfish.

---

*Bourbon may be used instead. This is a matter of personal taste.
†If fresh Shrimp Stock (made with shells) is unavailable, use a commercial shrimp base.
‡See page 73 for technique to avoid curdling.

Smitane Sauce

Yield: 1 gal (4 liter)   Prep time: 15 min
                                         Cook time: 20 min

Equipment
French knife, cutting board, whip, kitchen spoon, small brazier, strainer

Ingredients
onions, diced fine; 4
butter; as needed
white vinegar; 1 cup
*Chicken Stock; 1 gal (4 liter)
tarragon; 2 tbsp
bay leaves; 3
salt; to taste
black pepper; to taste
beurre manié; as needed
sour cream; 1½ cup (375 ml)

Method
1) Sauté onion in butter until transparent. Do not brown.
2) Add vinegar and simmer until total volume of liquid is reduced by half.
3) Add stock, tarragon, and bay leaves and simmer 10 minutes.
4) Adjust taste with salt and pepper as required.
5) Bring to boil. Thicken with beurre manié until consistency is sufficient to coat the back of a spoon and resembles pancake syrup in thickness. Do not make too thick.
6) Remove from heat and strain.
7) Finish with sour cream just before service.†

Uses
This is a very important sauce for chicken, cornish hen, and other poultry.

*If Chicken Stock is not available, make from a commercial chicken base.
†Once sour cream is added, do not heat to boiling. This will cause sauce to curdle. See page 73.

Soubise Sauce

Yield: ½ gal (2 liter)   Prep time: 15 min
                                          Cook time: 20 min

Equipment
French knife, cutting board, saucepan, whip, food mill or blender, kitchen spoon

Ingredients
onions, chopped; 6
*Chicken Stock; ½ gal (2 liter)
beurre manié; as needed
salt; to taste
black pepper; to taste
cayenne pepper; to taste
lemon juice; ½ oz (40 ml)

Method
1) Boil onions in stock until very tender.
2) Strain out onions and puree. Set onion puree aside.
3) Using the same stock, add beurre manié to make a good Béchamel Sauce (see page 81).
4) Add onion puree, salt, pepper, and cayenne.
5) Finish with a few drops of lemon juice.

Uses
This sauce is used on chicken and vegetables.

*If Chicken Stock is not available, good results can be obtained with commercial chicken base.

Stroganoff Sauce

Yield: 1 gal (4 liter)   Prep time: 15 min
                                    Cook time: 35 min

Equipment
French knife, cutting board, brazier, whip, kitchen spoon, strainer

Ingredients
butter; as needed
onions, medium, diced fine; 3
*demi-glace; 1 gal (4 liter)
beurre manié; as needed
sherry; ½ cup (125 ml)
Dijon mustard; 3 tbsp (60 ml)
lemon juice; 2 tsp (10 ml)
sour cream; 4 tbsp (80 ml)
salt; to taste
white pepper; to taste

Method
1) Sauté onions in butter until they are golden brown.
2) Add demi-glace and simmer for 30 minutes.
3) Remove from heat and strain.
4) Bring to boil. Add beurre manié until desired consistency is obtained.
5) Add sherry and simmer for 5 minutes more.
6) Remove from heat and add mustard, lemon juice, and sour cream.†
7) Adjust taste with salt and pepper.

Uses
This sauce is used for beef, especially Stroganoff-style dishes.

---

*If demi-glace is not available, make from commercial base. Thicken with beurre manié. Do not reduce, or sauce will be too salty.
†See page 73 for technique to avoid curdling.

Supreme Sauce

Yield: 1 gal (4 liter)

Prep time: 20 min
Cook time: 40 min

Equipment
French knife, cutting board, stock pot, kitchen spoon, strainer, whip

Ingredients
*Chicken Velouté; ½ gal (2 liter)
*Veal Velouté; ½ gal (2 liter)
mushrooms, chopped; 1½ lb (675 g)
mushroom base; ¼ cup (60 ml)
salt; to taste
black pepper; to taste
butter; ½ lb (225 g)
whipping cream; ½ cup (125 ml)

Method
1) Mix the two veloutés, mushrooms, and mushroom base.
2) Adjust heat to high simmer and reduce for 40 minutes or until the volume of liquid is reduced by half.
3) Adjust taste with salt and pepper as required.
4) Remove from heat and strain.
5) Whip in butter.
6) Finish with cream.†

Uses
This sauce is used for poultry, eggs, variety meats, and vegetables.

---

*See page 125.
†See page 73 for technique to avoid curdling.

Tortue Sauce

Yield: 1 qt (1 liter)

Prep time: 10 min
Rest time: 24 hr
Cook time: 15 min

Equipment
stainless steel, ceramic, or glass bowl (do not use aluminum), whip, small brazier, kitchen spoon

Ingredients

marjoram; 1 tsp
savory; 1 tsp
sage; 1 tsp
rosemary; 1 tsp
thyme; 1 tsp
bay leaves; 3
cayenne pepper; ½ tsp

essence of truffle; 1 tsp (5 ml)
  (when available)
Madeira wine; 1½ cup (375 ml)
*Madeira Sauce; 1 pt (½ liter)
tomato paste; ½ cup (125 ml)
salt; to taste
black pepper; to taste

Method
1) Mix marjoram, savory, sage, rosemary, thyme, bay leaves, cayenne, essence of truffle, and wine.
2) Allow this infusion to rest 24 hours, chilled.
3) Add Madeira Sauce and tomato paste and simmer 15 minutes.
4) Adjust taste with salt and pepper as required.
5) Strain.

Uses
In France, this is a favorite sauce for calf's head. It is an excellent choice for all variety meats.

Madeira Sauce is made by adding ¾ cup of Madeira wine to 3 pints of demi-glace and simmering about 10 minutes.

Velouté Sauce

Yield: 1 gal (4 liter)   Prep time: 10 min
             Cook time: 20 min

Equipment
saucepan, whip, kitchen spoon

Ingredients
Fish, Chicken, or Veal Stock; 1 gal (4 liter)
beurre manié; as needed
heavy cream; 1 cup (¼ liter)

Method
1) Bring stock to rolling boil.
2) Add beurre manié and thicken to desired consistency.
3) Finish with cream.*

Uses
In haute cuisine, Velouté Sauce is primarily used as an ingredient in other sauces. For this reason the recipe contains no seasonings. Alone, it can be used for meat, fish, shellfish, poultry, game, and vegetables. Of course, it should be made with a stock compatible with its intended use and seasoned appropriately. Use fish stock for fish, lobster stock for lobster, veal stock for veal, chicken stock for poultry or vegetables and so on.

Historically, Velouté Sauce always contains cream. However, if it is made as an ingredient for another cream sauce, no cream should be added until it is time to finish the final sauce.

Veloutés can, of course, be made with commercial bases. The on-going problem with this approach is the salt. Because of the large amount of salt in commercial bases (used as a preservative) the stock will be too salty if it is made strong and reduced. Thus, if velouté made with base is added to other ingredients to make another sauce, extreme caution must be used in reducing and seasoning.

It must be remembered that the quality of the final sauce depends upon the quality of the ingredients used as well as the skill of the saucemaker. Chicken Stock can be substituted for veal; Fish Stock, for lobster; and com-

*See page 73 for technique to avoid curdling.

mercial-based stocks, for the real thing. But you must ask yourself if the time and money saved by such practices justifies the loss of quality in the end result.

Made the same way, but not as strong, Velouté Sauce is also used to make soups.

Victoria Sauce

Yield: 1 qt (1 liter)   Prep time: 15 min
                                         Cook time: 30 min

Equipment
small brazier, kitchen spoon, whip, small strainer, cheesecloth

Ingredients
*Brown Sauce; 1 qt (1 liter)
red port wine; 3 cup (¾ liter)
red currant jelly; 12 tbsp (240 ml)
peppercorns; 30
cloves; 7
cinnamon bark, pieces; 2
orange zest; of 2 oranges
orange juice; 1 cup (¼ liter)
cayenne pepper; to taste

Method
1) Add wine, jelly, peppercorns, cloves, cinnamon, and orange peels to Brown Sauce.
2) Reduce liquid by one-third, simmering slowly, whisking frequently, and taking care to stir and clear the bottom of the brazier to preclude scorching.
3) Add orange juice.
4) Adjust seasoning with cayenne. Cook 5 minutes more.
5) Remove from heat and strain.

Uses
This sauce is used for *pâté*, pork, and game.

*See page 88.

❖

Watercress Sauce

Yield: 1 pt (½ liter)

Prep time: 15 min
Cook time: 10 min

Equipment
French knife, cutting board, sauté pan, whip, kitchen spoon, brazier

Ingredients
shallots, chopped fine; 25
butter; 2 oz (60 g)
watercress, leaves only; 5 bunches
tarragon, fresh; 3 tsp
garlic cloves, chopped fine; 5
white wine; 1½ cup (375 ml)
whipped cream, very cold; 6½ oz (185 g)
salt; to taste
white pepper; to taste
gelatin; 2 tbsp (20 g) (2 envelopes)
lemon juice; 3 tbsp (60 ml)

Method
1) Sauté the shallots in butter on low heat until tender and colorless, about 2 minutes.
2) Add watercress, tarragon, garlic, and wine and simmer 2 minutes.
3) Add cream, salt, and pepper and simmer for 10 minutes.
4) Remove from heat and add gelatin. Mix carefully with whip.
5) Add lemon juice and mix well.
6) Cool for 30 minutes.

Uses
This is an excellent sauce for mousse of fish.

❖

White Wine Sauce

Yield: ½ gal (2 liter)   Prep time: 15 min
                                    Cook time: 30 min

Equipment
saucepan, whip, kitchen spoon

Ingredients
dry white wine; 1 cup (¼ liter)
*Fish Stock; 1 cup (¼ liter)
peppercorns; 10
†Fish Velouté; ½ gal (2 liter)
heavy cream; ½ cup (125 ml)
egg yolks; 6
cayenne pepper; ¼ tsp or to taste
lemon juice; 1 tbsp (20 ml)
butter; 6 oz (170 g)
vermouth, dry; 2 oz (50 ml)

Method
1) Mix together wine, stock, and peppercorns. Over slow heat, reduce the volume of liquid by half.
2) Add velouté, cream, yolks, cayenne, and lemon juice and simmer for a few minutes.
3) Remove from heat and finish by whipping in butter and vermouth.

Uses
This is an outstanding sauce for fish.

*If Fish Stock is not available, make with either commercial clam base or commercial shrimp base.
†See page 125.

Yorkshire Sauce

Yield: 1 qt (1 liter)   Prep time: 15 min
                                   Cook time: 25 min

Equipment
saucepan, paring knife, kitchen spoon, strainer

Ingredients
port wine; 1 pt (½ liter)
orange zest, fine julienne; of 2 oranges
*Brown Sauce; 1 pt (½ liter)
currant jelly; 2 tbsp (40 ml)
cinnamon; ¼ tsp or to taste
cayenne pepper; ¼ tsp or to taste
red wine; 1 cup (¼ liter)
orange juice; ½ cup (125 ml)
salt; to taste
black pepper; to taste
sugar; to taste

Method
1) Simmer port wine and orange zest for 5 minutes.
2) Remove from heat and strain. Save zest.
3) Add Brown Sauce, jelly, cinnamon, and cayenne and simmer 10 minutes.
4) Add red wine and simmer 10 minutes more.
5) Remove from heat and strain. Add orange juice and zest.
6) Adjust taste with salt and pepper. If there is not an acceptable sweet-sour taste, add just a touch of sugar.

Uses
This sauce is perfect for ham, duck, or *pâté*.

*See page 88.

Summary

Sauces can be considered the soul of cuisine. In many cases, they are much more important than the foods they complement and enhance. The function of a sauce is to add to the appearance, flavor, and texture of food. But sauces are much more than that—they are magic and a delight. They transform an ordinary dinner into an evening of pure pleasure. Sauces are the primary reason the French have been the acknowledged leaders in world cuisine, probably since before the fourteenth century.

In the best establishments, sauces are made fresh every day. However, basic sauces can be made in quantity and frozen for use as required. Finished sauces, especially cream sauces, should be made fresh daily. Cream should not be added to sauces until just before service. The rule for sauces is: Fresh as possible is best.

Roux has historically been the thickening agent for most sauces. The authors prefer beurre manié because it gives the saucemaker more control over the final consistency of the sauce. Cornstarch is primarily used for dessert sauces and in oriental cooking. Other thickeners (sometimes called *liaisons*) are egg yolk, cream, blood (rarely used today), and arrowroot.

The mother sauces are so called because they are not really finished sauces but are primary ingredients in a large number of other sauces. They include Béchamel, Brown, Hollandaise, Marinara, and Velouté.

Discussion Questions*

1) If there were only two choices, would it be better to use Hollandaise Sauce from a can or to do without it entirely?
2) Aside from their overall excellence, what is the one specific thing that made the French the acknowledged leaders in world cuisine?
3) In top-of-the-line restaurants, when and how often are sauces usually prepared, and why?
4) Other than roux and beurre manié, what are some other thickening agents?

---

*Some discussion questions require culinary deductive reasoning. They may not be answered *directly* in the text, but enough information is given to deduce the answer logically.

5) Why is it important to avoid the use of salt when making sauces based on stocks made from commercial bases and concentrates?

Test Questions

1) List the ingredients in Hollandaise Sauce. Name two variations of Hollandaise Sauce.
2) List the ingredients of Dugléré Sauce. What is the sauce best used for?
3) List the ingredients of Mornay Sauce. How is it made?
4) What are the ingredients of beurre manié? What is it used for?
5) List the ingredients of American Sauce.
6) List the ingredients of Bordelaise Sauce. How is it made?
7) List the ingredients of Smitane Sauce. How is it made?
8) List the ingredients of Brown Sauce. How is it made?
9) List five sauces that use Brown Sauce as a basic ingredient.
10) List the ingredients of Béchamel Sauce. List two sauces that use it as a basic ingredient.

Chapter 8
✥ Soups

Hot Soups
Soup Thérèse
Soup Nicole
Potage Solferino
Soup Pistou
Garbure Soup
New England Clam Chowder
Borsch of Duck
Costa Rican Fish Soup
Beef Barley Soup
Tomato Onion Soup Catalane
Petite Marmite Champs Elysées
Manhattan Clam Chowder
Chef Chaton's Special Borsch
Shrimp Bisque
Leek and Potato Soup
Chef Chaton's Royal Mushroom
  Soup
Grandmother Clementine Soup
Guadeloupean Red Bean Soup
Gratinée Auvergnate Soup
Onion Soup
Consommé Colbert
Bouillabaisse Mère Terrats

Potage St. Thibery
Oxtail Soup St. Martin
Caribbean Conch Chowder "*La
  Frégate*"
French Riviera Soup
Tomato Consommé with
  Fennel
Velouté Maria
Wagon Train Soup
Cold Soups
Apricot Soup
Velouté of Tomato
Apple Vichyssoise Soup
Vichyssoise
Avocado Tomato Soup
Strawberry Soup
Mulligatawny
Carrots Vichyssoise
Mint Cucumber Soup
Andalusian Gazpacho
Cantaloupe Rum Soup
Hot or Cold Soups
Cream of Lettuce Soup
Watercress Soup

G|rimod de la Reynière, a famous eighteenth century French gastro-
nome, effectively described the role of the soup in the dinner: "It
is to a dinner what a portico or a peristyle is to a building; that is to say, it
is not only the first part of it, but it must be devised in such a manner as

to set the tone of the whole banquet, in the same way as the overture of an opera announces the subject of the work." This is just as true today.

The soup is one of the first impressions customers have. If the soup is well chosen, served appropriately and correctly, and looks and tastes marvelously, the stage is set for the rest of the dinner. The customers will be mentally (or actually) salivating for more marvelous things to come. If the soup is less than perfect or badly served, then the guests will tend to be mentally prepared for the worst. They will look for mistakes. They will notice any poor service. They will notice a careless garnish or drops of sauce on the edge of a plate. They will not return if they leave unhappy. But they will talk to their friends who will talk to their friends. One unhappy customer may result in ten or fifteen people who will never enter your restaurant. And your establishment will have taken the first tiny step on the journey to bankruptcy court.

Indeed, it is often far better that the entrée be mediocre than the soup. A memorable soup will dispose customers to overlook a borderline entrée or simply to have it changed for another. A bad soup is a disaster that is uncorrectable.

Planning Soups

When planning soups, there are two areas of concern. One is the soup itself and the other is the manner of service. Consider service first.

Serving the Soup

In an intimate type of restaurant, where the emphasis is on family style dining, a soup tureen may be placed on the table and the guests permitted to serve themselves. For more formal service, the waiter serves the soup from a tureen placed on a nearby table. For banquet service, the soup is ladled out in the kitchen and taken directly to the table. In all cases, care must be taken to insure that hot soup is served very hot, in preheated bowls or cups. Likewise, cold soups should be served very cold, in chilled dishes. They should always be correctly garnished, with the necessary condiments available.

Whether serving a banquet or filling orders a la carte, it is important that chefs and their serving staffs are aware of the necessary balance between soup and entrée. A thick soup (like oxtail) should never precede a heavy entrée (like lamb shank or prime rib). A delicate consommé or a light cream of vegetable soup would be more appropriate. A variety of flavors should be present on the menu. For example, if the entrée is beef, a chicken or fish soup would be appropriate. A beef soup would not allow the guests to enjoy this great variety of flavors. Waiters and banquet sales staff should be prepared to guide firmly and diplomatically the choices of the guests.

Preparing the Soup

Soups can be divided into three basic categories: the consommés and clear soups; the thickened soups and cream soups; and the purées and thickened vegetable soups. These categories, of course, are not written in stone. They are just a convenient way to classify them.

Consommé is essentially clarified and seasoned stock, whereas *clear soup* is this same stock with meat or vegetables added. There are many different types of *thickened soups*. Some are thickened naturally by dissolving some of the starchy ingredients during the cooking process (like barley soup). Others are thickened by adding the puree of some vegetable ingredient of the soup (like bean soup). Others are thickened by adding roux or beurre manié. *Cream soups* are thickened by adding a liaison of egg yolks and cream just before service or by adding Béchamel Sauce (as in the veloutés). In some *purees*, thickening is accomplished during cooking, which releases vegetable starch into the soup. In other purees (such as bisques), purees of fish, shellfish, vegetables, or meat along with a liaison of cream and egg yolk produce the thickening. Most of the *thickened vegetable soups* use a liaison of cream and egg yolk.

Good soups require much labor and time if they are to be memorable. There is nothing wrong with using leftovers for soup, provided they are appropriate and fresh. It is a grave mistake to use any ingredient that is of dubious quality or at the end of its shelf life. Good soups, like any other good food, require quality, fresh ingredients. Chefs must insure that as much care—and often as much expense—is lavished on the soup as on the rest of the menu.

Many chefs, for whatever reason, neglect to *dépouiller* (skim fat from) their soups at the end of cooking. This serious mistake should never be permitted to occur. As with stocks, if the fat is not skimmed, customers will see globules of fat floating in their bowls. If their eyes and palates miss this mistake, their stomachs will not.

The best rule of thumb to follow when preparing the soups is to simmer rather than boil. Boiling may make soup cloudy and release sharp unpleasant tastes that destroy a soup. Reduction caused by evaporation will cause the tastes to become too strong and too salty. Finished soups must be held very hot, but they cannot be allowed to simmer on the steamtable. When making soups that contain cream and egg yolk, add these ingredients just before service. This precludes curdling and also avoids the scorched taste that develops if cream is kept on the fire too long.

The Recipes

Most of the soups presented here can be considered classic because either they have been in use for many years (in some cases for centuries) in the best restaurants and hotels or they are regional classics.

The regional soups (like *Aïgo Saou* on the French Riviera, Conch Chowder in the West Indies, New England Clam Chowder in Maine and New Hampshire, Bouillabaisse in Marseille, or Garbure in the Pyrenees) have their origins in the pots of the householders in these areas. Most were routine items on peasant's tables long before anyone but the very rich dined outside their home hearths. Because they were good, such regional soups found their way onto fashionable tables in restaurants in Paris, London, Rome, Nice, and New York and eventually were praised by the popular press.

Other soups in this chapter are original creations of Chef Chaton. But as he says: "Really there is nothing new in cuisine. If we create a soup that is truly original and then dig long enough in the recipes of antiquity, we are likely to find a soup served long ago that is very close to our own invention. Cuisine is much like fiction and the dramatic arts in this sense. Love, hate, war, peace, fear, contentment, death, suffering, happiness—such themes were and are the building blocks of literature from the beginning of the written word to the present. So it is with cuisine, there are limitless variations—but really *new*—never!"

Our primary concern is with presenting soups that are delicious, marketable, and valuable to know. We are not especially concerned with their history and origin. All that is another field entirely. A whole book, for example, could be written on the historical origins of Onion Soup and its variations. We are concerned, however, that you learn these soups and sell them.

Soup Thérèse (Hot)

Yield: 2 gal (8 liter)

Prep time: 20 min
Cook time: 45 min

Equipment
French knife, cutting board, peeler, brazier, kitchen spoon, mixing bowl, whip, blender

Ingredients
butter; 1 cup or as needed
carrots, medium size, sliced thin; 8
leeks, including green stem, medium sized, well washed, sliced thin; 8
onions, medium sized, sliced; 8
turnips, peeled, sliced; 8
potatoes, medium, peeled, sliced; 6
Chicken Stock; 2 gal (8 liter)
salt; to taste
white pepper; to taste
crème fraîche; 1 qt (1 liter)

Method
1) Melt butter over medium heat. Add carrots, leeks, onions, and turnips and sauté until golden brown.
2) Add potatoes, stock, salt, and pepper and bring to boil.
3) Reduce heat and simmer until vegetables are tender.
4) Puree in blender. Return to pot and stir in *crème fraîche*.
5) Reheat until hot enough for service, stirring frequently. Do not allow to boil.
6) Adjust taste with salt and pepper as required.

---

*If commercial *crème fraîche* cannot be obtained, a good substitute can be made by adding 2 tablespoons (40 ml) of buttermilk to 1 quart (1 liter) of heavy cream and mixing well.

Soup Nicole (Hot)

Yield: 2 gal (8 liter)   Prep time: 30 min
                                          Cook time: 25 min

Equipment
French knife, cutting board, large brazier, mixing bowl, kitchen spoon, slotted kitchen spoon, strainer

Ingredients
Beef Stock, rich, clarified; 2 gal (8 liter)
olive oil; 6–7 tbsp (120 ml)
salt; 2 tsp or to taste
peppercorns, 12
garlic cloves, chopped very fine; 12
bay leaves; 3
parsley; ½ bunch
black pepper; to taste
eggs, poached; 30
thyme; 1 tsp

Method
1) Combine stock, oil, salt, peppercorns, garlic, bay leaves, and parsley and bring to a boil.
2) Reduce heat to simmer for 15–20 minutes.
3) Remove from heat and strain.
4) Adjust taste with salt and pepper as required.

Service
1) Garnish with poached egg and sprinkle with thyme.

Potage Solferino (Hot)

Yield: 1 gal (4 liter) Prep time: 25 min
Cook time: 45 min

Equipment
French knife, cutting board, brazier, fine strainer, kitchen spoon

Ingredients

butter; 2 oz (60 g)
bacon, diced small; 5 oz (150 g)
carrots, sliced; 5 oz (150 g)
leeks, well washed, sliced; 5 oz
 (150 g)
onions, sliced; 5 oz (150 g)
white turnips, sliced; 5 oz (150 g)
celery, sliced; 2 oz (60 g)
tomatoes, peeled, seeded, diced;
 5 oz (150 g)

Beef Stock; 1½ gal (6 liter)
potatoes, medium, diced small; 4
bay leaves; 2
thyme; 1 pinch
salt; to taste
white pepper; to taste
carrots, diced fine; as needed
turnips, diced fine; as needed
string beans, diced fine; as needed
parsley, fresh, chopped; 1 bunch

Method
1) Melt butter and cook bacon until slightly browned.
2) Add carrots, leeks, onions, turnips, and celery. Sauté for 10 minutes.
3) Add tomatoes and stock and simmer 15 minutes.
4) Add potatoes, bay leaves, thyme, salt, and pepper and cook until potatoes are done.
5) Remove from heat and strain.
6) Adjust taste with salt and pepper as required.

Service
1) Garnish with carrots, turnips, string beans, and parsley.

Soup Pistou (Hot)

Yield: ½ gal (2 liter)

Prep time: 30 min
Cook time: 1½ hr

Equipment
French knife, cutting board, grater, saucepan or small brazier, kitchen spoon

Ingredients
dry white navy beans, small, soaked
  overnight in 2-qt salted water; 1 lb
  (450 g)
salt; to taste
green beans, sliced; ¼ lb (115 g)
carrots, medium, sliced; 3
*kidney beans; ¼ lb (115 g)
vermicelli; ⅛ lb (60 g)

black pepper; ½ tsp or to taste
pistou
  garlic cloves, mashed; 4
  basil, fresh; 4 tbsp
  tomatoes, large, peeled, seeded,
   diced; 4
  olive oil; ¼ cup (60 ml)
Gruyère cheese, grated; 1 cup

Method
1) Bring beans and the water that the beans have soaked in to a boil.
2) Add salt, green beans, and carrots. Lower heat and simmer gently for 1½ hours or until navy beans are tender.
3) Add kidney beans, vermicelli, and pepper and cook 15 minutes more.
4) Place the garlic, basil, and tomatoes in a mortar and crush to a paste.
5) Add the oil drop by drop as for mayonnaise.
6) Add this paste to the soup. Bring back to a boil, stir well, and immediately remove from heat.
7) Adjust seasoning.

Service
1) Garnish with grated Gruyère cheese.

*If dried kidney beans are used, soak overnight and cook with navy beans.

Garbure Soup (Hot)

Yield: I gal (4 liter)

Prep time: 25 min
Cook time: 2 hr

Equipment
French knife, cutting board, 2 saucepans or braziers, kitchen spoon, food mill or blender, grater

Ingredients
carrots, medium; diced fine; 4
turnips, medium, diced fine; 4
potatoes, medium, diced fine; 6
white cabbage, sliced thin; 2.2 lb
 (I kg)
butter; as needed
dry white navy beans, small, soaked
 overnight in enough water to
 cover; 7 oz (200 g)

tomatoes, fresh, peeled, seeded,
 diced; 10 oz (300 g)
water; I gal (4 liter)
salt; to taste
black pepper; to taste
*croutons, small; as needed

Method
1) Cook carrots, turnips, potatoes, and cabbage in butter, covered, until tender.
2) In a separate brazier, cook beans and tomatoes in the water that the beans have soaked in. Simmer until beans are tender.
3) Pass everything in both pots through food mill or puree.
4) Add water, salt, and pepper and simmer about 30 minutes.

Service
1) Garnish with crouton.

*Make croutons by cutting sliced white bread with a cookie cutter into rounds slightly smaller than service cups. Dip the bread in beaten egg, drizzle with melted butter, sprinkle with grated Swiss cheese, and bake at 350°F until golden brown.

New England Clam Chowder (Hot)

Yield: 2½ gal (10 liter)   Prep time: 30 min
                                            Cook time: 1 hr

Equipment
heavy saucepan or brazier, kitchen spoon, French knife, cutting board

Ingredients
onions, diced; 1 lb (450 g)   clams, canned, drained, chopped;
green pepper, diced; ½ lb (225 g)   1 qt (1 liter)
celery, diced; 1 lb (225 g)   salt pork, small dice; ½ lb (225 g)
garlic cloves, minced; 4   thyme; 1 tsp
butter; 1 lb (450 g)   salt; to taste
flour; ½ lb (225 g)   white pepper; to taste
clam juice or Fish Stock; 1½ gal   light cream; 1 gal (4 liter)
 (6 liter)
potatoes, peeled, diced small; 2 lb
 (900 g)

Method
1) Sauté onions, green pepper, celery, and garlic in butter for about 10 minutes or until soft.
2) Add flour and cook about 5 minutes more or until roux is cooked, but not browned.
3) Add clam juice or Fish Stock and cook until the vegetables are slightly tender (al dente).
4) Add potatoes, clams, salt pork, thyme, salt, and pepper and continue to simmer until potatoes are tender.
5) Add cream and simmer briefly.
6) Adjust taste with salt and pepper as required.

Service
1) Serve with oyster crackers.

Borsch of Duck (Hot)

Yield: 3 gal (12 liter)

Prep time: 1 hr
Cook time: 3½ hr

Equipment
French knife, cutting board, paring knife, large kitchen spoon, grater, mixing bowl

Ingredients

onions, peeled, diced (medium brunoise); 4

carrots, peeled, cubed (medium brunoise); 6

cabbage, sliced fine; 2

parsley; 1 bunch

bay leaves; 5

Chicken Stock; 2 ½ gal (10 liter)

peppercorns, crushed; 25

ducks, 3-4; 12 lb (5 kg)

beets, raw, peeled, grated; 3

vinegar; ½ cup (125 ml)

flour; ½ cup

water; 1 qt (1 liter)

Italian sausage or kielbasa, cubed (medium brunoise); 2.2 lb (1 kg)

beets, raw, peeled, cubed (medium brunoise); 9

heavy cream or sour cream; as needed

Method
1) Place onions, carrots, cabbage, parsley, and bay leaves in a large pot. Cover with stock and peppercorns and cook.
2) When the liquid boils, cook for 1 hour.
3) Add ducks and simmer for 2 hours.
4) Mix grated beets and vinegar.
5) Mix flour and water until there are no lumps.
6) Remove the ducks, parsley, and bay leaves from the pot and remove fat from the broth.
7) Reheat the liquid until boiling and add the flour mixture. Mix very well to insure that there are no lumps.
8) Remove bones from the duck and cut meat into small pieces.
9) Add the duck, sausage, cubed beets, and vinegar mixture to the broth and boil 5 minutes.
10) Remove from heat and allow to rest 5 minutes.

Service
1) Garnish with a dollop of heavy cream or sour cream.

Costa Rican Fish Soup (Hot)

Yield: 2½ gal (10 liter)

Prep time: 20 min
Cook time: 45 min

Equipment
French knife, cutting board, large sauté pan or brazier

Ingredients

butter; 3½ oz (100 g)
onions, chopped fine; 18 oz (500 g)
celery, with leaves, chopped fine;
  14 oz (400 g)
garlic cloves, fresh, crushed; 6
plum tomatoes, canned, diced, without juice; 3 lb (1.35 kg)
Fish Stock; 2 gal (8 liter)

Chicken Stock; 3 cup (¾ liter)
dry white wine; 1 qt (1 liter)
salt; to taste
tabasco; 2 tsp (10 ml)
leaf thyme; 1½ tsp
parsley, chopped; 3 cup
*fish fillets, cut into 1-in. (8 cm)
  squares; 3 lb (1.35 kg)

Method
1) Melt butter and add onions, celery, and garlic.
2) Cook over medium heat about 5 minutes or until tender.
3) Add tomatoes, Fish Stock, Chicken Stock, wine, salt, tabasco, and thyme and simmer uncovered for 30 minutes.
4) Add parsley and fish and cook 5 minutes more. Do not overcook fish.†

---

*Any fish fillet will work, but we prefer cod or haddock.
†Overcooking will cause it to fall apart and become tasteless.

Beef Barley Soup (Hot)

Yield: 3 gal (12 liter)

Prep time: 30 min
Cook time: 2–2½ hr

Equipment
French knife, cutting board, brazier, kitchen spoon

Ingredients
mirepoix
    carrots, diced small; 3
    celery stalks, diced small; 3
    onions, medium, diced small; 3
vegetable oil; as needed
beef, chuck or round, raw or cooked, diced small; 3 lb (1.35 kg)
Beef Stock; 3 gal (12 liter)
tomatoes, fresh, peeled, seeded, diced; 4–5
barley; 1 lb (450 g)
parsley, chopped fine; ½ bunch
bay leaves; 3
salt and pepper; as needed

Method
1) Sauté mirepoix in oil until tender, but not brown.
2) Add beef, stock, tomatoes, barley, parsley, and bay leaves and simmer 2–2½ hours or until beef is tender.
3) Adjust taste with salt and pepper.

Tomato Onion Soup Catalane (Hot)

Yield: 2 gal (8 liter)   Prep time: 20 min
                                          Cook time: 45 min

Equipment
French knife, cutting board, brazier, whip, kitchen spoon

Ingredients
butter; ½ lb (225 g)
onions, halved, sliced very thin; 8
tomatoes, fresh, peeled, seeded, diced; 9 lb (4 kg)
thyme; 1 tbsp
allspice, ground; ½ tsp
salt; to taste
white pepper; to taste
Chicken Stock; 2 gal (8 liter)
tomato paste; 4 tbsp (80 ml)

Method
1) Sauté onions with butter about 15 minutes or until soft and transparent.
2) Add tomatoes, thyme, allspice, salt, and pepper and sweat about 10 minutes.
3) Add stock and tomato paste and simmer about 20 minutes.
4) Adjust taste with salt and pepper as required.

Service
1) Serve chilled.
2) Garnish with cube-shaped croutons.

1 Chicken cooked in banana leaves and served with coulis of pineapple is very popular in Thailand. (See page 211)

2 Petite Marmite Champs Elysées. This soup, topped with puff pastry, is a dramatic presentation. It was created by Chef Paul Bocusse for French President Giscard d'Estaing. (See page 147)

3 Royal Mushroom Soup, created by Chef Roland Chaton (See page 153)

4 A classic Escargot presentation (See page 44)

All Photos by Bill Freeland.

5 Dessert Crepes (See page 325)

6 *Jam of Onions is a good example of modern international cuisine. (See page 299)*

7 *Vol au Vent Financiére (See page 227)*

8 *Potato Voisin. This style of potato is well suited for beef or lamb. (See page 290)*

All Photos by Bill Freeland.

9 *Aigo Saou. Garnished with poached egg, this soup has been popular on the French Riviera for centuries. (See page 163*

10 Chef Chaton's version of classic Russian Borscht (See page 150)

11 Couscous Tunisian is a national dish in that country. (See page 256)

12 Ramekins of Shrimp and Scallops (See page 267)

13 Filet of Beef Wellington (See page 247)

14 Magret of Duck served with Coulis of Blackberry. The meat should be served slightly pink. (See page 217)

All Photos by Bill Freeland.

15 Eggplant Fulton was created by
Chef Roland Chaton for Admiral Fulton.
(See page 288)

16 Bird Casanova with Smitane Sauce
was created by Chef Roland Chaton.
(See page 221)

17 Pineapples with Black Pepper
was created by the Troisgros brothers, chefs and
restaurateurs in Roanne, France.
(See page 322)

18 Fresh Truffles
(See page 229)

All Photos by Bill Freeland.

Petite Marmite Champs Elysées (Hot)

Yield: 3 gal (12 liter)

Prep time: 1½ hr
Cook time: 2 hr

Equipment
French knife, cutting board, rolling pin, 5 saucepans, large braziers, pastry brush, china cap

Ingredients
Beef Stock, well seasoned; 3 gal (12 liter)
beef, diced small; 1 lb (450 g)
chicken, diced small; ½ lb (225 g)
onion, fine julienne; ½lb (225 g)
carrots, fine julienne; ½ lb (225 g)
celery, fine julienne; ½ lb (225 g)
cabbage, fine julienne; ½ lb (225 g)
turnips, fine julienne; ½ lb (225 g)
ham, cooked, fat removed, fine julienne; ½ lb (225 g)
puff pastry, rolled sheets; as needed

Method
1) Cook beef and chicken in stock about 1 hour or until tender.
2) Strain out all meat and reserve stock. Wash meat in running cold water to remove impurities and set aside.
3) Cook all vegetables by adding them to boiling salted water. They cannot be cooked together, for each vegetable has a separate cooking time: carrots, 6 min; and celery, onions, turnips, and cabbage, 4 min. Vegetables must be cooked al dente (firm, never mushy). When cooking is completed, add cold water immediately to stop cooking process.
4) In separate ovenproof-type ceramic serving cups, set up individual vegetables, individual meats, and puff paste.*
5) Using a saucer or a similar implement as a guide, cut round pieces of puff pastry about 2 inches wider in diameter than the diameter of serving cups.
6) Ladle each soup cup with reserved stock.† Add a pinch of beef, chicken, onion, carrots, celery, cabbage, turnips, and ham to each cup.

*If necessary, serving cups can be filled 1 day prior to service.
†Leave ½ inch (1 cm) clearance for dough from rim of cup; contact with liquid will prevent dough from rising.

7) Wet sides of cups with water and cover with pastry circle, sealing the edges to the wet sides of the cup. Egg wash center of top of the dough.

8) Bake in 400°F oven approximately 15 minutes or until pastry is golden brown. Because ovens vary, check pastry on a sample soup cup to insure that it is done. The pastry will puff up and form a beautiful pastry crown over the soup cup.

Service

1) Serve immediately. Once baked, this soup cannot be held long in a warmer. The soup vapors will cause the pastry to become mushy. Your guests will be pleased enough to forget any delay as these are cooked to order.

(See color plate 2)

Manhattan Clam Chowder (Hot)

Yield: 4 gal (16 liter)

Prep time: 30 min
Cook time: 1½ hr

Equipment
French knife, cutting board, large brazier, large whip, kitchen spoon

Ingredients
onions, diced small; 1¼ lb (560 g)
celery, diced small; 1¼ lb (560 g)
green peppers, diced small; 1¼ lb (560 g)
leeks, well washed, diced small; 4
butter or margarine; 12 oz (340 g)
flour; 10 oz (280 g)
*clam juice, canned; 4 gal (16 liter)
water; to taste (if needed)
tomatoes, canned, drained, diced; 20 oz (570 g)

potatoes, diced small; 4 lb (1.8 kg)
clams, diced small; 4 lb (1.8 kg)
curry powder; to taste (optional)
thyme; 2 tsp
salt; to taste
white pepper; 1 tsp or to taste
tabasco; ½ oz (15 g)
Worcestershire sauce; 2 oz (60 g)
parsley, fresh, chopped; 2 cup (1½ bunch)

Method
1) Sauté onions, celery, peppers, and leeks in butter until tender.
2) Sprinkle a little flour (*singer*) at a time on vegetables and mix well. Cook 3 minutes.
3) Add clam juice and water. Cover and cook for 5 minutes.
4) Add tomatoes, potatoes, clams, curry, thyme, salt, and pepper and cook 1½ hours, simmering slowly.
5) Add tabasco, Worcestershire sauce, and parsley and simmer 10 minutes.
6) Skim off fat if necessary.
7) Adjust taste with salt and pepper as required.

Service
1) Serve very hot with traditional oyster crackers on the side.

*If clam juice is not available, make with clam base and water.

Chef Chaton's Special Borsch (Hot)

Yield: 4 gal (16 liter)

Prep time: 40 min
Cook time: 1½ hr

Equipment
French knife, cutting board, large pot, large whip, kitchen spoon

Ingredients

Beef Stock; 4 gal (16 liter)
beef, diced small; 2½ lb (1.2 kg)
carrots, fine julienne; 2 lb (900 g)
celery, fine julienne; 2 lb (900 g)
tomato puree; 1 qt (900 g)
onions, fine julienne; 1½ lb (680 g)
dill, fresh, chopped; 3 bunches
potatoes, fine julienne; 1½ lb (680 g)
cabbage, shredded fine; 1
sugar; ¼ cup (60 g)

green peppers, fine julienne; 2½ lb
 (1.2 kg)
lemon juice; of 1 lemon
salt; to taste
peppercorns, well crushed; 15
bay leaves; 3
black pepper; to taste
beets, fresh, fine julienne; 4 lb
 (1.8 kg)
sour cream; as needed (1 tsp per
 serving)

Method
1) Bring stock to a boil. Add beef and simmer for 30 minutes. Skim off scum as required.
2) Add carrots, celery, tomato puree, onions, dill, potatoes, cabbage, sugar, peppers, lemon juice, salt, peppercorns, and bay leaves and simmer 45 minutes.
3) Adjust taste with salt and pepper as required.
4) Add beets and cook 15 minutes more.

Service
1) Serve hot.
2) Garnish with a dollop of sour cream.
3) May be accompanied by small portions of chicken feuilletage.

(See color plate 10)

Shrimp Bisque (Hot)

Yield: 1 gal (4 liter)

Prep time: 15 min
Cook time: 30 min

Equipment
French knife, cutting board, brazier, kitchen spoon, food mill or blender

Ingredients
mirepoix
    onions, diced small; 8 oz (225 g)
    celery, diced small; 8 oz (225 g)
    carrots, diced small; 6 oz (170 g)
leeks, cleaned well, diced; 12 oz (350 g)
butter; ½ lb (225 g)
cognac; 5 oz (150 ml)
*Shrimp Stock; 1 gal (4 liter)
thyme; 2 tsp

bay leaves; 3
salt; to taste
black pepper; to taste
chablis; 1 cup (¼ liter)
shrimp, unshelled, cooked; 5 lb (2.25 kg)
cognac; 1 tbsp (20 ml)
heavy cream; 1 pt (½ liter)
tomato paste; 1 tsp (5 ml)

Method
1) Sauté mirepoix and leeks for 5 minutes or until nearly tender.
2) Cover with cognac and ignite with a lighted match.
3) Add stock, thyme, bay leaves, salt, and pepper and simmer 30 minutes.
4) Add chablis and shrimp and simmer 3–5 minutes.
5) Puree. If good blender is used, puree shrimp with shells on to improve taste. If food mill is used, shell shrimp before using.
6) Add cognac, cream, and tomato paste. Do not bring to boil again after cream is added.
7) Adjust taste with salt and pepper as required.

Service
1) Serve quite hot.

*If Shrimp Stock is not available, use a commercial shrimp base.

Leek and Potato Soup (Hot)

Yield: 2 gal (8 liter)

Prep time: 10 min
Cook time: 30 min

Equipment
brazier, French knife, cutting board, kitchen spoon, food mill or blender

Ingredients
leeks, white only, cleaned well, diced; 5 lb (2.25 kg)
butter; ½ lb (225 g)
potatoes, sliced; 4 lb (1.8 kg)
Chicken Stock; 2 gal (8 liter)
bay leaves; 2
salt; to taste
white pepper; to taste
beurre manié; as needed
heavy cream; 1 pt (½ liter)
chives, chopped; as needed

Method
1) Sauté leeks in butter.
2) Add potatoes, stock, bay leaves, salt, and pepper and cook 30 minutes or until potatoes are tender.
3) Purée.
4) Return to brazier and bring to boil. Adjust consistency with beurre manié, if required. It should be the consistency of gruel.
5) Adjust taste with salt and pepper as required.
6) Add heavy cream.

Service
1) Garnish with chives.

Chef Chaton's Royal Mushroom Soup (Hot)

Yield: 2 gal (4 liter)

Prep time: 15 min
Cook time: 30 min

Equipment
French knife, cutting board, sauté pan, large brazier, kitchen spoon, buffalo chopper (if available)

Ingredients
mushrooms, chopped very fine; 4 lb (1.8 kg)
onions, chopped very fine; 2 lb (900 g)
butter; as needed
*Harvey's® Bristol Cream®; 2 cup (½ liter)
Chicken Stock, rich; 2 gal (8 liter)
Flour and water combined to consistency of Béchamel; as needed
paprika; touch
salt; to taste
black pepper; to taste
heavy cream; 1 qt (1 liter)

Method
1) Sauté mushrooms and onions in butter until tender.
2) Add Harvey's® Bristol Cream® and bring to boil.
3) While boiling, add stock.
4) Increase heat to bring soup to rolling boil and thicken with flour-water. When thickened, reduce heat again to simmer. Total cooking time from when the mushrooms, onions, and sherry were added to stock should be 20 minutes.
5) Add paprika and remove from heat.
6) Adjust taste with salt and pepper as required.
7) Add heavy cream. After cream is added do not bring to boil again.

(See color plate 3)

*Other dry sherries will not produce the desired taste.

Grandmother Clementine Soup (Cabbage Soup) (Hot)

Yield: 1 gal (4 liter)

Prep time: 40 min
Cook time: 2 hr

Equipment
French knife, cutting board, roast pan, kitchen spoon, brazier, skimmer, meat saw

Ingredients

beef bones, sawed into 1½-inch (40-mm) pieces; 5 lb (2.25 kg)
onions, diced fine; 2 cup
carrots, medium dice; 6
garlic cloves, chopped; 6
bay leaves; 3
short ribs; 5 lb (2.25 kg)
thyme; 2 tsp
paprika; 1 tsp
water; 3½ qt (3½ liter)
cabbage, shredded; 2

tomatoes, canned, drained, diced; 2 lb (900 g)
salt; to taste
tabasco; 1 tsp (5 ml)
parsley, chopped; as needed
lemon juice; 2 tsp (10 ml)
sauerkraut, canned, well rinsed, drained; 2 lb (900 g)
sugar; 2 tsp
black pepper; to taste
sour cream; as needed

Method
1) Place beef bones, onions, carrots, garlic, and bay leaves in roast pan. Put short ribs on top and sprinkle with thyme and paprika. Roast uncovered in 450°F oven 25 minutes, until meat is browned.
2) Transfer everything to a large brazier. Add water, cabbage, tomatoes, salt, and tabasco. Bring to boil then reduce heat and simmer 1½ hours.
3) Skim off fat well.
4) Add parsley, lemon juice, sauerkraut, and sugar and simmer uncovered 1 hour.
5) Remove bones and short ribs from brazier. Debone ribs; dice meat and discard fat.
6) Return meat to brazier and cook 5 minutes more.
7) Adjust taste with salt and pepper as required.

Service
1) Garnish with sour cream.

Guadeloupean Red Bean Soup (Hot)

Yield: I gal (4 liter)
Prep time: 40 min
Cook time: 3 hr

Equipment
French knife, cutting board, large brazier, kitchen spoon

Ingredients
bacon, diced small; 16 strips
celery stalks, diced small; 8
leeks, white part only, diced; 8
onions, small, diced; 4
turnips, peeled, diced; 4
carrots, sliced thin; 4
all purpose flour; 8 tbsp
Beef Stock; 1½ gal (6 liter)
dry red kidney beans, soaked in
  water overnight; 6 cup (1,000 g)
  (wet measure)
ham hocks, smoked; 2

dry red wine; 2 cup (½ liter)
tomato puree; 2 cup (400 g)
bouquet garni (tied in cheesecloth)
  peppercorns; 20
  bay leaves; 5
  cloves; 6
  garlic cloves; 12
oregano, dried; 2 tsp
hot pepper flakes; 1 tsp
salt; to taste
black pepper; to taste

Method
1) Brown bacon over medium heat. Remove and set aside.
2) Sauté celery, leeks, onions, turnips, and carrots in bacon fat, stirring frequently, about 10 minutes.
3) Sprinkle flour over vegetables, mix well, and sweat 5 more minutes.
4) Add stock, beans, ham hocks, wine, tomato puree, bouquet garni with garlic cloves, oregano, and pepper flakes. Heat to boiling and reduce to simmer.
5) Simmer covered, about 3 hours or until beans are tender. Remove from heat.
6) Discard bouquet garni. Remove ham hock and bone. Dice any useable meat and return to soup.
7) Skim off fat and correct taste.

Gratinée Auvergnate **Soup** (Hot)

Yield: 4 gal (16 liter)   Prep time: 25 min
                                           Cook time: 45 min

Equipment
French knife, cutting board, large soup pot, kitchen spoon, sauté pans

Ingredients
onions, medium, sliced thin; 15
butter; 23 oz (650 g)
Beef Stock, rich; 2 gal (8 liter)
Chicken Stock, rich; 2 gal (8 liter)
blue cheese; 1 lb (450 g)
walnuts, chopped; 14 oz (400g)
*croutons; as needed
Swiss cheese or Mozzarella cheese, sliced thin; as needed
salt; to taste
black pepper; to taste

Method
1) In butter, sauté onions until tender and golden. Drain butter when finished.
2) Bring stocks to a simmer. Add onions and simmer about 45 minutes.
3) Combine ½ pound of butter with the blue cheese, using more butter if required to make a heavy paste. Add 1 quart stock from the soup and mix very well.
4) Adjust taste with salt and pepper if required.
5) Add cheese mixture to the soup *after* it has simmered 45 minutes. Remove from heat.
6) Ladle soup into bowls. Add a pinch of chopped walnuts, crouton, and thin slices of cheese.
7) Place under broiler until cheese is bubbling and golden brown to dark brown. Serve at once.

*For croutons, cut stale slices of white bread slightly smaller than soup bowl using cookie cutter or similar device. Brush both sides with butter or margarine; brown in moderate oven until golden and quite dry.

Onion Soup (Hot)

Yield: 1¼ gal (5 liter)   Prep time: 20 min
                                   Cook time: 25 min

Equipment
French knife, cutting board, sauté pan, large saucepan, skimmer, kitchen spoon

Ingredients
onions, sliced thin; 10
butter; as needed
stock, ½ beef, ½ chicken, rich; 1¼ gal (5 liter)
sherry wine; 1 cup (¼ liter)
Worcestershire sauce; 1 tbsp (20 ml)
salt; to taste
black pepper; to taste
*croutons, slightly smaller than serving bowl; as needed
†Swiss cheese or Mozzarella cheese, sliced thin; as needed

Method
1) Sauté onions in butter until transparent, not brown.
2) Add to stock and simmer 20 minutes.
3) Add sherry and Worcestershire sauce and simmer 5 minutes.
4) Adjust taste with pepper and salt.
5) Fill soup bowls and add croutons. Put cheese on top of crouton, covering crouton and liquid.
6) Place under hot broiler until cheese is melted and golden to brown.

---

*Cut croutons from sliced stale French bread. Brush both sides with butter or margarine and brown in moderate oven until quite dry.
†Provolone cheese may also be used.

Consommé Colbert (Hot)

Yield: 2 gal (8 liter)   Prep time: 30 min
                                    Cook time: 45 min

Equipment
large saucepan, kitchen spoon, French knife, cutting board, small saucepan, small sauté pan

Ingredients
*Beef Stock, rich; 2½ gal (9 liter)
cabbage, medium, fine julienne; 1
carrots, small, fine julienne, 2
celery stalks, fine julienne; 6
onion, large, fine julienne; 1
rutabaga, fine julienne; 1 (or substitute 3 turnips)
salt; to taste
black pepper; to taste
mushrooms, fresh, sliced thin; 12
eggs, poached; 25
parsley, fresh, chopped; as needed

Method
1) Set stock to simmer.
2) Add cabbage, carrots, celery, onion, and rutabaga and simmer 45 minutes.
3) Add salt and pepper.
4) Sauté mushrooms.
5) Fill soup bowl and add handful of mushrooms and poached egg.

Service
1) Garnish with parsley.

*It is best to use a stock prepared from scratch and clarified in the usual way. If it is necessary to use a commercial base to boost the flavor of a weak natural stock, do so before clarification.

❊

Bouillabaisse Mère Terrats (Hot)

Yield: 1 gal (4 liter)

Prep time: 1 hr
Cook time: 40 min

Equipment
French knife, cutting board, medium brazier, small cleaver, stiff vegetable brush, kitchen spoon

Ingredients

carrots, diced small; ½ cup (100 g)
leeks, cleaned well, diced small; 3
onions, diced fine; ¾ cup (150 g)
olive oil; ½ cup (125 ml)
tomatoes, canned, drained, diced;
  1 qt (450 g)
garlic cloves, crushed; 6
orange slices; of 1 orange
parsley, chopped; 2 tbsp
fennel, chopped; 2 tbsp (1 tbsp substitute Pernod™) (20 ml)
bay leaves; 2
thyme; 1 tsp
salt; to taste
black pepper; to taste
water; ½ gal (2 liter)

lobster, 2-lb (900-g) size, cut in
  pieces, shell on; 2
eel, 1-in. slices; 1 lb (450 g)
sea bass, 1-in. cubes; 2 lb (900 g)
red snapper, 1-in. cubes; 3 lb
  (1.35 kg)
mussels, in shells, scrubbed, sand
  free; 2 doz.
clams, in shells, scrubbed, sand free;
  2 doz
shrimps, 10/15 size, shelled; 2 doz
butter, melted; ½ cup (100 g)
French bread, thick slices; as needed
saffron; 1 tsp
*Rouille Sauce; as needed

Method
1) Sauté carrots, leeks, and onions in oil for 8 minutes or until soft.
2) Add tomatoes, garlic, orange slices, parsley, fennel, bay leaves, thyme, salt, and pepper.
3) Add water, saffron, lobster, and eel and simmer 10 minutes.
4) Add bass and snapper and simmer 8 minutes more.
5) Add mussels, clams, and shrimp and simmer covered 18 minutes or until shells open. Remove from heat.
6) Butter both sides of bread and brown in moderate oven.

*See page 118.

Service
1) Serve with toast and Rouille Sauce in a separate dish.

Potage St. Thibery (Hot)

Yield: 2 gal (8 liter)   Prep time: 25 min
                                          Cook time: 1 hr, 20 min

Equipment
French knife, cutting board, blender, medium brazier, kitchen spoon

Ingredients
leeks, cleaned well, cut in large slices; 12
olive oil; 1 cup (250 ml)
tomato paste; 1 cup (250 ml)
Chicken Stock; 2 gal (8 liter)
potatoes, peeled, cut into medium cubes; 7
granulated sugar; 1 tbsp
salt; to taste
black pepper; to taste
saffron; ¼ oz (2 g)

Method
1) Sauté leeks using olive oil as needed. When soft and transparent, but not brown, add tomato paste.
2) Add stock and simmer for 40 minutes.
3) Add potatoes, sugar, salt, and pepper and simmer 30 minutes more.
4) Puree. Return soup to brazier, add saffron, and simmer 10 minutes more.
5) Make final taste adjustment if required.
6) Serve or cool and refrigerate.

❊

Oxtail Soup St. Martin (Hot)

Yield: 2 gal

Prep time: 40 min
Cook time: 3 hr

Equipment
French knife, cutting board, meat saw, large brazier, skimmer, kitchen spoon, heatproof plate

Ingredients

peanut oil; as needed
beef oxtails, 1-in. (2.5 cm) slices; 5
carrots, diced small; 8
turnips, diced small; 10
leeks, diced small; 6
onions, medium, diced small; 5
*flour, browned; ¾ cup
tomato paste; 1¼ cup (300 ml)
Beef Stock; 2 gal (8 liter)
dry white beans, soaked overnight in
  water; ¾ lb (340 g) dry weight

bouquet garni
  parsley; 1 bunch
  thyme; 1 tbsp
  bay leaves; 4
cinnamon bark; 3 pieces
salt; to taste
black pepper; to taste
cayenne pepper; to taste
red port wine; 1 cup, ½ pint
  (250 ml)

Method
1) Heat a large brazier with the bottom well covered with oil.
2) Sauté oxtails until golden brown.
3) Remove oxtails and set aside.
4) If needed, add more oil to brazier and sauté carrots, turnips, leeks, and onions until tender. During the cooking process, scrape the bottom of the brazier well with spatula (to use meat flavorings from sautéing).
5) When the vegetables are nearly tender, add flour and mix well. Cook a few minutes more until vegetables are tender.
6) Add tomato paste, stock, beans, and oxtails. Combine well. The meat must be well covered by liquid so add more stock if required.
7) Bring to boil, then reduce heat to simmer. Add bouquet garni, cinnamon bark, salt, pepper, and cayenne and simmer covered for 3 hours or until meat is very tender and nearly falling off the bones.
8) Remove all meat and bones from the soup. When the meat is cool, remove all bones and fat and discard. Dice meat into small cubes.

*Use bread flour browned on small sheet pan under boiler.

9) Remove all fat from the soup. Remove cinnamon bark and bouquet garni and discard. Adjust taste with salt, pepper, and cayenne.
10) Add port wine.

Caribbean Conch Chowder *"La Frégate"* (Hot)

Yield: 2 qt (2 liter)

Prep time: 45 min
Cook time: 1 hr

Equipment
French knife, cutting board, brazier, tenderizing mallet, kitchen spoon, paper towel

Ingredients

salt pork, rind removed, medium dice; ⅓ cup
vegetable oil; 2 tbsp (40 ml)
onion, large, diced fine; 1
garlic cloves, diced; 3
celery stalks, diced fine; 2
green peppers, diced fine; ½ cup
ham, cooked, diced fine; ½ cup
conch, cut in strips, tenderized with mallet, diced, blanched; 2 cup
tomatoes, peeled, seeded, chopped; 8

tomato paste; 1 heaping tbsp (25 ml)
thyme; ½ tsp
basil; ¼ tsp
water; 2 qt (2 liter)
carrots, ¼-in. slices; 2
potatoes, peeled, cubed; 3
Worcestershire sauce; 2 tbsp (40 ml)
tabasco; ½ tsp (3 ml)
salt; to taste
black pepper; to taste

Method
1) Sauté salt pork with oil until crisp and brown. Drain and set aside.
2) Sauté onion, garlic, celery, and peppers until tender.
3) Add ham, conch, tomatoes, tomato paste, thyme, and basil and sweat the mixture for 10 minutes.
4) Add water and simmer for 45 minutes.
5) Add carrots, potatoes, Worcestershire sauce, and tabasco and simmer 30 minutes more.
6) Add pork.
7) Adjust taste with salt and pepper as required.

French Riviera Soup *(Aïgo Saou)* (Hot)

Yield: 4 gal (16 liter)   Prep time: 45 min
                                            Cook time: 45 min

Equipment
French knife, cutting board, soup pot, small brazier, whip, kitchen spoon

Ingredients

onions, diced fine; 8 lb (3.6 kg)
leeks, white part only, diced; 12
butter; as needed
garlic cloves, diced; 40
bouquet garni
   bay leaf; 3
   thyme; 1 tsp
   parsley stems, chopped; ½ cup
orange peel; of 1 orange
fennel, fresh, sliced; 18 oz (500 g)
  (substitute 3 tbsp fennel seed)

tomatoes, canned, drained, diced;
  6½ lb (2.9 kg)
Chicken Stock, rich; 3 gal (12 liter)
salt; to taste
black pepper; to taste
potatoes, diced small; 8
Pernod™; 1 oz (25 ml)
*eggs, poached; 40
French bread croutons; 40

Method
1) Sauté onions and leeks in butter until tender.
2) Add garlic, bouquet garni, orange peel, fennel, and tomatoes and simmer 15 minutes.
3) Add stock and simmer 10 minutes more.
4) Adjust taste with salt and pepper.
5) Add potatoes and Pernod™ and simmer 10 minutes more or until tender.

Service
1) Garnish with poached egg floating on top of crouton.

(See color plate 9)

---

*Poach eggs with water and vinegar.

Tomato Consommé with Fennel (Hot)

Yield: 2 gal (8 liter)

Prep time: 15 min
Cook time: 60 min

Equipment
French knife, cutting board, kitchen spoon, soup pot, china cap, cheesecloth, skimmer

Ingredients
*fennel heart, fresh, diced; 2 cup (350 g)
Beef Stock; 1 gal (4 liter)
tomatoes, fresh, peeled, seeded, diced; 2 lb (1 kg)
tomato juice; 2 qt (2 liter)
carrots, diced small; 1
leeks, larger, cleaned well, diced small; 1

peppercorns; 8
cloves, whole; 2
salt; to taste
black pepper; to taste
egg whites, beaten; 6
ground beef, lean; 3 lb (1.35 kg)
fennel leaves, chopped; 4 tbsp

Method
1) Simmer fennel heart in stock for 5 minutes.
2) Add tomatoes, tomato juice, carrots, leeks, peppercorns, cloves, salt, and pepper. Bring to boil and then reduce to simmer.
3) Add egg whites and ground beef and simmer 1 hour. When raft forms on top of soup, do not stir.
4) Strain through cheesecloth, but do not force liquid. Allow to drain slowly to avoid forcing unwanted particles into soup.
5) Skim off all fat.
6) Adjust taste with salt and pepper as required.

Service
1) Garnish with chopped fennel leaves.

*If no fresh fennel is available use 2 tablespoons fennel seed.

Velouté Maria (Hot)

Yield: 2 gal (8 liter)   Prep time: 2 hr
                                          Cook time: 1½ hr

Equipment
French knife, cutting board, bowl, brazier, 3 saucepans, food processor or blender

Ingredients
leeks, white portion only, chopped fine; 1 lb (450 g)
butter; 10 oz (280 g)
white beans, soaked overnight, cooked; 2 lb (900 g)
*Chicken Velouté, very rich; 2 gal (8 liter)
white turnips, small, fine julienne; 5
carrots, fine julienne; 4
celery stalks, fine julienne; 4
mushrooms, fresh, fine julienne; 1 lb (450 g)
whipping cream; 1 qt (1 liter)
parsley, fresh, chopped; as needed

Method
1) Sauté leeks and mushrooms with butter a few minutes until tender. Reserve.
2) Blend white beans and add velouté.
3) Cook vegetables al dente. They must be cooked separately as they have different cooking times: turnips, 4 minutes; carrots, 6 minutes; celery, 4 minutes. When tender, plunge vegetables into ice water when they are done, to avoid overcooking.
4) Combine everything.
5) Finish with cream.

Service
1) Garnish with parsley.

*See page 125.

Wagon Train Soup (Hot)

Yield: 3 gal (12 liter)

Prep time: 30 min
Cook time: 2½ hr

Equipment
French knife, cutting board, kitchen spoon, medium brazier

Ingredients
mirepoix
  carrots, diced fine; 2
  celery stalks, diced fine; 4
  onions, diced fine; 1½
vegetable oil; as needed
beef, small cubes; 3 lb (1.35 kg)
Beef Stock; 3 gal (12 liter)

tomatoes, fresh, peeled, seeded,
  diced; 8
barley; 1 lb (450 g)
parsley; ½ bunch
bay leaves; 3
salt; to taste
black pepper; to taste

Method
1) Sauté mirepoix in oil about 15 minutes or until tender.
2) Add beef, stock, tomatoes, barley, parsley, and bay leaves and simmer 2–2½ hours or until barley is tender.
3) Adjust taste with salt and pepper as required.

Apricot Soup (Cold)

Yield: 1 qt (1 liter)

Prep time: 1¼ hr
Chill time: 3 hr

Equipment
stainless steel, glass, or ceramic mixing bowl, kitchen spoon, blender, whip, strainer

Ingredients
water, warm; as needed
apricots, dried; 2 lb (900 g)
dry white wine; 1 cup (¼ liter)
lemon juice; to taste
heavy cream; 2 cup (½ liter)
sour cream; as needed

Method
1) Soak apricots covered with warm water for 1 hour.
2) Puree apricots with the water they soaked in.
3) Strain and add wine.
4) Add lemon juice to taste and stir in cream. Mix well.
5) Chill overnight if time permits.*

Service
1) Serve chilled.
2) Garnish with a dollop of sour cream.

*Remember to chill only in stainless steel, glass, or ceramic bowl. Do not use aluminum.

Velouté of Tomato (Cold)

Yield: 2 gal (8 liter)   Prep time: 20 min
                                    Cook time: 1 hr
                                    Chill time: overnight

Equipment
French knife, cutting board, saucepan or brazier, mixing bowl, blender

Ingredients
Chicken Stock; 2 gal (8 liter)
rice; 14 oz (400 g)
tomatoes, fresh, peeled, seeded, diced; 4½ lb (2 kg)
salt; to taste
black pepper; to taste
cucumbers, seeded, sliced thin; 4
heavy cream; 1 cup (250 ml)

Method
1) Bring stock to a boil.
2) Add rice and cook for 20 minutes.
3) Add tomatoes, salt, and pepper and cook 30 minutes more.
4) Puree and return to the heat to simmer 5 minutes more.
5) Remove from heat and refrigerate for about 15 minutes.
6) Add cream, mixing well.
7) Adjust taste with salt and pepper as required.
8) Chill overnight.

Service
1) Serve very cold in chilled cups.
2) Garnish by floating thinly sliced cucumber on top of soup.

Apple Vichyssoise Soup (Cold)

Yield: 2 gal (8 liter)   Prep time: 25 min
                                              Cook time: 30 min

Equipment
French knife, cutting board, paring knife, apple corer, brazier, blender, stainless steel or ceramic bowl

Ingredients
Delicious apples, large, peeled, cored, diced; 12
Chicken Stock; 2 gal (8 liter)
beurre manié; as needed
heavy cream, chilled; 1 qt (1 liter)
salt; to taste
sugar; to taste
lemon juice, fresh; to taste
Delicious apples, large, fine julienne; 4

Method
1) Cook diced apples in stock for about 20 minutes or until tender.
2) Add beurre manié as needed for consistency.
3) Blend and chill.
4) Add cream and mix well.
5) Add salt, sugar, and lemon juice.

Service
1) Ladle cold soup into chilled bowls.
2) Garnish with julienne apples* and serve.

*If apples are prepared early, keep in bowl of cold water with lemon juice to prevent discoloration.

Vichyssoise (Cold)

Yield: 1¼ gal (5 liter)

Prep time: 20 min
Cook time: 45 min
Chill time: 6 hr

Equipment
French knife, kitchen spoon, brazier, blender, kitchen spoon

Ingredients
leeks, white part only, sliced thin; 4 lb (1.8 kg)
potatoes, peeled, chopped rough; 3 lb (1.35 kg)
Chicken Stock; 1 gal (4 liter)
milk; 5 cup (1¼ liter)
heavy cream; 2½ cup (625 ml)
salt; to taste
white pepper; to taste
chives, chopped; as needed

Method
1) Cover leeks and potatoes with stock and simmer until vegetables are very tender.
2) Puree everything a small amount at a time. Return to brazier and adjust heat to low.
3) Add milk, cream, salt, and pepper and simmer, stirring constantly just until blended.

Service
1) Serve well chilled.
2) Garnish with chopped chives.

Avocado Tomato Soup (Cold)

Yield: ¾ gal (3 liter)

Prep time: 15 min
Cook time: 20 min
Chill time: 4 hr

Equipment
French knife, cutting board, blender, whip, sauté pan, brazier

Ingredients
avocados, ripe, medium, peeled, pitted, cut in chunks; 6
lemon juice; 6 tbsp (120 ml)
Chicken Stock; ½ gal (2 liter)
butter; 3 tbsp (60 ml)
onions, medium, diced; 3
whole wheat flour; 3 tbsp

yogurt; 1 qt (1 liter)
tomatoes, peeled, seeded, diced; 9
cayenne pepper; ½ tsp or to taste
salt; to taste
black pepper, to taste
dill, parsley, or chives, fresh, chopped; as needed

Method
1) Blend avocados, lemon juice, and 1 cup stock until smooth.
2) Melt butter and cook onions until soft and transparent.
3) Add flour, mixing well with butter. Cook 2 or 3 minutes to create a roux.
4) Set remainder of stock to simmer.
5) Add onions and roux, stirring well with whip. Simmer and stir until mixture is well blended, about 5 minutes.
6) Remove from heat and add the avocado mixture.
7) Add yogurt, tomatoes, and cayenne.
8) Adjust taste with salt and pepper as required.
9) Chill about 4 hours or until very cold.

Service
1) Serve chilled.
2) Garnish with chopped fresh dill, parsley, or chopped chives.

Strawberry Soup (Cold)

Yield: 3 qt (3 liter)   Prep time: 5 min
                                         Cook time: 25 min

Equipment
blender, whip, kitchen spoon, large saucepan

Ingredients:
water; 1½ cup (375 ml)
red wine; 1½ cup (375 ml)
granulated sugar; 1 cup (125 ml)
lemon juice, fresh; 4 tbsp (80 ml)
cinnamon sticks; 2
strawberries, stemmed, pureed; 2 qt (1.1 liter)
whipped cream; 1 cup (2.5 dl)
sour cream; ½ cup (1.25 dl)
strawberries, sliced thin; as needed

Method
1) Combine water, wine, sugar, lemon juice, and cinnamon and simmer uncovered 15 minutes, stirring frequently.
2) Add strawberry puree and simmer 10 minutes more, stirring frequently.
3) Discard cinnamon sticks and chill about 4 hours or until very cold.
4) Gently combine whipped cream and sour cream and fold into strawberry mixture.

Service
1) Serve chilled.
2) Garnish with razor-thin slice of fresh strawberry.

Mulligatawny (Cold)

Yield: 1 gal (4 liter)

Prep time: 15 min
Cook time: 50 min

Equipment
French knife, cutting board, medium brazier, whip, kitchen spoon, strainer

Ingredients

onions, medium, sliced thin; 2
butter; 5 oz (150 g)
curry powder; 2 tsp
apricots, dried, chopped fine; 20
Chicken Stock; 1 gal (4 liter)
cornstarch; as needed
water; as needed

salt; to taste
black pepper; to taste
chicken breast, boneless, cooked,
 diced; 4
heavy cream, chilled; 2 cup (½ liter)
apricots, dried, fine julienne,
 blanched in salted water; as needed

Method
1) Sauté onions in butter until tender and transparent, but not brown.
2) Add curry, apricots, and stock and simmer for 20 minutes.
3) Make paste with cornstarch and water.
4) Adjust consistency of stock with cornstarch paste.
5) Add salt and pepper to adjust taste.
6) Strain. Add chicken.
7) Chill at least 4 hours or until very cold.
8) Mix in cream just before serving.

Service
1) Serve chilled.
2) Garnish with very fine julienne of dried apricot.

Carrots Vichyssoise (Cold)

1 gal (4 liter)

Prep time: 20 min
Cook time: 1 hr
Chill time: 4 hr

Equipment
French knife, cutting board, kitchen spoon, whip, blender

Ingredients
Chicken Stock, rich; 1 gal (4 liter)
ham hock; 1
sugar; 1 tbsp
potatoes, peeled, sliced; 8
carrots, peeled, sliced; 10
leeks, washed, sliced; 10
salt; to taste
black pepper; to taste
heavy cream; 1 qt (1 liter)
carrots, very fine julienne; 2

Method
1) Simmer ham hock with sugar in stock 30 minutes.
2) Add potatoes, carrots, and leeks and simmer 30 minutes more.
3) Remove ham hock and puree stock and vegetables.
4) Adjust taste with salt and pepper.
5) Chill at least 4 hours or until very cold.
6) Add cream.

Service
1) Serve chilled.
2) Garnish with julienne of carrots.

Mint Cucumber Soup (Cold)

Yield: 1 gal (4 liter)   Prep time: 10 min
Cook time: 10 min

Equipment
French knife, cutting board, brazier, blender, whip, kitchen spoon, large bowl

Ingredients
butter; 7 oz (200 g)
onion, medium, chopped fine; 5
garlic cloves; 3
cucumbers, peeled, sliced very thin; 15
rice flour; 5 oz (140 g)
Chicken Stock; 3 qt (3 liter)

mint, fresh, chopped fine; 10 tbsp
heavy cream; 1½ qt (1½ liter)
plain yogurt; ½ qt (½ liter)
salt; to taste
white pepper; to taste
cucumbers, sliced razor thin; as needed

Method
1) Melt butter over medium heat. Add onion and garlic and sauté until soft, but not brown.
2) Add cucumbers and cook slowly until soft.
3) Stir in flour.
4) Add stock, blending well, and simmer about 10 minutes.
5) Puree and transfer to large bowl.
6) Mix in mint, combining ingredients well.
7) Cover and chill at least 4 hours or until very cold.
8) Just before serving, stir in cream and yogurt and mix well.
9) Adjust taste with salt and pepper.

Service
1) Garnish with slices of cucumber.

Andalusian Gazpacho (Cold)

Yield: 1½ gal (6 liter)   Prep time: 45 min
                                           Chill time: 2 hr

Equipment
French knife, cutting board, large bowl, kitchen spoon, whip, ladle, bain marie, food mill or blender

Ingredients

tomatoes, large, peeled, seeded, chopped; 15

cucumbers, peeled, seeded, chopped; 6

green peppers, large, peeled, seeded, chopped; 6

onions, medium, chopped; 6

*dry white bread crumbs; 3 cup

parsley leaves, diced fine; 1½ cup

basil, fresh; 7 tbsp (or 3 tbsp dry basil)

tarragon, fresh, minced; 7 tbsp (or tarragon, dry; 3 tbsp)

chives, fresh, green part of leaf only, diced; 6 tbsp

garlic cloves, diced fine; 8

lemon juice, fresh; ¾ cup

salt; 5 tsp

Chicken Stock, cold, rich; 5 qt (5 liter)

tabasco; to taste

olive oil; 3–3½ cup (750–825 ml)

Method
1) Puree tomatoes, cucumbers, peppers, onions, bread crumbs, parsley, basil, tarragon, chives, and garlic.
2) Stir in lemon juice, salt, stock, and tabasco.
3) Add the oil in a stream, while whisking vigorously. Continue until oil is combined well.
4) Chill at least 2 hours. Mix again briskly.

Service
1) Serve cold.

*Little cubes of bread sautéed with butter can also be used.

Cantaloupe Rum Soup* (Cold)

Yield: ½ gal (2 liter)   Prep time: 20 min
                                Cook time: 20 min

Equipment
French knife, cutting board, saucepan, ladle, kitchen spoon, food processor or blender

Ingredients
butter; ½ cup (125 ml)
cantaloupes, medium, ripe, peeled, seeded, cubed; 4
orange marmalade; ½ cup (125 ml)
coconut milk, unsweetened; 4 tbsp (80 ml)
orange juice, fresh; 2 cup (500 ml)
whipping cream; 1 cup (250 ml)
dark rum; ½ cup (125 ml)
salt; to taste
black pepper; to taste
walnuts, toasted; as needed (optional)

Method
1) Melt butter over medium heat.
2) Add cantaloupe and sweat until soft, about 8 minutes.
3) Blend in marmalade and coconut milk.
4) Add enough orange juice to cover and simmer 12 to 15 minutes or until cantaloupe is very soft.
5) Puree cantaloupe mixture.
6) Return to saucepan and stir in cream and rum.
7) Adjust taste with salt and pepper as required.

Service
1) Serve cold.
2) Garnish with walnuts, if desired.

*An original Chef Chaton recipe.

Cream of Lettuce Soup (Hot or Cold)

Yield: 1½ gal (6 liter)   Prep time: 30 min
                                 Cook time: 30 min

Equipment
French knife, cutting board, brazier, strainer, kitchen spoon

Ingredients
Boston lettuce, heads, cored, quartered, shredded fine; 4
Chicken Stock; 1½ gal (6 liter)
onions, small, sliced; 4
celery, stalks, chopped; 4
butter; 1 cup or as needed
flour; 8 tbsp
heavy cream; 2 cup (½ liter)
salt; to taste
black pepper; to taste

Method
1) Boil lettuce in 1 cup stock for 5 minutes. Remove from heat.
2) Sauté onion and celery in butter until soft, but not browned.
3) Add flour and cook until flour and butter form a good roux, but not brown.
4) Add remaining stock and bring to boil. Boil uncovered 15 minutes.
5) Remove from heat and strain.
6) Add lettuce to stock in which it was cooked and reheat. Simmer 5 minutes.
7) Remove from heat. Add cream and mix well.
8) Adjust taste with salt and pepper as required.

Service
1) Serve hot or chilled.

Watercress Soup (Hot or Cold)

Yield: 1½ gal (6 liter)

Prep time: 20 min
Cook time: 45 min

Equipment
French knife, cutting board, saucepan, brazier, kitchen spoon, food mill or blender

Ingredients
Chicken Stock; 1½ gal (6 liter)
potatoes, diced; 4 lb (1.8 kg)
onions, sliced; 4 lb (1.8 kg)
watercress, leaves only, cleaned; 5 bunches
bay leaves; 3
light cream; 1 pt (500 ml)
chives, fresh; ¼ cup
salt; to taste
black pepper; to taste

Method
1) Bring stock to boil and reduce to simmer.
2) Add potatoes, onions, watercress, and bay leaves and cook about 45 minutes or until the potatoes are tender.
3) When cooked, strain or puree.
4) Heat cream, almost to boiling, and add to soup.
5) Add chives.
6) Adjust taste with salt and pepper as required.

Service
1) Serve hot or chilled.
2) Garnish with 1 leaf of watercress per cup.

Summary

The importance of the soup cannot be overemphasized. Especially in America, where customers often skip the appetizer, many times the soup is the customers' first impression of the meal to come. It not only whets the appetite, it also provides the customers with subtle cues of what is to follow.

Hot soups must be served hot, in heated cups or bowls. Cold soups must be served cold, in chilled containers.

It is very important that the correct soup is paired with the entrée. A light soup is followed by a heavy entrée; a heavy soup is followed by a light entrée.

Soups can be divided into three basic categories: the consommés and clear soups; the thickened soups and the cream soups; and the purees and thickened vegetable soups.

Soups must be made with top-quality, fresh ingredients. They should not be viewed as a means of disposing of leftovers. Most soups will keep three days under refrigeration; however, they should not be reheated more than once (heating and cooling destroys flavor).

The *dépouiller* (skimming off the fat) step must never be overlooked if high standards of appearance, taste, and digestibility are to be maintained.

It is important to simmer rather than boil soups when cooking.

Because of the very small temperature difference, there is no significant time saved by boiling a soup. Also, boiling tends to break up foods and increases the risk of scorching.

Discussion Questions*

1) If you were the chef in a good restaurant that usually carried at least three soups on the menu, how often would you make fresh soup?
2) How important are the garnishes on the soup?
3) Soup is usually perceived by customers to be a low-cost item. In reality, is it cheap to make a good soup (in terms of food cost)?
4) Why is it important to have a trained front-of-the-house staff to encourage customers to match the appropriate soups to their entrées?
5) What would be an appropriate soup to serve with Beef Shortribs and Horseradish Sauce? (Name two possibilities.)

*Some discussion questions require culinary deductive reasoning. They may not be answered *directly* in the text, but enough information is given to deduce the answer logically.

6) What would be an appropriate soup to serve when the entrée is Mushroom Soufflé? (Name two possibilities.)

Test Questions

1) Are there any significant differences in the ingredients of Leek and Potato Soup (a hot soup) and Vichyssoise (a cold soup)?
2) The recipe for Cold Strawberry Soup calls for fresh strawberries. If frozen strawberries, which are usually sweetened, are used, what adjustments must be made of the other ingredients?
3) In the recipe for *Petite Marmite Champs Elysées*, the method indicates that all vegetables must be cooked separately. Why?
4) *Petite Marmite Champs Elysées* must be finished to order and once ready to serve, cannot be held for long. Why?
5) In Chef Chaton's Special Borsch, the beets are not added until the very end. Why?
6) What two stocks are used in the onion soup recipe?
7) For banquet service, what adjustment would you make in the method of finishing the onion soup?
8) Why is clarification a required step in the preparation of Consommé Colbert?
9) Why is bouillabaisse so rarely found on the menus of cheaper establishments?
10) In Oxtail Soup St. Martin, how thick should the oxtails be cut?

Chapter 9

✤ **Salads**

Currently salad is very much in vogue in this country. Constantly touted by the popular press to a health-conscious public, salad is perceived to be healthful by the customers and, as such, has become big business. Americans daily consume uncountable tons of lettuce, tomatoes, onions, garbanzo beans, potatoes, celery, green peppers, scallions, cold beans, cauliflower, broccoli, and so on. Raw vegetables have become chic as appetizers and the crunch of raw broccoli being munched can be heard from coast to coast.

We have come a long way from the gelatinized carrots and pink French dressing of the 1950s. The National Executive Chef of a major hotel chain says their most popular salad consists of half the heart of a Boston lettuce garnished with a piece of artichoke heart, a black olive, a cherry tomato, and a piece of Camembert. It is dressed slightly with vinaigrette.

Preparing the Vegetables

Carefully preparing the vegetables that become a part of the salads is essential. In fact, most of your prep time will be consumed cleaning and cutting vegetables.

Cleaning salad vegetables is very important. No customer wants to bite into a piece of lettuce only to find some hidden grains of garden dirt. All vegetables, especially the leafy variety, must be cleaned and rinsed and dried. If moist vegetables are tossed in a salad, the dressing will become diluted and the taste will not be as impressive as it might have been.

Garnishes like basil and parsley leaves should be trimmed with small scissors to insure the most appetizing appearance.

Tomatoes, too, must be handled with special care. They will peel easily if you dip them in boiling water for 10 seconds before you try to remove their skins.

The Recipes

In this chapter we present a large number of salad items that are rarely seen in this country but are widely served in Europe and can be considered "classic." The classic salads have been popular for generations—some into antiquity. Most are relatively simple and easy to prepare and serve. All have pleased the palates of international customers in fine restaurants around the world for many years.

Note that, although the ingredients are the same as found in the fast-food salad bars, the combinations and juxtapositions of tastes will strike many customers and salad chefs as "new." With the possible exception of Old Monk Salad, they are not new. Some are slightly altered to accommodate American ingredient availability. All have been chosen with the tastes of the American customer in mind.

We urge you to try them all.

Pasta, Tomato, and Tuna Salad

Yield: 12 portions   Prep time: 30 min

Equipment
French knife, cutting board, small saucepan, colander, small scissors, mixing bowl, kitchen spoon

Ingredients
eggs, hard-cooked; 3
heavy cream; 8 tbsp (160 ml)
cider vinegar; 3 tbsp (60 ml)
ketchup; 3 tbsp (60 ml)
Dijon mustard; 1½ tbsp (30 ml)
salt; to taste
black pepper; to taste
pasta, cooked; 1 lb (450 g)

tomatoes, medium, firm, peeled, seeded, diced; 10
white tuna, water packed; 2.2 lb. (1 kg)
Italian parsley, leaves only, chopped; as needed (substitute leftover cooked rice)
chives (*ciboules*), fresh, chopped; ¼ bunch

Method
1) To make dressing, separate egg yolks and whites and set whites aside. Crush yolks and mix well with cream, vinegar, ketchup, mustard, salt, and pepper.

Service
1) Put pasta in center of bowl and top with tomatoes and chunks of tuna. Pour dressing on top. Garnish with chives, parsley, and finely diced egg whites.

Smoked Trout Salad

Yield: 12 portions   Prep time: 10 min

Equipment
French knife, cutting board, paper towels, rubber spatula, small scissors, mixing bowl, kitchen spoon

Ingredietns

Granny Smith apples, small, un-peeled, cored, sliced; 3
lemon juice; of 1½ lemons
egg yolks, hard-cooked; 3
cider vinegar; 3 tbsp (60 ml)
Dijon mustard; 1 tbsp (20 ml)
salt; to taste
black pepper; to taste
plain yogurt or *crème fraîche*; 1 cup

Belgian endives, medium, cut in 1-in. rounds ; 6
lamb's foot (*mâche*), washed, well dried; 20 oz (600 g)
walnuts, crushed; 3 tbsp (60 ml)
smoked fillet of trout, sliced thin; 14 oz (400 g) (substitute smoked herring or salmon)
fresh chives, cut fine; ½ bunch

Method
1) Coat apples with lemon juice.
2) To make dressing, mix yolks with vinegar, mustard, salt, and pepper.
3) Add yogurt and mix well. Set aside.
4) Combine endive, lamb's foot, walnuts, and trout.
5) Add dressing.

Service
1) Garnish with chives.

Salade Taboulé

Yield: 12 portions

Prep time: 25 min
Chill time: 3 hr

Equipment
French knife, cutting board, small scissors, small saucepan, mixing bowl,
  kitchen spoon

Ingredients
couscous semolina; 10 oz (300 g)
water, salted, boiling; 1 cup (¼ liter)
lemon juice; 4
Boston lettuce, medium, torn in pieces; 3
tomatoes, firm, medium, peeled, seeded, cut in large brunoise; 10
salt; to taste
black pepper; to taste
mint leaves, fresh; 4 tbsp
olive oil; 3 tbsp (60 ml)

Method
1) Put semolina in bowl. Add boiling salted water. Rest 15 minutes until
   volume increases and liquid is absorbed.
2) Add half the lemon juice to the semolina.
3) Combine lettuce, tomatoes, salt, and pepper.
4) Add semolina and mint.
5) Mix remaining lemon juice and oil and add to taboulé.
6) Cover and chill for 3 hours.
7) Adjust taste and mix well.

Sevillan Salad

Yield: 12 portions   Prep time: 20 min

Equipment
French knife, cutting board, small scissors, paring knife, mixing bowl, kitchen
 spoon

Ingredients
Vinaigrette
   corn oil; 6 tbsp (120 ml)
   white vinegar; 3 tbsp (60 ml)
   grapefruit juice, fresh squeezed from segmented grapefruit; 1 tbsp (20 ml)
   orange juice, fresh squeezed; 1 tbsp (20 ml)
   salt; to taste
   black pepper; to taste
Boston lettuce, hearts; 12
grapefruit, segmented; 6
oranges, segmented; 6
mint leaves, fresh; as needed

Method
1) To prepare vinaigrette, mix oil, vinegar, grapefruit juice, and orange juice
    well.
2) Adjust taste with salt and pepper.

Service
1) Place lettuce hearts in center of plate; make a ring around the lettuce
    hearts, alternating orange and grapefruit segments.
2) Garnish with mint.
3) Serve with vinaigrette on the side.

Spanish Salad

Yield: 12 portions   Prep time: 20 min

Equipment
French knife, cutting board, small saucepan, mixing bowl, kitchen spoon

Ingredients
French beans (very small string
  beans), cleaned, cooked 7 min in
  boiling salted water, cut in 2-in. (5-
  cm) diagonal slices; 2.2 lb (1 kg)
tomatoes, peeled, seeded, quartered;
  4–5
Vinaigrette
  peanut oil; 6 tbsp (120 ml)
  tarragon vinegar; 2 tbsp (40 ml)
  chives (*ciboules*), fresh, chopped;
    ½ bunch
  salt; to taste
  black pepper; to taste

sweet pimientos, red or yellow,
  broiled, peeled, julienne cut; 4
Spanish onions, sliced thin in rounds;
  2
mushrooms, fresh, washed, dried,
  sliced lengthwise; 6

Method
1) Mix beans and tomatoes.
2) To make vinaigrette, mix well oil, vinegar, and chives. Add to vegetables.
3) Adjust taste with salt and pepper.

Service
1) Garnish with pimiento, onion rings, and mushrooms.

Three Colors Salad

Yield: 12 portions   Prep time: 20 min

Equipment
French knife, cutting board, small scissors, small saucepan, mixing bowl, kitchen spoon, small baking pan

Ingredients
Vinaigrette
    sunflower oil; 6 tbsp (120 ml)
    cider vinegar; 3 tbsp (60 ml)
    Dijon mustard; 1 tbsp (20 ml)
salt; to taste
black pepper; to taste
green peppers, baked, browned, seeded, fine julienne; 3
corn, cooked; 2 lb (900 g)
tomatoes, medium, peeled, seeded, quartered; 12
Italian parsley, leaves only; as needed

Method
1) To make vinaigrette, combine vinegar, mustard, and oil. Mix well.
2) Adjust taste with salt and pepper.

Service
1) Put a scoop of corn in the center of the plate; circle with tomato quarters; and make an outer ring of julienne of green pepper.
2) Sprinkle with vinaigrette.
3) Garnish with parsley.

Watercress Salad

Yield: 12 portions   Prep time: 20 min

Equipment
French knife, cutting board, 2 small pots, mixing bowl, kitchen spoon

Ingredients
Vinaigrette
 crème fraîche; 1 tbsp (140 ml)
 Dijon mustard; 2 tbsp (40 ml)
 salt; to taste
 black pepper; to taste
Italian parsley, leaves, chopped; ¼ bunch
chervil, leaves, chopped; ¼ bunch
baking potatoes, medium, Idaho preferred, cooked, peeled, sliced; 5
watercress leaves; 4 bunches
eggs, hard-cooked, chopped; 4

Method
1) Prepare vinaigrette by combining *crème fraîche*, mustard, salt, and pepper.
2) Mix parsley and chervil together.
3) Combine potatoes, watercress, and vinaigrette.

Service
1) Garnish with parsley, chervil, and chopped egg.

*If unavailable, substitute 2 tablespoons buttermilk well-mixed with 1 quart (1 liter) whipping cream.

Old Monk Salad*

Yield: 24 portions   Prep time: 1 hr

Equipment
French knife, cutting board, large jar, assorted bowls, kitchen spoon

Ingredients
olive oil; 3 cup

red wine vinegar; 1 cup (¼ liter)

egg yolks; 8

parsley, chopped; 6 tbsp

onions, chopped; 3 tbsp

garlic cloves, fresh, minced; 4

shallots, shopped; 3

Dijon mustard; 3 tbsp (60 ml)

tarragon; ½ tsp

black pepper; dash

Lea & Perrins™ Worcestershire
  Sauce; 4 tbsp (20 ml)

mushrooms, fresh, sliced; 3 cup

Boston lettuce, heads; 4

spinach, fresh, stems removed; 1 gal
  (4 liter)

romaine lettuce; 2 heads

watercress; 2 bunches

hearts of palm, canned (14 oz each),
  drained, bite size; 4 cans

artichoke hearts, canned (14 oz
  each), drained, quartered; 4 cans

avocado, fresh, peeled, seeded, sliced
  lengthwise; 4

walnuts, coarsely chopped; 8 tbsp

Method
1) In a large jar, prepare dressing by combining oil, vinegar, egg yolks, parsley, onion, garlic, shallots, mustard, tarragon, pepper, and Worcestershire sauce. Cover and shake vigorously.
2) Add mushrooms.
3) Place lettuce, spinach, romaine, and watercress in salad bowl.
4) Add hearts of palm, artichoke hearts, and avocado.
5) Sprinkle walnuts on top.
6) Toss with dressing.

*This recipe was a Lea & Perrins™ cooking contest winner.

Spaghetti Salad with Fresh Basil

Yield: 12 portions   Prep time: 25 min

Equipment
large pot, colander, mixing bowl, kitchen spoon, 2 large forks

Ingredients
egg yolks; 3
Parmesan cheese, grated; 3 oz (85 g)
lemon juice; 3 tbsp (60 ml)
yogurt; 1 pt (½ liter)
salt; to taste
*basil, leaves; 1 bunch
spaghetti, cooked al dente; 1½ lb (600 g) [7½ oz (210 g) uncooked]

Method
1) To make dressing, combine egg yolks, Parmesan cheese, and lemon juice until they are creamy.
2) A little bit at a time, add yogurt, salt, and basil.
3) Mix spaghetti and dressing and fold together until well combined.

*The basil leaves will look best if they are trimmed from their stalks with a small scissors.

Classic Vinaigrette Dressing

Yield: 30 portions   Prep time: 10 min

Equipment
French knife, cutting board, mixing bowl, kitchen spoon

Ingredients
olive oil or other vegetable oil; 1 cup (¼ liter)
wine vinegar; 7 tbsp (140 ml)
salt; to taste
black pepper; to taste
Dijon mustard; 2 tbsp (40 ml)
shallots, crushed, chopped fine; 6 cloves
chervil or parsley, chopped fine; ½ bunch

Method
1) Mix all ingredients together.*

Uses
Use on almost any salad vegetable combination.

---

*For cost effectiveness when making large quantities, some water is often added. If adding water, insure that vinaigrette is well mixed to attain a good emulsion.

Gypsy Tomato Salad

Yield: 12 portions

Prep time: 20 min
Cook time: 45 min

Equipment
French knife, cutting board, small scissors, blender or food mill, mixing bowl, baking pan

Ingredients
eggplants, medium; 6
lemon juice; of 1 lemon
onions, medium, peeled, diced; 3
garlic cloves, peeled, diced; 4
olive oil; 3 tbsp (60 ml)
salt; to taste
black pepper; to taste
tomatoes, medium, firm; 12
basil, fresh, leaves; ½ bunch

Method
1) Cut off stalk of eggplants and bake in 350°F oven for about 45 minutes.
2) Allow eggplants to cool before cutting them in half, lengthwise.
3) Spoon out the centers and puree.
4) Put eggplant puree in bowl and add lemon juice. Mix well.
5) Add onions, garlic, oil, salt, and pepper and combine well. Chill.
6) Wash and dry tomatoes. Cut off tops and spoon out meat. Finely chop the meat and discard the juice and seeds. Salt inside the tomatoes and set aside, cut side down, to drain.
7) Combine tomato meat, basil, and eggplant puree.

Service
1) Fill tomatoes with tomato-eggplant mixture.
2) Garnish with basil leaves.

Niçoise Salad

Yield: 12   Prep time: 45 min

Equipment
French knife, cutting board, assorted pots, assorted bowls, kitchen spoon

Ingredients
Vinaigrette
   virgin olive oil; 6 tbsp (120 ml)
   red wine vinegar; 2 tbsp (40 ml)
   salt; to taste
   black pepper; to taste
   shallots, chopped; 2
eggs, boiled, peeled, quartered; 6
tuna, white, drained, crumbled;
   1½ lb (675 g)
French beans (very small string
   beans), cleaned, cooked 3 min in
   boiling salted water; 1½ lb (675 g)

tomatoes, peeled, seeded, quartered;
   4
new potatoes, medium, cooked,
   sliced; 4
black olives, oil packed, pitted; 5 oz
capers; 1 oz (30 g)
radishes, washed, bits of leaf at-
   tached; 1 bunch
Spanish onions, sweet, sliced in
   rounds; 2
romaine lettuce; 1 head
anchovy fillets; 24

Method
1) Make vinaigrette by combining oil, vinegar, salt, pepper, and shallots.
2) In large bowl, combine eggs, tuna, beans, tomatoes, potatoes, olives, capers, radishes, onions, lettuce, and vinaigrette, taking care not to bruise lettuce.

Service
1) Garnish with anchovy fillets.

Maria Salad

Yield: 12 portions   Prep time: 25 min

Equipment
French knife, cutting board, assorted small pots, kitchen spoon, large bowl

Ingredients
Vinaigrette
    walnut oil; 6 tbsp (120 ml)
    white wine vinegar; 2 tbsp (40 ml)
    Dijon mustard; 1 tbsp (20 ml)
    salt; to taste
    black pepper; to taste
Belgian endive; 6
red beets, medium, cooked, fine julienne; 4

roots of celery (celeriac), fine julienne; 28 oz (800 g)
tomatoes, peeled, seeded, quartered; 4
egg yolks, chopped very fine; 6
chervil or Italian parsley, leaves, chopped; 1 bunch

Method
1) Prepare vinaigrette by mixing oil, vinegar, and mustard.
2) Adjust taste with salt and pepper.

Service
1) Place endive leaves in the center, beets around the endives, celery root around the red beets, and tomatoes in the outer and final ring.
2) Garnish with egg yolk and parsley or chervil.
3) Pour vinaigrette on top just before service.
4) Serve individually or family style.

Louisette Salad

Yield: 12 portions   Prep time: 20 min

Equipment
French knife, cutting board, small saucepan, mixing bowl, kitchen spoon

Ingredients
Vinaigrette
   olive oil; 2 tbsp (40 ml)
   corn oil; 2 tbsp (40 ml)
   wine vinegar; 2 tbsp (40 ml)
   Dijon mustard; ½ tbsp (10 ml)
   salt; to taste
   black pepper; to taste
romaine lettuce, hearts, very young and tender; 6
tomatoes, medium, peeled, seeded, julienne; 6
muscat grapes, washed, seeded; 9 oz (250 g)
chives, fresh, chopped fine; 1 bunch

Method
1) To make vinaigrette, mix olive oil, corn oil, vinegar, and mustard.
2) Adjust taste with salt and pepper.
3) Combine lettuce, tomatoes, and grapes.
4) Pour vinaigrette on top.

Service
1) Garnish with fresh chives.

Andalouse Salad

Yield: 12 portions   Prep time: 30 min

Equipment
French knife, cutting board, saucepan, mixing bowl, kitchen spoon

Ingredients
Vinaigrette
  olive oil; 6 tbsp (120 ml)
  wine vinegar; 2½ tbsp (50 ml)
  shallots, chopped fine; 4
  salt; to taste
  black pepper; to taste
  tarragon leaves, chopped; 8
rice; 8 oz (250 g)
tomatoes, peeled, seeded, quartered;
  4

sweet pimientos, broiled, peeled,
  seeded, fine julienne; 3
garlic cloves, crushed, chopped very
  fine; 5
onions, medium, chopped very fine;
  2
Italian parsley leaves, chopped fine;
  ¼ bunch

Method
1) Prepare vinaigrette by mixing oil, vinegar, shallots, salt, pepper, and tarragon together.
2) Rinse the rice three or four times or until the water becomes clear.
3) Bring rice to boil in 16 ounces of water. Reduce to simmer. Cover and cook about 15 minutes or until rice is tender and water is absorbed.
4) Combine rice, tomatoes, pimientos, garlic, and onions.
5) Add vinaigrette.

Service
1) Garnish with chopped parsley.

Salad with Roquefort

Yield: 12 portions   Prep time: 30 min

Equipment
French knife, cutting board, small pot, assorted bowls, food mill, rubber spatula

Ingredients
Dressing
  egg yolks, hard-cooked; 6
  Dijon mustard; 1½ tbsp (30 ml)
  Roquefort cheese; 7 oz (200 g)
  yogurt; 1 qt (1 liter)
  crème fraîche; 2 tbsp (40 ml)
  cider vinegar; 4 tbsp (80 ml)
  salt; to taste
  black pepper; to taste

endive, cleaned, torn in bite-sized
  pieces; 1 head
escarole, cleaned, torn in bite-sized
  pieces; 1 head
Boston lettuce, cleaned, torn in bite-
  sized pieces; ½ head
romaine, cleaned, torn in bite-sized
  pieces; ½ head
egg whites, hard-cooked, diced
  small; 6

Method
1) Prepare dressing by combining egg yolks, mustard, and cheese into a smooth paste.
2) Add yogurt, *crème fraîche*, and vinegar. Using a whip, beat the dressing until it is light and approximately the consistency of mayonnaise. Adjust taste with salt and pepper.
3) In a large bowl, mix endive, escarole, lettuce, romaine, and fold in dressing well but slowly, so as not to bruise the lettuce. Chill.

Service
1) Garnish with fine-chopped egg whites.

---

*If unavailable, substitute 2 tablespoons buttermilk well mixed with 1 quart (1 liter) whipping cream.

Country Salad (Salade Campagnarde)

Yield: 12 portions

Prep time: 20 min
Cook time: 20 min

Equipment
French knife, cutting board, assorted pots, mixing bowls, kitchen spoon

Ingredients
Vinaigrette
    vegetable oil; 6 tbsp (120 ml)
    dry white wine; 3 tbsp (60 ml)
    vinegar; 3 tbsp (60 ml)
    lemon juice; 3 tbsp (60 ml)
    Dijon mustard; 1½ tbsp (30 ml)
    salt; to taste
    black pepper; to taste
escarole, cleaned, cut in bite-sized
    pieces; 3

Italian parsley, leaves only, chopped
    fine; 1 bunch
beef, boiled, fine julienne; 1½ lb
    (600 g)
potatoes, medium, cooked, sliced
    thin; 6
eggs, hard-cooked; 3
Spanish onions, medium, peeled, ½
    diced fine; ½ sliced thin; 3

Method
1) Prepare vinaigrette by mixing oil, wine, vinegar, lemon juice, mustard, salt, and pepper.
2) Put the escarole and half of parsley in a large bowl and add the vinaigrette.
3) Add beef, potatoes, eggs, and onions.

Service
1) Garnish with chopped parsley.

Summary

An increasingly large portion of the American restaurant market perceives salads as healthful. Restaurants are selling salads in ever increasing quantities because of this perception.

This chapter introduces "new" salads that can increase salad sales by greatly pleasing customers who may not be familiar with European taste juxtapositions. Even the most avid salad lovers must get bored with the offerings on the average menu.

In this chapter we have presented a change of style and a challenge to the student and the salad chef.

Discussion Questions*

1. What is one factor that has caused an increasing interest in salads among American customers?
2. Why are the cheese-flavored and sugar-filled prepared commercial salad dressings not appropriate for haute cuisine menus?
3. What could be one reason why American salad menus are rarely innovative?
4. Is the American perception of salads as "healthful" always true? Give an example of when this might not be true. From a marketing point of view, does it matter whether this perception is accurate or not?
5. Pick two salad recipes from this chapter that might be considered new to the average American customer.
6. Find, among the recipe ingredients in this chapter, two items that probably would be difficult to obtain in American rural areas.

Test Questions

1. What are *ciboules*?
2. Describe the correct procedure for peeling tomatoes.
3. List two recipes for vinaigrette.
4. What are pimientos? How are they prepared?
5. List the ingredients for Spanish Salad.
6. What part of the celery plant is used in Maria Salad?
7. What cheese is used in Spaghetti Salad with Fresh Basil?

*Some discussion questions require culinary deductive reasoning. They may not be answered *directly* in the text, but enough information is given to deduce the answer logically.

8. How are the pimientos cut in Spanish Salad?
9. List the ingredients for Sevillan Salad.
10. In Pasta, Tomato, and Tuna Salad, could fresh tuna be used instead of canned?

Chapter 10
The Entrées

Chicken Columbo Creole
Chicken *Cordon Bleu*
Chicken *Papillote* Jean Jeannin
Chicken Wrapped in Banana
  Leaves
Coq au Vin
Fricassee of Chicken with Vinegar
Chicken Soufflé
Boneless Breast of Duck
Coulis of Blackberry
Cornish Hens Moscovite
Bird Casanova
Mushroom Soufflé
Classic Quiche Lorraine
Pâté en Croûte
French Liver *Pâté*
Frog Legs Riesling
Vol au Vent Financière
Truffles in Turnovers
Pork Cutlets Paprika
Brochettes of Pork Marinade
Pork Chops with Watermelon
Alsatian Sauerkraut
Beef Burgundy
Short Ribs with Horseradish
  Sauce
Hungarian Beef Goulash
Steak Diane

Estouffade Provençale
Pot Roast of Beef with Mustard
  Sauce and Vegetables
Filet of Beef Wellington
Blanquette of Veal
Veal Marengo
Osso Buco
Quenelles of Veal (or Chicken)
Lamb Shank *Jardinière*
Classic Couscous Tunisian with
  Lamb and Two Sauces
Rack of Lamb Persillé
Côte d'Agneau à la Nelson
Cuisine Moderne: Grouper
  Renée Flament
Panade
Sole, Salmon, and Scallop
  Mousse
Mousse of Fish
Ramekins of Shrimp and
  Scallops
Jambalaya
Lobster fra Diavolo
Quenelles of Fish
Fish Soufflé
Seafood Stuffing for Crepes
Crab Imperial

C ooking is a fine art, a science, but it is also show business. The meal is the show; the Chef, the director and producer; the entrée, the star.

In a full French menu the entrée follows the *relevé* and is the third course. On American menus, the entrée is usually preceded by soup and salad and often by appetizers. It is never the first course. Nevertheless, in America's "get down to the nitty-gritty" atmosphere of the 1980s, the entrée is sometimes eaten alone with only bread and salad as an accompaniment. Despite current practices, the fact remains: Whenever the entrée is served, it is the critical part of the meal.

The Perfect Entrée

Even the most inexperienced chef knows that the entrée must, first of all, taste good. But taste is not enough. It must look beautiful, and it must be served well.

Appearance

A chef in New York decided to dye his mashed potatoes *green* in honor of St. Patrick's Day. His green potatoes, and most of the food served with them, came back to his kitchen untouched. This chef learned an important lesson and hastily prepared a fresh batch of potatoes. He consigned the green batch to the garbage can! The entrée, then, must look good.

Care must be taken to garnish the dish, to arrange the contents of the plate in an artistic manner, to use the sauce above or below the meat (depending on the style desired), to arrange the vegetables aesthetically. The portion size must be determined with an eye to reality and not just the cost sheet.

Let's look at two plates, each with the same basic contents but each presented with styles that are worlds apart. The first plate is an oval china white platter. A six-ounce piece of baked sole fillet is on the left side of the plate. A paper cup of tartar sauce and a lemon wedge sit on top of the fish. Just to the right of the fish is a baked potato, uncut, with a chip of melted margarine on the plate oozing from a little piece of cardboard. Next to that is a pile of carrot rounds.

We have the same oval platter and the same contents for the second plate. But there is a subtle and important difference. The baked fish is positioned precisely in the center of the plate. The tartar sauce has been sparingly spooned over the center of the fish. It has a pink tinge from the addition of a touch of tomato puree and contrasts nicely to the white of the fish. A thin twist of lemon rests at each end of the fish. The potato, now to the left of the fish, has been opened at the top with an X-shaped cut and a pat of butter is just beginning to melt inside the potato. To the right of the fish are precisely cut, matchstick-size pieces of julienne carrot, piled together like firewood stacked in an orderly manner. A perfect twig of parsley sits on a corner of the pile of carrots.

It makes no sense to slave for hours preparing a perfect entrée, only to have it arrive on the customer's table looking like something dished up in an army field kitchen. The chef must insure that somewhere, someone in the serving process is checking each and every plate before it goes to the dining room. If necessary, the waiters can be trained to do this. Good waiters check their plates by reflex anyway, since they know that the size of their tips is directly related to their customers' satisfaction.

Chefs must use common sense. They can leave nothing to chance. Care and constant vigilance is required. Good chefs will be sure that no dish leaves the kitchen with even a spare drop of sauce on the edge of a plate to detract from the appearance of the food. They will check to be sure both the plates and the food are hot. They will also check to be sure the waiters deliver the food from the kitchen promptly.

The Perfect Menu

Chefs must use a great deal of care and hard-thinking when they prepare their menus.

There are many factors to consider. What are the tastes of his customers? Fancy dishes, for example, do not sell well in rural areas. What is selling and what is not? From the beginning, chefs must keep track of this data. They must adjust their menus accordingly. What are the limitations of the staff? Entrées that require a great deal of preparation are impossible if there are no motivated, capable prep people. What about food cost? The rule of thumb is menu price equals the food cost multiplied by five. If the menu price of an item costs out to fifty dollars, it may not be practical to run the item. How the entrée is cooked is a factor also. If a menu is overloaded with sauté items (which must be cooked to order), even the best sauté cook will fall behind during a rush.

Safety note: Many of the entrées require a step to "ignite with match." Be sure to use a long fireplace match or twist of paper. Stand back from pan!

Chicken Columbo Creole

Yield: 36 portions

Prep time: 65 min
Cook time: 30 min

Equipment
French knife, cutting board, brazier, kitchen spoon

Ingredients
Marinade
  water; 1 gal (4 liter)
  wine vinegar; 1½ cup (375 ml)
  garlic cloves, crushed, chopped
    fine; 40
  cayenne pepper; 1 tsp
  salt; to taste
  black pepper; to taste
chickens; 2½–3 lb (1.5 kg), cut in 8
  pieces; 12

green peppers, diced fine; 4
potatoes, diced medium; 10
scallions, diced fine; 12
olive oil; 1 cup (¼ liter)
parsley, chopped fine; ½ cup
thyme; 1 tbsp
curry powder; 8 tbsp
lemon juice; of 2 lemons

Method
1) Make marinade by combining water, vinegar, garlic, cayenne, salt, and pepper.
2) Put mixture in brazier and add chicken pieces. Marinate 45 minutes at room temperature.
3) Add peppers, potatoes, scallions, oil, parsley, thyme, and curry and cook covered about ½ hour or until chicken is tender.
4) Add lemon juice to the cooking liquid just before serving.

Service
1) Serve moistened with its own cooking juices.

Suggested Wines
Rosé de Provence "les Demoiselles" or California Cabernet Rosé

Chicken *Cordon Bleu*

Yield: 24 portions

Prep time: 40 min
Cook time: 13 min

Equipment
mallet, French knife, cutting board, boning knife, mixing bowl, sheet pan

Ingredients
pink salt
  paprika; as needed
  salt; as needed
  black pepper: as needed
chicken breasts, boned, skin on, flat-
  tened; 24
ham, cooked, sliced thin; 24

Swiss cheese, sliced thin; 24
bread flour; as needed
eggs; 16
milk; 1 qt (1 liter)
cracker meal; as needed

Method
1) Sprinkle pink salt over inside of chicken breasts.
2) Position chicken breast skin side down. Place ham and cheese slices on chicken. Roll from both sides to center. Handle carefully; when cooked, chicken will harden slightly and retain its shape.
3) Roll in bread flour. Coat with egg wash and then cracker meal. Repeat process.*
4) Deep fry until golden brown. Then bake in 400°F oven about 10 minutes.

Service
1) Serve with Cherry Sauce,† Bigarade Sauce,‡ or a simple white sauce.

Suggested Wines
Vin Blanc du Marmandais Côtes de Birac or California White Chianti

---

*Some cooks partially freeze the product at this stage to insure perfect shape.
†See page 91.
‡See page 85.

Chicken *Papillote* Jean Jeannin

Yield: 4 portions

Prep time: 20 min
Cook time: 30 min

Equipment
French knife, cutting board, small brazier, sauté pan, kitchen spoon, large sheets of parchment paper, cookie sheet, scissors

Ingredients
chicken, 2½–3 lb (1.1–1.35 kg); 1
butter, melted; 3 tbsp
vegetable oil; 3 tbsp
shallots, chopped fine; 1 tbsp
dry vermouth; ½ cup (125 ml)
dry white wine; ½ cup (125 ml)
mushrooms, fresh, chopped; 4 tbsp

butter, fresh; 1 oz (30 g)
ham, chopped; 2 tbsp
tarragon, chopped; ¼ tsp
butter, melted; as needed
bacon, fried crisp; 4 slices
salt; to taste
black pepper; to taste

Method
1) Cut chicken in four pieces and sauté slowly in butter and oil until golden brown and cooked. Remove chicken and set aside.
2) Add shallots and sweat very slowly until tender.
3) Remove shallots. Discard fat in pan. Deglaze pan with vermouth and wine.
4) Add stock and shallots and boil until reduced by a third.
5) Sauté mushrooms slightly in butter and add to sauce.
6) Return chicken pieces to sauce and steep (without heat) for 10 minutes.
7) Finish sauce with ham and tarragon.
8) Cut four sheets of parchment paper to a large heart shape.
9) Butter paper. Layer with a little sauce, then the chicken piece, a little more sauce, and finally bacon.
10) Fold the paper over and seal edges very well, making a series of accordion pleats along the seam, very small pleats are the best. Place bags on greased cookie sheet.
11) Bake in 350°F oven until puffed up, about 10 minutes.
12) Cut open bags with scissors, leaving bottom part of paper and edges on serving plate. Trim to present pleasing appearance.

Suggested Wines
Rosé Tavel or California Rosé

Chicken Wrapped in Banana Leaves
(Poulet en Feuilles de Bananiers)

Yield: 16 portions

Prep time: 30 min
Marinating time: 5 hr
Cooking time: 5 min

Equipment
French knife, cutting board, toothpicks or butcher's string, mixing bowl, whip, kitchen spoon, flat plastic or stainless steel pan

Ingredients
Marinade
    soy sauce; 1 cup (¼ liter)
    wine vinegar; 1 cup (¼ liter)
    honey; ½ cup (125 ml)
    coriander; 3 tbsp
    parsley, fresh, chopped fine; 3 tbsp
    Lea & Perrins™ Worcestershire Sauce; 4 tbsp (80 ml)
chicken, boned, cut into large cubes; 8
banana leaves; 10
palm oil or good-quality deep fryer liquid oil; as needed
*Coulis of Pineapple

Method
1) Mix soy sauce, vinegar, honey, coriander, parsley, and Lea & Perrins™ for marinade.
2) Place chicken in a small container and cover with marinade.
3) Refrigerate for at least 5 hours, turning meat at least three times to insure maximum contact with the marinade.
4) Wrap chicken with banana leaves, making tight little packets secured with toothpicks or butcher's string.
5) Deep fry in 375°F fat for 5–8 minutes or until done.

*To make Coulis of Pineapple, puree canned pineapple and cook with just enough cornstarch to thicken to the consistency of Coulis of Blackberry (page 218).

Service

1) Serve the leaf packets open and trimmed so that they look good on the plate.
2) Garnish with Coulis of Pineapple.

Suggested Wines

Bordeaux Blanc Sauterne or California Sauterne

(See color plate 1)

Coq au Vin

Yield: 18 portions   Prep time: 30 min
                                      Cook time: 1 hr

Equipment
French knife, cutting board, heatproof casserole or brazier with lid, kitchen
spoon, slotted spoon

Ingredients
salt pork, diced; 1 cup
butter; 1 lb (450 g)
olive oil; 1 cup (¼ liter)
pearl onions; 36
mushrooms, fresh; 36
chicken, 2½–3 lbs (1.1–1.35 kg)
  each, cut into 8 pieces; 6
flour; as needed
salt; to taste
black pepper; to taste
garlic cloves, chopped fine; 10

thyme; 1 tsp
bay leaves; 3
parsley sprigs; ½ bunch
cognac, warm; 1½ oz (3 ml)
burgundy or other dry red wine;
  1½ qt (1½ liter)
sugar; 1 tsp
Chicken Stock; 1 qt (1 liter)
beurre manié; as needed
parsley, chopped fine; ½ bunch

Method
1) Sauté salt pork in butter and oil until golden brown.
2) Add onions and cook 3 minutes; add mushrooms and cook 2 minutes more.
   Remove onions and mushrooms from pan and set aside.
3) Roll chicken in flour seasoned with salt and pepper.
4) Sauté chicken in the same fat used for onions and mushrooms until golden
   on all sides.
5) Put onions and mushrooms back into casserole with chicken.
6) Add salt, pepper, garlic, thyme, bay leaves, and parsley. Add chicken stock
   and cook covered in 350°F oven until almost tender.
7) Remove chicken and all vegetables. Set aside and keep warm.
8) Skim off excess fat from pan juices and discard.
9) Bring remaining juices to boil and add cognac and wine.
10) Add sugar and bring to boil. If there is insufficient sauce, add stock. Reduce
    to half the original quantity by boiling.
11) Thicken with beurre manié if required.

12) Return chicken and vegetables to casserole and bake covered in 350°F oven until chicken is very tender.

Suggested wines
Vin Blanc du Marmandais Côtes de Birac or California White Chianti

Fricassee of Chicken with Vinegar

Yield: 20 portions

Prep time: 15 min
Cook time: 30 min

Equipment
French knife, cutting board, large brazier, spatula, tongs, kitchen spoon

Ingredients
chicken, fryers, 2½–3 lb (1.5 kg) each, cut into 8 pieces; 7
flour; as needed
chicken fat; 7 oz (200 g)
salt; to taste
black pepper; to taste
shallots, chopped fine; 9 oz (250 g)
white wine vinegar; 1½ pt (625 ml)

white wine; 1 pt (½ liter)
tomatoes, peeled, seeded, diced; 18 oz (500 g)
currant jelly; 8 tbsp (160 ml)
green peppers; 6
Chicken Stock; 1½ qt (1½ liter)
beurre manié; as needed
parsley, chopped; as needed

Method
1) Sprinkle chicken with flour and sauté in chicken fat until brown. Season with salt and pepper.
2) Discard fat.
3) Add shallots and sweat a few minutes.
4) Add vinegar, wine, tomatoes, jelly, and peppers* and reduce about 10 minutes.
5) Add stock and cook about 15 minutes or until tender.
6) Remove chicken and set aside.
7) Thicken liquid in brazier with beurre manié and use as sauce.

Service
Serve garnished with parsley.

Suggested Wines
Vin Blanc de Savoie or California White Colombard

---

*Often, as a variation, instead of tomatoes and green peppers, we add eighteen green peppercorns (*poivre vert*) to the vinegar, wine, and current jelly.

Chicken Soufflé

Yield: 4 portions   Prep time: 30 min
                                     Cook time: 15 min

Equipment
French knife, cutting board, grinder with fine screen, sieve or strainer, kitchen spoon, whip or portable mixer, 4 soufflé cups, wood skewer

Ingredients
*chicken breasts, cooked; 1¼ cup
†Béchamel Sauce, thick; ½ cup (125 ml)
butter; 1 tsp (5 ml)
egg yolks; 3
egg whites; 3
salt; to taste
black pepper; to taste

Method
1) Grind chicken and then press through a fine sieve or strainer.
2) Mix chicken with Béchamel Sauce. Adjust taste with salt and pepper.
3) Mixing well, bind chicken mixture with egg yolks. At this point, the mixture can be held overnight in the refrigerator.
4) Beat egg whites to the consistency of meringue (without, of course, the sugar).
5) Fold egg whites into chicken mixture, combining well.
6) Pour into lightly buttered and floured cups and bake in 375°F oven about 15 minutes. Soufflé should be brown on top and should test clean with a wooden skewer.

Service
1) Serve at once. This entrée cannot be held more than a few minutes.

Suggested Wines
Rosé de Savoie "les Violettes" or California Cabernet Rosé

---

*This recipe may be applied to such fowl as pigeon, turkey, and guinea fowl.
†See page 81.

Boneless Breast of Duck (Magret de Canard)*

Yield: 10 portions

Prep time: 40 min
Cook time: 10 min

Equipment

boning knife, broiler pan, saucepan, kitchen spoon, French knife, cutting board

Ingredients

ducks, 5 lb (2 kg, 250 g) average weight; 5
†Coulis of Blackberry; 1½ cup (375 ml)
†Coulis of Strawberry; 1½ cup (375 ml)
pink salt
  salt; as needed
  black pepper; as needed
  paprika; as needed
butter or margarine; ½ lb (225 g)
bread, white; 10 slices

Method

1) Remove duck breasts from carcasses. Leave skin on, but prick with fork every inch or so, so that fat in skin will drain away during cooking.
2) Sprinkle inside and out with pink salt.
3) Broil about 8 minutes, turning at least once. When duck is finished, it will still be pink inside.
4) Prepare croutons by removing crusts from bread and brushing both sides with butter or margarine. Bake in 400°F oven, turning once, until both sides are golden brown. Cut into wedges and use as a base for the duck on the serving plate (like toast points).
5) Slice duck diagonally and arrange carefully on croutons.
6) Mix Coulis of Blackberry and Coulis of Strawberry together and use as a sauce on top of duck. The sauce can also be in the bottom of the plate.

Suggested Wines

Cahors or California Gamay Red

(See color plate 14)

*This entrée should be cooked to order and served immediately. Holding cooked duck tends to make meat dry and rubbery.

†See page 218.

Coulis of Blackberry*

Yield: 1 pt (½ liter)   Prep time: 5 min
                                         Cook time: 10 min

Equipment
blender, saucepan, kitchen spoon

Ingredients
blackberries, washed; 1 pt (250 g)
lemon juice; 1 tbsp (20 ml)
cornstarch; as needed
water; as needed

Method
1) Puree blackberries and lemon juice and simmer a few minutes.
2) Make a thin paste of cornstarch and water and add little by little to puree until it is the consistency of cold pancake syrup.

Service
1) Serve hot.

(See color plate 14)

*This recipe can also be used for strawberries and raspberries.

Cornish Hens Moscovite

Yield: 6 portions

Prep time: 20 min
Cook time: 40 min

Equipment
French knife, cutting board, clean cloth, roast pan or large casserole, sauté pan

Ingredients
cornish hens; 6
cognac; ½ cup (125 ml)
salt; as required
black pepper; as required
sweet butter; as needed
shallots, chopped; 8
chives, chopped; ½ cup (substitute scallions)
mushrooms, fresh, chopped; 6

tomatoes, peeled, seeded, diced; 3
thyme; ½ tsp
bay leaves; 2
savory; ½ tsp
paprika; 1 tsp
*Smitane Sauce; 1 pint (½ liter)
mushroom caps, broiled with seasoned oil; 6

Method
1) Open cornish hens from the back and remove backbone. Flatten slightly, being careful not to break bones or tear meat.
2) Wipe with clean cloth soaked in brandy and then rub with salt, pepper, and paprika.
3) Melt ½ cup butter.
4) Add birds and bake at 350°F for 35 mintues or until tender. Turn frequently and baste with melted butter and juices. When birds are finished, remove, keep warm.
5) Remove the juices and butter from roast pan and put into sauté pan. Add shallots, chives, mushrooms, and tomatoes and simmer this mixture 4 minutes, stirring constantly.
6) Add thyme, bay leaves, savory, and paprika and simmer 5 minutes more.
7) Stirring constantly, add Smitane Sauce and bring to boil.
8) Pour boiling sauce over warm birds.

*See page 120.

Service
1) Garnish with mushroom caps.

Suggested Wines
Rosé d'Arbois (Jura) or California Grignolino Rosé

Bird Casanova

Yield: 8 portions

Prep time: 20 min
Cook time: 35 min

Equipment
French knife, cutting board, sheet pan, cleaver or heavy spatula

Ingredients

cornish hens; 8
pink salt
  salt; as needed
  black pepper; as needed
  paprika; as needed
Dijon mustard; 10 oz (280 g)
garlic cloves, chopped fine; 20

ham, chopped fine; 8 oz (225 g)
parsley, chopped fine; 1 bunch
bread crumbs; 1 lb (450 g) or as
  needed
butter, melted; as needed
*Smitane Sauce

Method
1) Split bird from the back and remove backbone. Flatten bird with cleaver or heavy spatula.
2) Season inside and out with pink salt.
3) Place the bird on the buttered sheet pan, skin side down. Brush the inside with mustard.
4) Add first the garlic, then ham, then parsley, then bread crumbs. These ingredients are added in layers and when finished should create a low mound. Baste with melted butter.
5) Bake in 350°F oven 35 minutes. Take care not to overcook.†

Service
1) Serve with Smitane Sauce.

Suggested Wines
Lancer's Rosé or California Rosé Zinfandel

(See color plate 16)

*See page 120.
†Do not attempt to hold this entrée very long as it will dry out quickly.

Mushroom Soufflé

Yield: 18 portions

Prep time: 25 min
Cook time: 15 min

Equipment
French knife, cutting board, grater, whip, kitchen spoon, mixing bowl, saucepan, soufflé dishes

Ingredients
*Béchamel Sauce; 3 cup (¾ liter)
salt; to taste
black pepper; to taste
†Swiss cheese, grated; 1½ cup (250 g)
eggs; 15
mushrooms, fresh, chopped fine; 1½ lb (675 g)

Method
1) Add salt, pepper, and Swiss cheese to Béchamel Sauce.
2) Separate the egg whites from the yolks. Whip the whites until they are the consistency of a good meringue.
3) Fold the yolks into the sauce after insuring sauce is not too hot.
4) Add mushrooms to Béchamel Sauce and then gently fold in the egg whites.
5) Pour into buttered soufflé dishes and cook in 400°F oven for 15 minutes, until puffed and well browned.

Suggested Wines
California Gamay Rosé or Côtes du Marmandais Rosé

---

*See page 81.
†If desired, a different taste can be obtained by substituting 1½ teaspoon thyme for Swiss cheese.

Classic Quiche Lorraine*

Yield: 6 portions

Prep time: 15 min
Cook time: 25 min

Equipment
French knife, cutting board, mixing bowl, sauté pan, mixing bowl, whip,
kitchen spoon, strainer, pie tin

Ingredients
bacon, slices, cut in half; 6
Swiss cheese, sliced thin; 12
eggs, lightly beaten; 6
light cream; 2 cup (½ liter)
flour; 1 tbsp
nutmeg, ground; 1 pinch
cayenne pepper; 1 pinch
black pepper; 1 pinch
9-in. pie shell, unbaked, made with unsweetened pie dough; 1

Method
1) Sauté bacon until slightly brown, cooked but not crisp.
2) Cover bottom of pie shell with overlapping bacon and cheese slices.
3) Combine eggs, cream, flour, nutmeg, cayenne, and pepper and beat well.
4) Strain and fill pie shell with mixture.
5) Bake in hot oven (400°F) for 25 minutes. Do not cut for at least 10 minutes after removing from oven.

Suggested Wines
Alsace Gewürztraminer or California Gewürztraminer

---

*Quiche Lorraine may be prepared in advance if the pastry and the filling are refrigerated separately. It is unwise to prepare more than a day ahead, as the pie dough and cut cheese will dry out. Allow dough and filling to stand at room temperature for 30 minutes before combining and baking.

*Pâté en Croûte**

Yield: 6 portions   Prep time: 20 min

Equipment
sifter, mixing bowl, rolling pin, baker's work table or work board

Ingredients
bread flour; 18 oz (500 g)
salt; ½ oz (15 g)
butter; 5½ oz (150 g)
olive oil; 4 tbsp (80 ml)
egg yolks; 4
cold water; ½ qt (½ liter) or as needed

Method
1) Sift flour and salt together.
2) Add butter and oil and blend with hands.
3) Blend in egg yolks
4) Add cold water until pie dough-like consistency is attained.
5) Roll dough to ¼-inch thickness and encase cold *pâté*.
6) Bake in 400°F oven, ½ hour per pound of meat. After dough browns, cover with aluminum foil to prevent burning.

Suggested Wines
Red Bordeaux Château de Chevalier or California Gamay Red

*Any *pâté*, partially cooked, may be used.

French Liver *Pâté*

Yield: 3½ lb (1.5 kg)

Prep time: 45 min
Cook time: 1½ hr
Chill time: overnight

Equipment
meat grinder, French knife, cutting board, mixing bowl, kitchen spoon, electric mixer, loaf pan, large shallow pan

Ingredients
pork liver or calf liver; 1½ lb (675 g)
whipping cream; ½ cup (125 ml)
onion, large, chopped fine; 1
butter; 1 tbsp (20 ml)
pork fat; ½ lb (225 g)
pork; 1½ lb (675 g)
garlic cloves, crushed; 2
parsley, chopped; 2 tbsp
thyme; 1 tsp

basil; 1 tsp
flour; 1 tbsp
eggs; 2
cognac; ½ cup (125 ml)
salt; 1 tsp
black pepper; 1 tsp
bay leaves; 3
pork fat, ¼-inch (6-mm) slices; 3

Method
1) Grind liver and mix with cream. Let stand for 1 hour.
2) Sauté onion in butter until tender but not brown.
3) Grind pork fat with pork.
4) Combine liver mixture, sautéed onions, ground pork and pork fat, garlic, parsley, thyme, basil, flour, eggs, cognac, salt, and pepper and mix very well. (An electric mixer will insure complete blending of all ingredients.)
5) Line loaf pan with pork fat slices.
6) Fill loaf pan with meat mixture, put bay leaves on top, and seal with foil.
7) Bake in water bath for 1½ hours at 350°F. Place loaf pan in shallow pan of boiling water and put both pans in oven. Water should cover half the depth of loaf pan.
8) Remove the foil 20 minutes before the end of cooking so the top of *pâté* will be golden brown and attractive.
9) Cool overnight before serving.

Suggested Wines
Beaujolais Chiroubles or California Gamay Red

Frog Legs Riesling

Yield: 24 portions   Prep time: 20 min
                                      Cook time: 25 min

Equipment
French knife, cutting board, brazier, kitchen spoon, whip

Ingredients
shallots, chopped fine; 24   Chicken Stock, rich; 1 qt (1 liter)
scallions, chopped fine; 4 bunches   salt; to taste
butter or margarine; 18 oz (500 g)   black pepper; to taste
frog legs, split into individual legs; 96   heavy cream; 1½ qt (1½ liter)
garlic cloves, chopped fine; 6   butter; as needed
Riesling wine; 1 qt (1 liter)   lemon, sliced thin; as needed

Method
1) Sauté shallots and scallions in melted butter about 2 minutes.
2) Add the frog legs and garlic and sauté until the legs are light golden brown.
3) Add wine, stock, salt, and pepper and bring to a boil. Simmer uncovered for about 10 minutes or until frog legs are tender.
4) Remove legs and keep warm.
5) Boil liquid about 10 minutes to reduce.
6) Add cream and butter if desired, after removing from heat. Using whip, mix very well to produce a medium consistency.

Service
1) Arrange legs attractively on plate and cover with sauce.
2) Add parsley to sauce just before serving.
3) Garnish with lemon.

Suggested Wine
Riesling Alsace or Riesling California

Vol au Vent Financiére

Yield: 24 portions

Prep time: 1 hr
Cook time: 20 min

Equipment
French knife, cutting board, brazier, sauté pan, bowls, kitchen spoon, pastry brush, sheet pan, parchment paper

Ingredients
*sweetbreads, poached, diced small; 2 lb (.9 kg)
chicken breast, boned, poached, diced small or *veal brains, poached, diced small; 2 lb (.9 kg)
†veal tongue, poached, diced small; 2 lb (.9 kg)
Financiére Sauce
 ‡Chicken Velouté, thick; 5 qt (5 liter)
 Madeira wine; 1 cup (250 ml)
 mushrooms, fresh, sliced thin, sautéed; 2 cup

olives, black, pitted, sliced; 1½ cup
olives, green, pitted, sliced; 1½ cup
thyme; 1 tsp
salt; to taste
pepper; to taste
beurre manié; as needed
beaten egg white; of 5 eggs
whipping cream; 1 cup (250 ml)
**Puff Pastry shells and lids, baked; 24

Method
1) Combine diced meats and set aside.
2) Bring Velouté to simmer in brazier. Add Madeira, mushrooms, olives, and thyme. Simmer 20 minutes and adjust taste with salt and pepper.
3) If not thick, add beurre manié as required. Sauce should be thicker than pancake syrup. Finish with cream.
4) When desired thickness is reached, add meats. Combine well. Insure mixture is quite hot.

*Placing sweetbreads or brains in pot of salted cold water. Begin heating. When water comes to a boil, meats are done.
†Veal tongue is cooked by simmering about 3 hours in salted water with mirepoix and bouquet garni.
‡See page 125.

5) Fill warmed shells (not quite to top of pastry) and cover with pastry lid.

Service

1) Serve at once. Do not hold for more than 10 minutes or pastry will become soggy.
2) For classic service, detach pastry lid enough so customer may partially view contents.

Suggested Wines

Bordeaux Blanc or California Chenin Blanc

(See color plate 7)

**Pastry shells, usually smaller than traditional *Vol au Vent* shells, can be purchased in pre-baked form, usually without lids.

To make from scratch:

1) Roll puff pastry to ¼-inch (5-mm) thickness.
2) Cut a round of dough, 6-inch (12-cm) in diameter. Place on sheet pan lined with parchment paper.
3) Cut another round of the same size. From this, cut and discard a 4½-inch (9-cm) diameter circle, leaving a doughnut shape.
4) Brush the first pastry piece with egg white. Place the doughnut-shaped round on top and press lightly to seal.
5) Cut a 6-inch (12-cm) diameter round for lid.
6) Brush the doughnut-shaped round with egg white, avoiding the edges, and seal on lid.
7) Bake at 400°F about 20 min, or until puffed and golden brown.
8) To fill, detach lid. Replace before service.

Truffles in Turnovers (Truffes en Chaussons)

Yield: 8 portions

Prep time: 30 min
Cook time: 30 min

Equipment
French knife, cutting board, rolling pin, parchment paper, sheet pan, table fork, pastry brush

Ingredients
truffles, fresh; 8 (canned truffles *cannot* be substituted)
salt; to taste
black pepper; to taste
fatback, sliced very fine; 8
*Puff Pastry; 18 oz (500 g)
goose liver mousse; 8 oz (230 g)
armagnac; 2 tbsp (40 ml)
eggs; 2
milk; 1 tbsp (20 ml)

Method
1) Wash and scrub truffles carefully. Dry truffles and salt and pepper them.
2) Wrap each truffle in a slice of fatback.
3) Roll puff pastry to ⅛–⅙ inch thickness and cut dough into circles.
4) Cover the inside of each circle with goose liver mousse and sprinkle a few drops of armagnac on top of mousse.
5) Add the truffle wrapped with fatback.
6) Wet the outside of the puff pastry circle with finger to insure a good seal. Fold into half-moon shape and seal again with fork.
7) Brush with egg wash† (except on seals) and puncture dough with fork.
8) Bake at 400°F about 25 minutes.

Suggested Wines
Pommard or Taylor Baco Noir Burgundy

(See color plate 18)

---

*See pages 40–41.
†For egg wash, whip eggs and milk together.

Pork Cutlets Paprika

Yield: 24 portions   Prep time: 20 min
                                            Cook time: 20 min

Equipment
French knife, cutting board, small brazier, kitchen spoon, mallet, parchment paper sheets, large sauté pan, spatula, whip

Ingredients
Sauce
    bacon, chopped; 2 cup
    onions, chopped fine; 2 cup
    sweet paprika; 10 tbsp
    cayenne pepper; ½ tsp
    *Brown Sauce; 1½ qt (1½ liter)
    sour cream; 10 tbsp (200 ml)
    salt; to taste
    black pepper; to taste
pork loin cutlets, boned, 5 oz (150 g) each; 24
flour; 4 cup
peanut oil; as needed
lemon wedges; as needed
parsley sprigs; as needed

Method
1) Prepare sauce, sauté bacon and onion until bacon is crisp and onion is tender and transparent.
2) Pour off fat. Add paprika and cayenne and stir constantly over medium heat for 1 minute.
3) Stir in Brown Sauce and continue to heat to boiling point.
4) Remove pan from heat and add sour cream, salt, and pepper.
5) Keep sauce warm on steam table or in hot water bath. Do not boil.
6) Use a mallet to flatten cutlets between parchment paper sheets until they are ¼ inch thick. Sprinkle with salt and pepper and dredge in flour, shaking off excess.
7) Sauté cutlets in oil with moderately high heat, about 2 minutes on each side or until they are light golden in color.

*See page 88.

8) Drain well and add sauce.

Service
1) Garnish with lemon and parsley.

Suggested Wines
Bourgogne Rouge, Nuits-St.-Georges, or California Corignane

Brochettes of Pork Marinade

Yield: 12 portions

Prep time: 15 min
Marinate time: 24 hr
Cook time: 15 min

Equipment
French knife, cutting board, mixing bowl, shallow dish, metal skewers, broiler pan

Ingredients
Marinade
   olive oil; 2 cup
   peppercorns, crushed; 20
   thyme; 1 tbsp
   garlic cloves, fresh, crushed, chopped; 10
   cumin powder; 1½ tsp
   Lea & Perrins™ Worcestershire Sauce; 6 tbsp
pork tenderloin, cut in 1-inch (2.5-cm) cubes; 6 lb (2.7 kg)
salt pork, smoked, cut in 1-inch (2.5-cm) cubes; 4.4 lb (2 kg)
onions, blanched in salted water, quartered, layers separated; 3
peaches, sliced; as needed
melon, sliced; as needed

Method
1) Prepare marinade by combining the oil, peppercorns, thyme, garlic, cumin, and Lea & Perrins™.
2) Cover tenderloin cubes with marinade and refrigerate 24 hours.
3) Prepare brochettes by alternating on skewer one cube of salt pork, one cube of tenderloin, and one piece of onion. There should be four pieces of tenderloin for each brochette.
4) Broil 15 minutes in preheated medium broiler, turning frequently.

Service

1) Serve on a bed of rice.
2) Garnish with peaches or melons.
3) Use either Robert Sauce* or Cider Sauce.†

Suggested Wines

Beaujolais-Brouilly or California Gamay Red

*See page 117.
†See page 92.

Pork Chops with Watermelon
(Côtes de Porc à la Pastèque)

Yield: 12 portions   Prep time: 15 min
                                        Cook time: 25 min

Equipment
French knife, cutting board, large sauté pan, kitchen spoon

Ingredients
pork chops; 12
butter; 11 oz (300 g)
watermelon, rind removed, seeded, cut in medium cubes; 11 lb (5 kg)
*crème frâiche
cinnamon; 1 tsp
salt; to taste
black pepper; to taste

Method
1) Sauté pork chops with about half the butter for about 18 minutes or until done.
2) Drain cubed watermelon.
3) After draining excess fat from pork chops, set aside and keep warm.
4) Discard most of the fat in the sauté pan and sweat about half of the watermelon cubes for 15 minutes.
5) Crush melon cubes with fork and add *crème frâiche*. Mix well.
6) Add cinnamon, salt, and pepper and simmer very slowly for 10 minutes.
7) Very quickly, sauté the rest of the watermelon with the remaining butter over high heat.
8) Add to the sauce.
9) Place pork chops on warmed plates and sauce, insuring that each chop has a few chunks of melon.

Suggested Wines
Beaujolais Fleurie or California Gamay Red

---

*If commercial version is unavailable, substitute by mixing well 1½ quart (1½ liter) of heavy cream with 2 tablespoons (40 ml) of buttermilk.

Alsatian Sauerkraut (Choucroute Garnie)

Yield: 24 portions   Prep time: 30 min
                                           Cook time: 1½ hr

Equipment
French knife, cutting board, large brazier, kitchen spoon

Ingredients
pork butt, fresh, parboiled 10 minutes, sliced; 2 lb (.9 kg)
sauerkraut, canned, well washed, squeezed dry; 6 lb (2.7 kg)
green apples, peeled, sliced; 4
onions, medium, studded with 4 cloves each; 2
carrots, peeled, quartered; 2
juniper berries; 36
bouquet garni
   parsley, chopped; ½ cup
   thyme; 1 tsp
   bay leaf; 3
dry white wine; 3 cup (¾ liter)
Chicken Stock or White Stock; 2½ qt (2½ liter)
salt; to taste
black pepper; to taste
lard, melted; 1½ cup (375 ml)
bacon or lean salt pork, cut in ¼-in. (.6-mm) slices, parboiled for 10 min.;
   1½ lb (675 g)
boiled ham, sliced; 1½ lb (675 g)
Polish sausage; 18 (substitute any cooked smoked sausage or even
   frankfurters)
potatoes, boiled; 24

Method
1) Line the bottom of brazier with slices of pork butt and place sauerkraut on top.
2) Add apples, onions, carrots, berries, bouquet garni, wine, and sufficient stock to cover sauerkraut. Season lightly with salt and pepper.
3) Add lard, cover, and simmer 1½ hours.
4) Add bacon, folding into the other ingredients and cook 15 more minutes.

5) Add ham and sausages and cook an additional 10 minutes.
6) Discard onions and bouquet garni.

Service
1) Make bed of sauerkraut on warmed platter. Insure that each portion includes a piece of pork, ham, sausage, and apple.
2) Serve with piece of boiled potato on same plate.
3) Moisten with a little of the cooking liquid.

Suggested Wines
Blanc de Moselle, California Riesling, or California Barbera

Beef Burgundy

Yield: 24 portions

Prep time: 45 min
Cook time: 3 hr

Equipment
French knife, cutting board, large sauté pan, large heatproof casserole with lid, kitchen spoon

Ingredients
olive oil; 1 cup (250 ml)
butter; as needed
salt pork, small julienne; 2 lb (900 g)
bread flour; as needed
beef, top round or chuck, well
  trimmed, cleaned, cut into 1¼-in.
  (3 cm) cubes; 12 lb (5.4 kg)
salt; to taste
black pepper; to taste
cognac, warm; 1 cup (250 ml)
carrots, chopped (medium brunoise);
  2
leeks, chopped; 3
shallots, diced small; 12
Spanish onions, chopped (medium
  brunoise); 2

garlic cloves, crushed; 4
bouquet garni
  bay leaves; 3
  thyme; 1½ tsp
  parsley, chopped; 1½ cup
burgundy wine; 2 qt (2 liter)
Beef Stock; as needed
beurre manié; 8 tbsp or as needed
pearl onions; 24
red wine; as needed
sugar; 1 tsp
mushroom caps; 24
lemon juice; 1 tsp (5 ml)
parsley, chopped fine; as needed

Method
1) Heat 8 tablespoons olive oil and 8 tablespoons butter and sauté salt pork until golden brown. Transfer pork to casserole.
2) Using the remaining oil, brown beef cubes on all sides and season with salt and pepper. Add cognac.
3) Ignite beef and cognac with a lighted match and transfer to casserole.
4) Brown carrots, leeks, shallots, Spanish onions, and garlic in remaining fat. Transfer to casserole.
5) Add bouquet garni, burgundy wine, and enough stock to cover the contents and cook covered in slow oven (300°F) for 1 hour.
6) Remove casserole from oven. Skim off fat. Stir in little pieces of beurre manié.

7) Return to oven and cook 1¾ hours more or until beef is very tender. Set aside and keep warm.
8) Brown pearl onions in 4 tablespoons butter. Add a little red wine and sweat until onions are tender.
9) Sauté mushroom caps in butter with lemon juice.
10) Remove bouquet garni from casserole and discard. Correct seasoning with salt and pepper if required.

Service
1) Garnish with pearl onions, mushroom caps, and a sprinkle of parsley.

Suggested Wines
Volnay or Taylor Baco Noir Burgundy

Short Ribs with Horseradish Sauce

Yield: 30 portions

Prep time: 30 min
Cook time: 2½ hr

Equipment
French knife, cutting board, large brazier, kitchen spoon, strainer, bowls, whip

Ingredients

short ribs, well trimmed; 30
olive oil; ½ pt (¼ liter)
mirepoix
   carrots, diced small; 4
   celery stalks, diced small; 4
   onions, medium, diced small; 3
bay leaves; 4
thyme; 2 tbsp
caraway seeds; 1 tbsp
cognac; 1 cup (250 ml)
red wine; 1 qt (1 liter)

garlic cloves, crushed; 2
salt; to taste
black pepper; ½ tsp
Beef Stock; 2 gal (8 liter)
parsley, fresh, chopped; 1 cup
  (175 g)
tomato paste; 3 tbsp (60 ml)
sour cream; ½ pt (¼ liter)
horseradish; ½ pt (¼ liter)
beurre manié; as needed
parsley, fresh, chopped; as needed

Method
1) Brown all sides of short ribs with oil. Set ribs aside.
2) In remaining oil, sauté mirepoix, bay leaves, thyme, and caraway seeds about 10 minutes.
3) Add cognac and ignite with match.
4) When flame stops, add wine and simmer 3 minutes.
5) Add garlic, salt, pepper, stock, parsley, and tomato paste and bring to boil. Add ribs. Simmer about 2½ hours or until beef is tender, nearly falling off the bone.
6) Carefully remove ribs and set aside.
7) Strain cooking liquid and return to heat.
8) Bring to a rapid boil and thicken with beurre manié. Sauce should be somewhat thicker than pancake syrup at this point. Remove from heat.
9) Combine sour cream and horseradish.
10) Spoonful by spoonful, add the hot sauce to the sour cream mixture until it is approximately the same temperature as the liquid in brazier. Use whip constantly.

11) Combine the sour cream mixture with sauce in brazier.

Service
1) Serve sauce on top of ribs.
2) Garnish with chopped parsley.
3) Noodles are a good accompaniment.

Suggested Wines
Médoc Rouge or California Barbera

Hungarian Beef Goulash

Yield: 25 portions

Prep time: 25 min
Cook time: 2½ hr

Equipment
French knife, cutting board, large brazier, spatula, kitchen spoon

Ingredients
bacon fat; ½ pt (¼ liter)
beef chuck, well trimmed, 1½-in. (3 cm) cubes; 10 lb (4.5 kg)
onions, chopped fine; 8 lb (3.6 kg)
Beef Stock; 2 qt (2 liter)
garlic cloves, chopped; 12
caraway seeds; 4 tsp
sweet paprika; 8 tbsp
salt; to taste
black pepper; as needed
tomato puree; 2 cup (500 ml)

Method
1) Heat bacon fat until it begins to smoke. Sear beef in fat and reduce heat to low.
2) Sauté onions with beef and fat about 10 minutes.
3) Add stock, garlic, caraway seeds, paprika, salt, and pepper and heat to boiling. Reduce to simmer and simmer covered about 2 hours or until beef is tender.
4) Stir in tomato puree and simmer uncovered another 30 minutes to reduce. Liquid should be consistency of syrup.

Service
1) Serve with potato croquettes or noodles.

Suggested Wines
Bordeaux Rouge Château Las-Cases or California Red Zinfandel

Steak Diane

Yield: 12 portions   Prep time: 15 min
                                      Cook time: 10 min

Equipment
French knife, cutting board, large sauté pan, spatula, kitchen spoon

Ingredients
unsalted sweet butter; 2 cup (440 g) | Beef Stock; 3 cup (750 ml)
mushrooms, sliced; 3 lb (1.36 kg) | beurre manié; 2 tbsp
shallots, minced; ½ cup | *Robert Sauce; ¾ cup (180 ml)
parsley, chopped; ½ cup | Worcestershire sauce; 2 tbsp (40 ml)
Madeira wine; 1½ cup (3 dl) | salt; to taste
filet of beef, about 4 lb, cut in | black pepper; to taste
  ⅜-in. slices; 2 | wild rice, hot, cooked; 3 lb (1.35 kg)
cognac, warm; ½ cup (125 ml) | cooked weight

Method
1) Heat butter. Add mushrooms, shallots, and parsley and sauté about 3 minutes or until shallots are transparent.
2) Deglaze pan with wine. Add beef and cook until medium rare, turning once (about 3 minutes).
3) Pour cognac over beef and ignite. When flame dies, remove beef and set aside, keeping warm.
4) Add stock.
5) Add buerre manié and bring to boil for 2 to 5 minutes or until desired thickness is obtained.
6) Stir in Robert Sauce and Worcestershire sauce. Adjust taste with salt and pepper if required.
7) Return beef to pan just long enough to moisten and reheat.

Service
1) Serve beef over wild rice with sauce.

Suggested Wines
St. Emilion Château Croque-Michotte or California Merlot

*See page 117.

Estouffade Provençale

Yield: 30 portions

Prep time: 30 min
Cook time: 3 hr

Equipment
French knife, kitchen knife, cutting board, large brazier, kitchen spoon

Ingredients
salt pork, cut in lardons*; 2½ lb (1.1 kg)
beef from short ribs or chuck, well trimmed, 1½-in. (3-cm) cubes; 15 lb
  (6.8 kg)
onions, medium, sliced; 8
garlic cloves, crushed; 8
flour; 1 cup (110 g)
Beef Stock; 1 gal (4 liter)
red wine; 2½ cup (625 ml)
orange zest; of 1 orange
bouquet garni
  bay leaf; 4
  thyme; 4 tbsp
  parsley, stems; ½ cup
tomatoes, diced, canned, drained; 2½ lb (1.1 kg)
tomato paste; 1 tbsp (20 ml)
olives, black or green, pitted, sliced; 60
mushrooms, fresh, sliced; 1½ lb (671 g)
butter; as needed
parsley, chopped; as needed

Method
1) Sauté salt pork until golden brown. Remove and set aside.
2) Sauté beef, onions, and garlic in salt pork fat.
3) Sprinkle the beef and onions with flour and sweat a few minutes, mixing
   well.
4) Add stock, wine, orange zest, bouquet garni, tomatoes, tomato paste, and
   olives and bring to boil. Simmer 2½ to 3 hours or until beef is quite tender.

*A lardon is the thickness of a french fry, but about 1½ inches (40 mm) long.

5) While beef is cooking, sauté fresh mushrooms in butter and set aside. Mix into Estouffade 10 minutes before end of cooking.

Service
1) Garnish with a few sautéed lardons and parsley.
2) Serve with noodles.

Suggested Wines
Bandol Rouge or California Red Sebastiani

Pot Roast of Beef with Mustard Sauce and Vegetables
(Pot au Feu avec la Sauce Moutarde et les Petits Légumes de Jardin)

Yield: 6 portions

Prep time: 25 min
Cook time: 3 hr

Equipment
French knife, boning knife, cutting board, butcher's string, large heavy skillet, large casserole or pot roast pan with tight-fitting lid, aluminum foil, sauce pans, ovenproof platter, wooden spoon

Ingredients
beef chuck roast, bone out; 4 lb (1.8 kg)
all-purpose flour; ½ cup
salt; ½ tsp
black pepper; ½ tsp
sugar; 1 tsp
vegetable oil; 2 tbsp (40 ml)
onions, medium, sliced; 2
dry red wine; ½ cup (125 ml)
milk; ½ cup (125 ml)

Beef Stock; 1 cup (250 ml)
bay leaf; 1
parsley, chopped; 2 tbsp
carrots, tiny Belgian, peeled, with 1-in. green tops; 12
leeks, small, trimmed; 12
new potatoes, small; 24
Dijon mustard; 2 tbsp (40 ml) or to taste
milk or cream; 4–6 tbsp

Method
1) Trim roast very well, insuring that all fat is removed.
2) Tie roast securely with string at 1-inch intervals.
3) Combine flour, salt, pepper, and sugar and dredge meat in it on all sides to coat well. Shake off excess.
4) Heat oil over medium high heat almost to smoke point and brown meat lightly on all sides.
5) Remove meat and set aside. Pour off all but 1 tablespoon of fat.
6) Add onions and cook over low heat 8 to 10 minutes or until onions are soft and transparent. Then add half of wine to deglaze skillet.

7) Place beef in foil-lined casserole* with onions and liquid in skillet. Add remaining wine, milk, and stock. Spread onions over meat and add bay leaf and parsley. Fold sides of foil together over top of meat to form an airtight envelope. Place cover on casserole.†

8) Roast in preheated 325°F oven for 3 hours or until meat is tender when pierced with skewer.

9) Toward end of cooking time, heat medium saucepan of salted water to boiling over medium heat. Add carrots and cook covered until just tender, about 6 to 8 minutes. Drain, set aside, and keep warm.

10) Add leeks to boiling salted water and cook covered until just tender, about 15 minutes. Drain, set aside, and keep warm.

11) Add potatoes to boiling salted water and cook covered until just tender, about 15 minutes. Drain, set aside, and keep warm.

12) Remove casserole from oven and transfer meat to ovenproof platter. Broil for a few minutes. This is done only long enough to brown the meat slightly and to bring the onions to a golden brown color.

13) Pour cooking juices from casserole into small heavy saucepan or brazier and skim off fat from surface.

14) Add mustard and milk or cream (depending on desired thickness of sauce) and heat through over low heat. *Do not allow to boil*! Boiling will cause sauce to curdle.

15) Remove from heat and season with salt and pepper to taste.

16) Discard string from roast. Slice meat for service.

Service

1) Arrange carrots, leeks, and potatoes around sliced meat on platter.

2) Sprinkle potatoes with chopped parsley.

3) Sauce meat‡ as it is served, with cooking juices.

Suggested Wines
Burgundy Vergelesses Red or California Gamay Noir

---

*Foil must be large enough to enclose roast completely.

†Any variation of this procedure (such as the use of the widely available plastic "roast bags") is acceptable as long as the meat is tightly sealed so that it can cook in its own steam and juices.

‡As a variation, Horseradish Sauce (page 101) may be used.

❖

Filet of Beef Wellington

Yield: 10 portions

Prep time: 30 min
Cook time: 1 hr

Equipment
French knife, cutting board, butcher's string, sauté pan, rolling pin, fork, sheet pan

Ingredients
tenderloin of beef; 5 lb (2.25 kg)
salt; to taste
black pepper; to taste
paprika; to taste
butter; as required
truffled goose liver; 1 lb (450 g)
*Puff Pastry; 2½ lb (1.1 kg)
egg yolk, beaten; 1
†Madeira Sauce or ‡Bordelaise Sauce; 1 pt (½ liter)

Method
1) Clean tenderloin.
2) Season with salt, pepper, and paprika.
3) Spread a generous amount of butter over the meat.
4) Brown and partially cook tenderloin 5 minutes on each side. Allow to cool. Dry well.
5) When cold, spread goose liver over the entire surface.
6) Roll out the pastry into an oblong ⅛-inch (3-mm) thick. Place tenderloin in the center. Prepare another oblong piece, slightly longer, for a top to completely enfold with pastry. Moisten edges with water, trim the edges, and seal together.
7) Decorate with strips of pastry, brush with beaten egg yolk, and prick top of pastry with fork. Place on sheet pan.
8) Bake in preheated 400°F oven about 40 to 45 minutes or until the pastry is well browned. Cooking time depends on whether medium or rare meat is desired. Internal temperature is 110°F for rare.

*See page 40–41.
†See pages 124.
‡See page 87.

Service

1) Serve accompanied with sauce in a sauce boat.

Suggested Wines

California Red Cabernet Sauvignon or Côtes-du-Rhône Gigondas

(See color plate 13)

Blanquette of Veal

Yield: 20 portions

Prep time: 30 min
Cook time: 1½ hr

Equipment
French knife, cutting board, kitchen spoon, brazier

Ingredients
veal shoulder, well trimmed, cut into 1½-in. (3 cm) cubes weighing 2 oz
  (60 g); 8 lb (3.6 kg)
Chicken Stock; 1½ gal (6 liter)
onion, whole, studded with 4 cloves; 1
mushrooms, fresh; 7
bouquet garni
    bay leaves; 3
    parsley stems, chopped; ½ cup
    thyme; 1 tbsp
carrot, sliced; 1
garlic cloves, diced; 4
celery leaves; from 2 stalks
salt; to taste
black pepper; to taste
onion, sliced; 1
beurre manié; as needed
nutmeg; ½ tsp
egg yolks; 7
heavy cream; 1 qt (1 liter)
lemon juice; 2 tsp (40 ml)
mushrooms, canned; 1 lb (450 g)
parsley, chopped; 1 bunch

Method
1) Place veal in pot with cold water and bring to boil to blanch. Wash again in cold water and drain.
2) Simmer veal with stock, cloved onion, fresh mushrooms, bouquet garni, carrots, garlic, celery leaves, salt, and pepper about 1½ hours or until veal is tender.
3) Sauté sliced onion.

4) When veal is tender, remove from sauce and drain.
5) Thicken sauce with beurre manié.
6) Add nutmeg and simmer about 5 minutes.
7) Finish with egg yolks and cream and adjust taste with lemon juice, salt, and pepper as required.

Service

1) Garnish veal and sauce with sautéed onions, canned mushrooms, and chopped parsley.

Suggested Wines

Côtes-du-Rhône Rosé des Baumes-de-Venise or California Cabernet Rosé

Veal Marengo*

Yield: 20 portions

Prep time: 20 min
Cook time: 1½ hr

Equipment
French knife, cutting board, large brazier, kitchen spoon

Ingredients

veal, well trimmed, cubed; 5 lb
  (2.25 kg)
flour; 1½ cup (175 g)
paprika; 1 tbsp
salt; to taste
black pepper; to taste
onions, diced small; 2 lb (900 g)
garlic cloves, crushed; 5
olive oil; ½ cup (125 ml)
cognac, warm; 1½ oz (44 ml)

Chicken or Veal Stock; 1 qt (1 liter)
mushrooms, sliced; 2 lb (900 g)
tomatoes, peeled, seeded, diced;
  1⅓ qt
olives, pitted, mixture of green and
  black, sliced; 50
parsley, chopped; ½ cup
thyme; 1 tsp
bay leaf; 2

Method
1) Dust veal with flour, paprika, salt, and pepper.
2) Sauté veal, onions, and garlic in oil until veal is slightly brown and onions are transparent.
3) Add cognac and ignite with lighted match.
4) Add stock, mushrooms, tomatoes, olives, parsley, thyme, bay leaf and bring to boil. Reduce to simmer and simmer for 1½ hours.
5) Adjust taste with salt and pepper if necessary.

Service
1) Serve over spaghetti.

Suggested Wines
Rosé de Callas or California Zinfandel

Chicken Marengo is made in exactly the same manner. Simply substitute chicken for veal and cook only 1 hour.

Osso Buco (New Style)

Yield: 24 portions   Prep time: 40 min
                                             Cook time: I hr, 45 min

Equipment
French knife, cutting board, meat saw, large brazier, sauté pan, kitchen
spoon.

Ingredients

veal shank, bone-in, I-in. (2.5-cm)   bouquet garni
  slices; 17 lb (7.65 kg)   parsley, stems, chopped; ½ cup
olive oil; I cup (250 ml)   bay leaves; 3
butter; 3½ oz (100 g)   thyme; I tbsp
carrots, medium, sliced; 12   tomato paste; I cup (250 ml)
onions, medium, diced; 6   white wine; 2 cup (½ liter)
shallots, diced; 15   salt; to taste
orange juice; of 8 oranges   black pepper; to taste
orange zest; of 3 oranges   heavy cream; I qt (I liter)
garlic cloves, diced; 10   orange slices; as needed

Method
1) Using brazier, sauté veal slices a few minutes on each side in a mixture of
   oil and butter. Remove from heat.
2) Sauté carrots, onions, and shallots until golden. Add to meat and return brazier to heat.
3) Add orange juice, orange zest, garlic, bouquet garni, tomato paste, wine,
   salt, and pepper and simmer I½ hours or until meat is tender.
4) Remove meat and keep warm.
5) Add cream, blend sauce, and simmer very slowly for 5 minutes.

Service
1) Serve veal shanks in sauce.
2) Garnish with orange slices.

Suggested Wines
Lancer's Rosé or California Rosé Zinfandel

Quenelles of Veal (or Chicken)
(Old Recipe—100 years old)

Yield: 8 portions

Prep time: 30 min
Cook time: 5–10 min

Equipment
boning knife, cutting board, meat grinder with very fine screen, large mixing bowl, brazier, kitchen spoon, whip

Ingredients
veal or chicken breast; 18 oz (500 g)
white bread, crust removed; 9 oz (250 g)
milk; 3 cup (¾ liter)
butter; 9 oz (250 g)
salt; to taste
black pepper; to taste
egg yolks; 4
egg whites; 4
water, salted; 2 gal (8 liter)
flour; as needed
*Sauce Portugaise; as needed

Method
1) Remove all skin and fat from meat. Grind in meat grinder, two to three times if necessary to obtain a fine paste.
2) Soak bread in milk and squeeze out as much moisture as possible.† Discard milk or save for soup.
3) Mix well the meat, bread, and butter.
4) Season with salt and pepper and mix again.
5) Add egg yolks and mix again.
6) Fold in egg whites and mix well.
7) Bring water to boil. Reduce heat to simmer.
8) Shape quenelle mixture into small balls or little sausage shapes and dip in flour.

*See page 111.
†This is called Panade (see also page 262).

9) Drop quenelles into water and poach 5 to 10 minutes, depending on size. Insure that each quenelle is same weight so that cooking time will be same for all.
10) Drain well.

Service
1) Serve with Portugaise Sauce.

Suggested Wines
Burgundy Morey-St.-Denis Rosé or California Gamay Rosé

Lamb Shank *Jardinière*

Yield: 30 portions

Prep time: 20 min
Cook time: 2 hr

Equipment
French knife, cutting board, large brazier, kitchen spoon

Ingredients
lamb shanks; 30
olive oil; I cup (250 ml)
salt; to taste
black pepper; to taste
Chicken Stock; I gal (4 liter)
garlic cloves, chopped; 12
dry white wine; I qt (I liter)
bay leaves; 3
thyme; I tsp

parsley, chopped; to taste
nutmeg; ½ tsp
onions, diced fine; 2
tomato sauce; 3 cup (750 ml)
Madeira wine; I cup (¼ liter)
carrots, diced medium; 4
celery stalks, diced medium; 12
potato, diced medium; 7

Method
1) Sauté lamb in oil until they are brown on all sides. Add salt and pepper.
2) Add stock, garlic, white wine, bay leaves, thyme, parsley, and nutmeg and simmer about 15 minutes.
3) Add onions, tomato sauce, and Madeira wine and simmer 15 minutes more.
4) Add carrots and celery and continue to simmer for I hour more.
5) Add potatoes and cook for 30 minutes more or until meat is tender, almost falling off the bone.

Service
1) Serve well moistened with natural cooking liquid. Usual portion is one shank per person.

Suggested Wines
Beaujolais Fleurie or California Petite Sirah

Classic Couscous Tunisian with Lamb and Two Sauces

Yield: 30 portions

Prep time: 3 min
Cook time: 3 hr

Equipment
French knife, cutting board, couscousier,* large mixing bowl, large brazier

Ingredients
lamb shoulder, well trimmed, cut in
  2-in. (7-cm) cubes; 30 lb (13.5 kg)
couscous semolina; 6 lb (2.7 kg)
margarine; 1 lb (450 g)
olive oil; as needed
onions, diced fine; 2
Chicken Stock; 2 gal (8 liter)
tomatoes, canned, diced, drained;
  2½ lb (1.1 kg)
cumin; 3 tsp
carrots, peeled, cut lengthwise; 15
turnips, peeled, cut in half; 15

green peppers, trimmed, cut in half;
  15
celery stalks, leaves removed; strings
  removed, cut in half; 30
zucchini, cut in 3 pieces; 10
cabbage, heads, cut in 8 pieces; 4
potatoes, peeled, cut in half; 15
garbanzo beans, canned, drained;
  2½ lb (1.1 kg)
bananas, peeled just before serving,
  cut lengthwise; 15
scallions, trimmed; 30
†Harissa Sauce; 1 tsp

Method
1) Inspect lamb cubes and insure that all fat and gristle have been removed.
2) Fill couscousier with salted water and bring to a boil.
3) Moisten couscous in large bowl with salted water.
4) Spoon couscous into top of couscousier and cook covered for 20 minutes.
5) Return couscous to bowl and moisten with salted water.
6) Return couscous to couscousier and cook covered for 20 minutes.
7) Return couscous to bowl and blend in margarine to coat the grains.
8) Set aside couscous and keep warm.
9) Sauté lamb in oil until brown. Set lamb aside and discard fat.
10) Sauté onion in oil.

*A couscousier is similar to a double boiler except the upper part of the device is perforated
  on the bottom.
†Harissa (hot) sauce is available in concentrated form and should be mixed with water. Or it
  can be prepared by mixing 6 ground cayenne peppers, 20 crushed cloves of garlic, 1
  teaspoon of coriander, salt, pepper, olive oil, and a little bit of water.

11) Combine lamb and onion.
12) Add stock, tomato, cumin, and garlic and bring to a boil. Reduce to a simmer and cook 1½ to 2 hours or until lamb is tender.
13) Boil or steam carrots, turnips, peppers, celery, zucchini, cabbage, and potatoes until tender but not mushy.
14) Remove lamb from brazier and boil liquid about 15 minutes to reduce.

Service
1) Cover plate with two large serving spoons of couscous. Place lamb cubes on top and arrange vegetables around plate. Add garbanzo beans.
2) Garnish with bananas and scallions.
3) Moisten everything with cooking liquid from lamb.
4) Serve Harissa Sauce and lamb broth in different dishes when presenting this entrée.

Suggested Wines
Thé à la menthe (mint tea) or robust dry red wine

(See color plate 11)

Rack of Lamb *Persillé*

Yield: 8 portions   Prep time: 20 min
                                               Cook time: 45 min

Equipment
boning knife, French knife, cutting board, roasting pan, stock pot

Ingredients

racks of lamb; 2

salt; to taste

black pepper; to taste

prepared mustard or Dijon mustard;
 2 tbsp (40 ml)

white bread crumbs, fresh; 1 cup

parsley, chopped; 2 tbsp

garlic cloves, chopped fine; 4

mirepoix
 carrots, diced; ⅓ cup
 celery, diced; ⅓ cup
 onions, diced; ⅓ cup

Veal Stock or Chicken Stock; 3 cup
 (750 ml)

Method
1) Trim racks and season with salt and pepper.
2) Place in roasting pan without fat and roast at 350°F for 30 minutes.
3) Remove racks from oven and brush with mustard.
4) Combine bread crumbs, parsley, and garlic and sprinkle generously over
   racks. At the same time add mirepoix and cook 10 to 15 minutes more.
5) Deglaze pan with stock.
6) Reduce stock, strain, and skim off fat. Use as sauce for service.

Suggested Wines
Beaujolais Brouilly St. Amour or California Pinot St. Georges Red

❧

Côte d'Agneau à la Nelson*

Yield: 12 portions

Prep time: 45 min
Cook time: 30 min

Equipment
French knife, boning knife, cutting board, meat saw, bowl, sauté pan, pastry brush

Ingredients
rack of lamb; cut in 1½-in. (40-mm) thick chops; 1
butter; 8 oz (225 g)
†Puff Pastry; 3 lb (1.35 kg)
duxelles; 1 lb (450 g)
boiled ham, ⅛-in. slices; 24
salt; as needed
black pepper; as needed
egg yolks; 2
‡Madeira Sauce or **Soubise Sauce; 1 pt (½ liter)

Method
1) Cook the chops in butter over moderate heat for about 7 minutes on each side. Allow to cool.
2) Roll the pastry into rectangles 6 × 5 × ⅛ inches thick.
3) Place 1 teaspoon of duxelles in the center of each rectangle of puff pastry. Cover with a slice of ham. Delicately (so as not to damage the dough) put the chop on top of the ham. Cover the chop with another slice of ham and then put another teaspoon of duxelles on top of the ham. Season lightly with salt and pepper.
4) Roll out more puff pastry and cut into rectangles 9 × 7 × ⅛ inches. Use this as the top piece of pastry over the chop.
5) Moisten all edges with water to insure a perfect seal.
6) Brush the top of the pastry with beaten egg yolks. Take care not to brush the edges (this could damage the seal).
7) Prick tops of pastry with fork and bake at 400°F for about 20 minutes.

*This is a very old Chaton family recipe, probably about 150 years old.
†See page 40–41.
‡See page 124.
**See page 121.

Service

1) Serve with sauce in sauce boat.

Suggested Wines

Beaujolais Brouilly St. Amour or California Pinot St. Georges Red

❧

Cuisine Moderne: Grouper Renée Flament*

Yield: 12 portions   Prep time: 30 min
                                      Cook time: 15 min

Equipment
French knife, cutting board, medium pot, 2 sauté pans, large saucepan, 6 ovenproof plates, china cap

Ingredients

green cabbage, halved, separated
  into leaves; 2
grouper, fresh, cut into finger-size
  (*goujonettes*) pieces; 3 lb (1.35 kg)
flour; as needed
butter; 4 oz (100 g)
salt; as needed
black pepper; as needed
cayenne pepper; as needed
lime juice; 6 tsp

boiled ham, sliced; 12
Sauce
  onion, chopped fine; 1
  olive oil; 2 tbsp (40 ml)
  tomatoes, ripe, peeled, seeded,
    diced; 8
  sugar; ½ tsp
  parsley, chopped; 1 tbsp
  boiled ham, diced fine; 4 oz
    (100 g)

Method
1) Blanch cabbage in boiling salted water. Remove cabbage and immerse in cold water to stop cooking.
2) Dust grouper with a little flour.
3) Sauté grouper in butter for about 2 minutes.
4) Add salt, pepper, cayenne, and lime juice.
5) Wrap each piece of grouper first with a piece of cabbage and then with a slice of ham.
6) Prepare sauce by sautéing onion with oil until tender and transparent.
7) Add tomatoes, sugar, and a touch of pepper and sweat 15 minutes.
8) Add the diced ham and parsley and cook 3 minutes more.
9) Cover bottom of plate with sauce.† Place a serving of fish in the sauce. Cover with a little sauce, a leaf of cabbage and a little more sauce on top of the cabbage.

---

*I consider Renée Flament one of the best Chefs in the French Riviera and have used her name for this plate.

†Bonne Femme Sauce (page 86), Dugléré Sauce (page 96), or Fernand Point Sauce (four parts American sauce [page 77] and one part Hollandaise Sauce [page 99]) before beurre manié may be substituted. For me the best choice is Dugléré Sauce.

10) Heat in a very hot 475°F oven for 5 to 7 minutes.

Service
1) Serve very hot.
2) Remove top leaf of cabbage and add fresh sauce just before serving.

Suggested Wines
Blanc de Cassis (produced in Cassis, France, near Toulon) or California Riesling

Panade*

Yield: 18 oz   Prep time: 10 min

Equipment
large mixing bowl, whip, kitchen spoon

Ingredients
bread flour; 4½ oz (125 g)
butter; 3 oz (90 g)
milk; 1 cup (250 ml)
egg yolks; 4

Method
1) Combine flour and butter very well.
2) Combine milk and yolks.
3) Combine flour and milk mixtures.

*Panade is a liaison used to bind forcemeat and fish. It is used for mousse and quenelles. The quantity in this recipe is sufficient for 1 kilogram of forcemeat. It should be added to forcemeat until desired consistency is obtained. Quantities needed will vary, depending on forcemeat used.

Sole, Salmon, and Scallop Mousse

Yield: 25 portions

Prep time: 1 hr
Cook time: 1 hr, 15 min

Equipment
meat grinder with fine screen, stainless steel mixing bowls, hotel pan, kitchen spoon, whip, small sauté pan, 9 × 5 in. loaf pans, parchment paper, spatula, cheesecloth, sheet pan

Ingredients

sole fillets, pureed, well chilled; 2 lb (900 g)

whipping cream; 2¼ cup (560 ml)

egg whites; 2

salt; 1½ tsp

white pepper; ½ tsp

nutmeg, grated; ½ tsp

salmon fillets, pureed, well chilled; 2 lb (900 g) (reserve 4 pieces, about 3 × 8 × ⅛ in. [7.6 cm × 20 cm × 5 mm])

whipping cream; 1¾ cup (½ liter)

egg whites; 2

salt; 1 tsp

red pepper, ground; ¾ tsp

nutmeg, grated; ¾ tsp

scallops, pureed, well chilled; 1½ lb (675 g) (reserve 18)

whipping cream; 2¼ cup

egg whites; 2

salt; 1½ tsp

white pepper, ground; ½ tsp

nutmeg, grated; ½ tsp

spinach, well washed, stems removed, blanched; 2 bunches

Method
1) Transfer chilled sole puree to a stainless steel bowl set in a hotel pan filled with ice.
2) Whisking constantly, gradually add cream in a slow steady stream until well blended.
3) Fold frothy beaten egg whites into sole mixture and season with salt, white pepper, and nutmeg.
4) For purposes of taste adjustment, sauté two spoons of sole mixture until opaque. Using taste of cooked fish as an indicator, adjust seasoning of the uncooked mixture.
5) Transfer chilled salmon puree to a stainless steel bowl set in a hotel pan filled with ice.
6) Whisking constantly, gradually add cream in a slow steady stream until well blended.

7) Fold egg whites into salmon mixture and season with salt, red pepper, and nutmeg.

8) For purposes of taste adjustment, sauté two spoons of salmon mixture until opaque. Using taste of cooked fish as an indicator, adjust seasoning of the uncooked mixture.

9) Transfer chilled scallops puree to a stainless steel bowl set in a hotel pan filled with ice.

10) Whisking constantly, gradually add cream in a slow steady stream until well blended.

11) Fold egg whites into scallop mixture and season with salt, white pepper, and nutmeg.

12) For purposes of taste adjustment, sauté two spoons of scallops mixture until opaque. Using taste of cooked fish as an indicator, adjust seasoning of the uncooked mixture.

13) Line the loaf pans with oiled parchment paper.

14) Divide the sole mousse in half and put it in the two loaf pans. Pat it evenly and firmly in the bottom of the loaf pans, smoothing the top evenly with a spatula.

15) Center one piece of the reserved salmon on top of the sole mousse. Cover with three or four large spinach leaves.

16) Divide the salmon mousse in fourths. Spread a quarter of the salmon mousse evenly over the spinach leaves in each pan, smoothing carefully.

17) On a piece of cheesecloth, spread out five or six large spinach leaves end to end, with the edges overlapping slightly.

18) Arrange nine of the reserved whole scallops down the center of the leaves.

19) Using the cheesecloth as a sort of sleeve to hold everything together, carefully roll the leaves into cylinders. Remove cheesecloth.*

20) Using a spatula, transfer the "sausage" to the center of loaf pan.

21) Repeat the process for the other loaf pan.

22) Spread another quarter of salmon mousse around and on top of the "sausage" in each loaf pan. Smooth top with spatula.

23) Cover the salmon mousse in each loaf pan with a single layer of spinach leaves. Then cover the spinach leaves in each pan with another piece of salmon. (Loaf pans at this point should be about two-thirds full.)

24) Divide scallop mousse in half and put in the two loaf pans.

25) Cover the loaf pans with cut pieces of oiled parchment paper flush against the contents.

*Here is the tricky part, especially if you have never done it before. First of all visualize a sausage, the skin consisting of blanched leaves of spinach and the stuffing whole scallops. This will be the end product of your labors.

26) Set the loaf pans in a hotel pan filled with boiling water so that the water is about halfway up the sides of the loaf pans.
27) Bake in a preheated oven at 350°F until mousse is set and thermometer inserted in the center registers 120°F, about 1 to 1¼ hours.
28) Remove from oven and allow to stand until room temperature. Place a light weight (such as a dish) over each mousse and refrigerate overnight.
29) To remove mousse from loaf pan, dip pan momentarily in hot water and invert on sheet pan. The mousse, because of the parchment paper, should slide easily out of the pan.
30) Slice cold to order and heat in microwave.

Service
1) Cut in about 1-inch (2.5 cm) slices and serve two slices to the order.
2) Serve with Nantua Sauce* or American Sauce.†

Suggested Wines
California Emerald Riesling or Pouilly-Fuissé

*See page 108.
†See page 77.

Mousse of Fish

Yield: 25 portions

Prep time: 20 min
Cook time: I hr minimum
Chill time: I hr

Equipment
mixing bowl, kitchen spoon, loaf pan, sheet pan, meat grinder with fine screen

Ingredients
fish, raw, without skin or bones; 36 oz (I kg)
egg whites; 5
cognac; ½ cup (125 ml)
heavy cream; I qt (I liter)
salt; as needed
pepper; as needed
eggs; 3
*Panade; 18 oz (500 g)

Method
1) Grind fish in meat grinder.
2) Add egg whites, cognac, cream, salt, pepper, and eggs and mix well.
3) Grind mixture again in meat grinder.
4) Combine very well panade and fish mixture and place mixture in greased loaf pan. Shake pan to remove air bubbles.
5) Bake in water bath at 350°F for about I hour.
6) Chill at least I hour before removing from loaf pan.

Service
1) Slice and serve with appropriate sauce.†

Suggested Wine
Vin Blanc de Bandol or California Chenin Blanc

*See page 262.
†Either Princess Sauce (page 113) or Watercress Sauce (page 127) is ideal.

Ramekins of Shrimp and Scallops

Yield: 12 portions

Prep time: 30 min
Cook time: 10 min

Equipment
saucepan, sauté pan, 12 individual ramekins or casserole dishes, spatula, kitchen spoon

Ingredients
spinach, fresh, well cleaned, chopped rough; 6 lb (2.7 kg)
scallops, fresh; 3 lb (1.35 kg)
shrimp, uncooked, shelled, deveined; 3 lb (1.35 kg)
clarified butter; 9 oz (250 g)
olive oil; ½ cup (125 ml)

salt; to taste
black pepper; to taste
*Béarnaise Sauce; as needed
tomatoes, fresh, medium, peeled, seeded, chopped rough; 6
wild rice, cooked, hot; 3 lb (1.35 kg) cooked weight

Method
1) Blanch spinach in boiling water until barely tender. Drain well.
2) Line bottoms of the individual ramekins with spinach. Be careful to leave enough room for the scallops and shrimp.
3) Sauté scallops and shrimp in a mixture of butter and oil for about 4 minutes or until scallops are opaque and shrimp is pink.
4) Remove from heat and season with salt and pepper.
5) Place equal portions of shrimp and scallops in each ramekin and top with Béarnaise Sauce.
6) Broil under medium heat in preheated broiler until top is golden brown. Watch carefully to prevent burning.

Service
1) Garnish with sautéed tomato.
2) Serve with wild rice.

Suggested Wines
Alsace Riesling and California Riesling

(See color plate 12)

*See page 80.

Jambalaya

Yield: 20 portions   Prep time: 50 min
                                      Cook time: 1½ hr

Equipment
French knife, cutting board, brazier, roast pan, kitchen spoon

Ingredients
butter; ¼ cup (60 ml)

olive oil; ¼ cup (60 ml)

scallions, chopped fine; 6 cup (about 6 bunches)

onions, chopped fine; 5 cup (about 4 onions)

celery, chopped fine; including leaves; 1½ cup (about 3½ stalks)

green peppers, chopped fine; 1½ cup (about 3)

shrimp, raw, chopped fine; 1 lb (450 g)

ham, cooked, chopped fine; ¾ lb (350 g)

garlic cloves, chopped fine; ⅓ cup (about 12)

tomatoes, canned, diced, drained; 2 qt (750 g)

tomato paste; ½ cup (125 ml)

basil; 2 tbsp

marjoram; 2 tbsp

thyme; 1½ tbsp

oregano; 1½ tbsp

cayenne pepper; 1 tsp

cloves, ground; ¾ tsp

bay leaves; 2

Chicken Stock; 2 qt (2 liter)

rice, converted, uncooked; 4 cup

ham, cooked, cut into ¾-in. (20-mm) chunks; 2¼ lb (1,000 g)

salt; to taste

black pepper; to taste

shrimp, medium, uncooked, shelled, deveined; 6 lb (2.7 kg)

Method
1) Heat butter and oil.
2) Add scallions, onions, celery, green peppers, chopped shrimp and ham and sauté over medium heat for about 5 minutes or until vegetables are soft.
3) Add garlic and cook 1 more minute.
4) Stir in tomatoes, tomato paste, basil, marjoram, thyme, oregano, cayenne, cloves, and bay leaves and simmer 10 minutes.
5) Add stock and bring to boil. Stir in rice, cover, and simmer 30 minutes or until rice is tender.
6) Stir in ham chunks and season with salt and pepper.

7) Add additional cayenne, basil, and thyme if required at this point. If holding for future service, refrigerate now and finish on day used.
8) Transfer Jambalaya to roast pan. If cold, heat in oven at 350°F for 40 minutes.
9) Stir in whole shrimp and bake until shrimp are firm, about 6 minutes. Do not overcook shrimp or they will become tough and rubbery.

Suggested Wines
Pouilly-Fuissé or California Chablis

Lobster fra Diavolo

Yield: 6 portions   Prep time: 15 min
                                     Cook time: 35 min

Equipment
French knife, cutting board, large sauté pans, kitchen spoon, large roast pans

Ingredients
lobsters, split; 1¼ lb (675 g)
olive oil; ¾ cup (180 ml)
tomato sauce; 3 cup (750 ml)
parsley, chopped fine; 6 tbsp
garlic, chopped fine; 3 tbsp
oregano, ¾ tsp
salt; to taste
black pepper; to taste
lemon, wedges; as needed
parsley; as needed

Method
1) Sauté lobsters, cut side down, in oil for 5 minutes.
2) Arrange lobsters cut side up in large roasting pan.
3) Deglaze sauté pan with tomato sauce. Add parsley, garlic, oregano, salt, and pepper and simmer 3 minutes.
4) Pour mixture over lobsters. Add ¼-inch of water to bottom of pan, cover pan tightly, and bake at 300°F for 30 minutes.

Service
1) Moisten with cooking juices before serving.
2) Garnish with lemon and parsley.

Suggested Wines
Mâcon Blanc Villages Latour or California Chablis

Quenelles of Fish
(Old Recipe—100 years old)

Yield: 8 portions

Prep time: 30 min
Cook time: 5–10 min

Equipment
meat grinder with very fine screen, large mixing bowl, kitchen spoon, brazier

Ingredients
fish, any type, raw, skinned, boned; 18 oz (500 g)
white bread, crusts removed; 18 oz (500 g)
milk; 3 cup (¾ liter)
butter; 18 oz (500 g)
salt; to taste
black pepper; to taste
egg yolks; 6
egg whites; 4
flour; as needed
parsley, chopped very fine; as needed

Method
1) Grind fish meat in grinder as many times as necessary to obtain a fine paste.
2) Soak bread in milk and squeeze out as much moisture as possible. Discard milk or save for soup.
3) Mix well the fish paste, bread, and butter.
4) Season with salt and pepper and mix again.
5) Add egg yolks and mix well.
6) Fold in egg whites and mix.
7) Shape quenelles mixture into small balls or little sausage shapes. Insure that they are the same size so they will require the same cooking time. Dip in flour.
8) Drop quenelles gently into 2 gallons (8 liters) of simmering salted water and poach 5 to 10 minutes.
9) Drain well.

Service
1) Serve with either Nantua Sauce* or American Sauce.† Either is ideal.

Suggested Wines
Entre-Deux-Mers Château Bourdieu or California Chablis

*See page 108.
†See page 77.

Fish Soufflé

Yield: 4 portions   Prep time: 30 min
                                           Cook time: 15 min

Equipment
French knife, cutting board, fine sieve or strainer, 4 soufflé cups, kitchen spoon, whip or portable mixer, wooden skewers

Ingredients
fish, any type (including leftovers); 1¼ cup
butter; as needed
*Béchamel Sauce, thick; ¾ cup (180 ml)
egg yolks; 3
egg whites, beaten; 4
salt; to taste
black pepper; to taste

Method
1) Cook fish in butter. Cool and press through a fine sieve or strainer.†
2) Mix the fish with the Béchamel Sauce.
3) Bind the mixture with the egg yolks, mixing well. Adjust taste with salt and pepper. At this point the mixture can be held overnight in the refrigerator.
4) Fold egg whites beaten to the consistency of meringue into mixture.
5) Lightly butter and flour soufflé cups and fill them two-thirds full.
6) Bake in 375°F oven, about 15 minutes. Soufflé should be brown on top and test clean with a wooden skewer.‡

Suggested Wines
Wine of Cassis (French Riviera) or California Chablis

---

*See page 81.
†Use grinder for large quantities.
‡This entrée cannot be held for more than a few minutes.

Seafood Stuffing for Crepes

Yield: 15 portions (2 crepes per
       portion)

Prep time: 30 min
Cook time: 10 min

Equipment
French knife, cutting board, sauté pan, mixing bowl, kitchen spoon

Ingredients
mushrooms, chopped; 20
shallots, chopped; 18
celery stalks, chopped very fine; 6
butter; as needed
crab meat, chopped; 1 lb (450 g)
shrimp, chopped; 1 lb (450 g)
fish, chopped; 1 lb (450 g)
chablis; 1 cup (¼ liter)

dry white vermouth; ½ cup (125 ml)
salt; to taste
black pepper; to taste
cayenne pepper; 1 tsp
beurre manié; as needed
parsley, chopped fine; 1 bunch
bread crumbs, fine; as needed
crepes, prepared in advance; 35

Method
1) Sauté in butter the mushrooms, shallots, and celery until tender.
2) Add crab meat, shrimp, fish, chablis, vermouth, salt, pepper, and cayenne
   and sauté 10 minutes, mixing often with spoon.
3) Thicken with beurre manié and remove from heat.
4) Mix in a little parsley.
5) Add bread crumbs until the mixture is thick enough to hold a shape.
6) Chill.

Service
1) Reheat in oven or microwave.
2) Roll into hot crepes.
3) Serve with Nantua Sauce* or American Sauce.†

Suggested Wines
Riesling or Moselle White

*See page 108.
†See page 77.

Crab Imperial

Yield: 50 portions

Prep time: 25 min
Cook time: 10 min
Chill time: 2 hr

Equipment
buffalo chopper, French knife, cutting board, cheesecloth, kitchen spoon, brazier, china cap, cookie cutter

Ingredients
onions, chopped fine; 7 lb (3.15 kg)
green peppers, chopped fine; 7 lb (3.15 kg)
margarine; 1 lb (450 g)
dry mustard; 4 tbsp
dry sherry wine; 2 cup (½ liter)

snow crab meat, all traces of shell removed, squeezed dry in cheesecloth; 15 lb (6.75 kg)
white roux; as needed
yellow egg coloring; 3 drops
white bread crumbs; 1½ cup (200 g) or as needed
pimientos, canned, chopped fine; 3

Method
1) Chop the onions and the green peppers separately using a buffalo chopper if available. Drain the juice of both vegetables in a china cap.
2) Sauté onions and peppers in margarine until transparent, but not brown. Mix together well.
3) Add mustard, sherry, and crabmeat.
4) Thicken with white roux.
5) Add a few drops of egg coloring.
6) Finish with the bread crumbs for consistency and the pimientos for color.
7) Refrigerate for at least 2 hours.
8) After shaping with appropriate cookie cutter, sauté or reheat in pastry shells.

Suggested Wines
Puligny-Montrachet White or California White Folle Blanche

Summary

The entrée, be it simple or complex, must taste good, but taste is not enough. It must not just look good, it must look *perfect*. It must be a work of art, a show in itself. No matter how good the taste, customers will not be happy if the plate looks like the product of an army field kitchen.

Consider color when choosing vegetables and sauces. Position of the items on the plate must be considered. Appropriate garnishes must be chosen and used.

When each entrée is ready to be served, someone must check each and every plate before it goes out into the dining room.

Many factors come into play in the choice of entrées for the menu. Tastes and preferences of the customer, what sells and what does not, abilities of the kitchen staff, physical limitations of the kitchen, and food costs must be an integral part of the evaluation process when choosing entrées for the menu.

Discussion Questions*

1) Would a menu heavy with fish items and fancy sauces be likely to go over big in a rural area in the Midwest?
2) If the food cost for an entrée is $10.00, what should the menu cost be?
3) Who should check plates before they leave the line and go to the dining room?
4) What are some factors to consider when choosing entrées for the menu?
5) Why would it be a mistake to overload a menu with sauté items?
6) Besides taste, what else is important in entrée preparation?

Test Questions

1) List the ingredients for *Coq au Vin*.
2) When Boneless Breast of Duck (*Magret de Canard*) is finished, what color should the flesh be?
3) In Fricassee of Chicken with Vinegar, how is the chicken cut?
4) Describe the ingredients and method in the preparation of Coulis of Blackberry.
5) Describe the ingredients and method in preparing Bird Casanova.

*Some discussion questions require culinary deductive reasoning. They may not be answered *directly* in the text, but enough information is given to deduce the answer logically.

6) What dough is used in the preparation of Classic Quiche Lorraine?
7) Is salt pork used in the preparation of French Liver *Pâté*?
8) In the preparation of Frog Legs Riesling, what must be done to the legs before cooking?
9) What meats are used in Alsatian Sauerkraut (*Choucroute Garnie*)?
10) What cut of beef is the best to use for Beef Burgundy?

Chapter 11

✣ The Vegetables

T raditionally, fund raiser banquets or retirement dinners serve low-cost fare such as cold dehydrated mashed potatoes, canned peas and carrots mixed together, and a piece of baked chicken covered with a nondescript white sauce. Today, no banquet chef worthy of the name would offer dehydrated potatoes or canned peas and carrots. Perhaps, twenty years ago, the excuse was that fresh vegetables were out of season. But this excuse is no longer valid.

Availability

Now, right now, is the best time in history to be a chef. Fresh vegetables and fruits are available year round. In most locations, it is possible to get daily deliveries. In fact, most good produce houses not only provide daily delivery but are quite happy to locate whatever exotic produce you require, despite whether they routinely stock it.

In addition to the fresh vegetables, an unlimited variety of frozen pre-prepared vegetables are available. Some of these are even better than the fresh. French fries are a perfect example. The modern processors of French fries wash the fries and leach out most of the starch. The starch is then sprayed back on the outside of the fries, resulting in a crispy outside and a mealy inside. They have created the perfect French fry. It is not possible to duplicate this result in "scratch" French fries.

Also available are freeze-dried and dehydrated vegetables and fruits that are excellent in quality, reasonable in price, and very convenient.

"OK, OK," you say. "I know that there are a lot of products out there. I know that even the fast food houses are jumping on the fresh fruit and produce bandwagon and smiling all the way to the bank. But what should *I* do?"

Menu Updates

Something Different
First of all, review the vegetables already on your menu. Perhaps you already are using mostly fresh produce. Perhaps you constantly get raves about your salads. But what about the potatoes that go out of your kitchen next to the beef filets? What about the vegetables that share the plate with your scallops?

Are your vegetables like the interstate highways—dependable but boring and exactly the same wherever you go? Do you serve baked potatoes wrapped in foil? Steamed rounds of carrots? Frozen corn that sits on the steam table until someone notices that it has turned brownish green and throws it away?

Read all our recipes in this chapter. Experiment with a few of them. You should get a lot of happy faces in the dining room.

Most importantly, think *different* (not necessarily fancy). You will come up with plenty of unusual ways to serve vegetables. After all, why expect customers to come to you, when they can get the same thing across the street? Think *different* and smile all the way to the bank.

Something Fresh
It is also important to become familiar with the prices of seasonal produce. There is nothing wrong with frozen produce, but it is *not* as good as the fresh. Frozen produce, of course, is usually preferable to poor-quality fresh produce.

Some of these frozen products are indistinguishable from fresh. Because of savings in labor, they may be far more practical to use. French fries are a perfect example. Making them from scratch requires blanching and cooling before the final frying step (in addition to peeling and cutting). Modern potato processors do all of this, including blanching, so they simply have to be tossed in the deep fryer. Perfect French fries require controlled conditions for preparation, something most cooks don't have time to worry about.

Finding a good produce supplier is important. They can help you select appropriate seasonal produce. But you must also learn these things for yourself.

Remember that modern customers are concerned about health. They perceive fresh produce as being the most healthful (whether it is or not is irrelevant). Their perceptions are what determine whether or not they return to your restaurant.

If you can truthfully say that you serve *only* fresh produce, in these times that is a strong motivation to keep that customer coming back. Here is another smile on the way to the bank!

Brussel Sprouts St. Malo

Yield: 12 portions

Prep time: 10 min
Cook time: 20 min

Equipment
French knife, cutting board, steamer or saucepan, sauté pan, kitchen spoon

Ingredients
brussel sprouts; 3 lb (1.35 kg)
onion, chopped fine; 1 cup
butter; 4 tbsp (80 ml)
sour cream; 1 qt (1 liter)
salt; to taste
white pepper; to taste

Method
1) Steam brussel sprouts for 10 minutes or until tender.*
2) Sauté onion in butter until tender and transparent, but not brown.
3) Stir in sour cream and heat, stirring constantly. As soon as sour cream begins to simmer, remove from heat.
4) Add brussel sprouts and mix gently, but well. Adjust taste with salt and pepper.

---

*American guests prefer brussel sprouts cooked al dente (cooked but still firm). Europeans prefer this vegetable to be served mushy.

❖

Spinach Flan with Fresh Tomato
(Darioles d'Epinards à la Tomate Fraîche)

Yield: 8 portions   Prep time: 20 min
                                      Cook time: 35 min

Equipment
French knife, cutting board, sauté pan, kitchen spoon, mixing bowl, 8 dariole molds,* aluminum foil

Ingredients
spinach, cleaned very well, stems removed; 1½ lb (675 g)
garlic cloves, minced; 6
butter, unsalted; ½ cup (125 ml)
milk; 1 cup (250 ml)
heavy cream; 1 cup (250 ml)
eggs, beaten; 6
salt; 2 tsp
black pepper; to taste
nutmeg; pinch
shallots, minced; 4
tomatoes, peeled, seeded, diced; 12

Method
1) Sauté the spinach and garlic in butter for 5 minutes, mixing well while cooking.
2) Transfer the mixture to a cutting board and chop. Set aside.
3) Combine milk, cream, eggs, salt, pepper, and nutmeg.
4) Add the sautéed spinach and mix well.
5) Butter the dariole molds. Fill them with the spinach mixture and cover with buttered foil.
6) Place the molds in a water bath of boiling water and bake in an oven preheated to 400°F for 25 minutes or until they are firm to the touch.
7) Sauté shallots in butter for 1 minute.
8) Add tomatoes and reduce until liquid is evaporated.

*A dariole mold is a ceramic, ovenproof mold, like a custard dish. It is standard in French kitchens. Although they are available in specialty shops, we have found that the most practical substitute for commercial use is the muffin tin.

9) Season to taste with salt and pepper. Reserve and keep warm.

Service
1) Demold the darioles onto heated plates.
2) Garnish with the sautéed tomatoes on the side.
3) A variation is to top the darioles with a poached egg and surround them with chopped tomatoes.

Potato Croquettes Carême*

Yield: 12 portions

Prep time: 30 min
Cook time: 20 min

Equipment
French knife, cutting board, saucepan, food mill or grinder, mixing bowls, kitchen spoon, whip, sauté pan, deep fryer

Ingredients
potatoes, medium, peeled, quartered; 14
Beef Stock; ½ gal (2 liter)
Chicken Stock; ½ gal (2 liter)
salt; to taste
black pepper; to taste
sugar; to taste
nutmeg; to taste

butter; 4½ oz (125 g)
eggs, separated; 6
heavy cream; 9 tbsp (180 ml)
bread crumbs; 7½ cup
eggs, whole; 6
Parmesan cheese, grated; 5 cup
peanut oil; as required

Method
1) Place potatoes in sauce pan and add equal parts of Beef Stock and Chicken Stock to cover. Add salt, pepper, sugar, and nutmeg to taste. Cover and bring to boil. Reduce to simmer and cook 20 minutes.
2) When potatoes are tender, they will have absorbed all, or nearly all, the cooking stock. If not, drain potatoes.
3) Grind potatoes in food mill or grinder.
4) Place mashed potatoes in buttered sauté pan and cook over low heat, stirring constantly to prevent burning. The purpose of this operation is to remove excess liquid and to intensify (by reduction) the flavors absorbed from the cooking liquid. When potatoes are the consistency of damp sawdust, remove from heat.
5) Stir in egg yolks and cream.
6) Prepare three bowls as follows: #1 containing half the bread crumbs; #2 containing beaten eggs; #3 containing a mixture of the remaining bread crumbs and cheese.
7) Form the mashed potatoes into small croquettes, the size of a small egg that is more oblong than round. Insure that each croquette weighs the same.

*From a recipe by Master Chef Carême, circa 1833.

8) Roll the croquettes in bread crumbs, then in the beaten eggs, and finally in the mixture of bread crumbs and cheese.

9) Test fry a few croquettes to insure that they are not being made too large. If they are too large, the outside will become too dark before the inside is hot. At this point the croquettes may be refrigerated until needed.

10) Deep fry in 375°F oil, in deep fryer, until the outsides are golden brown and the insides are steamy hot; about 3 minutes.

11) Drain excess fat.*

*Holding time is less than for French fries. Croquettes tend to become mushy on the outside if held hot too long.

Tomatoes Florentine

Yield: 12 portions   Prep time: 20 min
                                      Cook time: 10 min

Equipment
French knife, cutting board, small sheet pan, spatula, kitchen spoon, sauté
pan

Ingredients
tomatoes, large, sliced thick; 12 slices
garlic salt; as needed
salt; as needed
black pepper; as needed
onion, chopped fine; 1 cup
butter; 2 tbsp (40 ml)
spinach, frozen, chopped, thawed, drained; 20 oz (560 g)
*corn bread stuffing; ⅔ cup
eggs, lightly beaten; 2
Parmesan cheese, grated; 4 tbsp
parsley, fresh, chopped; 2 tbsp

Method
1) Place tomato slices on greased sheet pan and sprinkle with garlic salt, salt,
   and pepper.
2) Sauté onion in butter until tender.
3) Mix onion with spinach that has been blanched in salted water.
4) Add corn bread stuffing, eggs, cheese, and parsley. Season with salt and pepper and mix together well.
5) Put even amounts of the spinach mixture on top of tomatoes until it is all
   used up. Sprinkle with additional cheese.
6) Bake in 350°F oven for about 5 minutes until quite hot and cheese is
   melted.

---

*Corn bread moistened with Chicken Stock and mixed with a touch of sage, a bit of finely
diced celery, salt, and pepper.

Eggplant Fulton

Yield: 40 portions   Prep time: 25 min
                                       Cook time: 7 min

Equipment
French knife, cutting board, sauté pan, sheet pan, kitchen spoon

Ingredients
eggplants; 120 slices
margarine; as needed
tomatoes; 120 slices
*croutons; 40
†tomato sauce; 1 qt (1 liter)
provolone or Mozzarella cheese; 40 thin slices
paprika; as needed

Method
1) Sauté eggplant in margarine. Drain on absorbent paper.
2) If tomatoes are green or hard, sauté the tomato slices slightly in margarine.
3) On greased sheet pan, place crouton, a slice of eggplant, a slice of tomato, a slice of eggplant, a slice of tomato, a slice of eggplant, a slice of tomato, and a liberal spoonful of tomato sauce. Top with a slice of cheese and sprinkle with paprika. Repeat this procedure until you have forty portions.
4) Bake in 350°F oven about 7 minutes or until cheese is melted and vegetables are hot.
5) Serve as soon as possible. Cheese tends to become rubbery if held too long.

(See color plate 15)

---

*Prepare croutons with white bread, crusts removed. They may be square (cut with knife) or round (cut with cookie cutter). Brush both sides of bread with melted margarine or butter and bake until crisp and golden brown. Do not overbake.
†See page 105 for Marinara Sauce or substitute any other tomato sauce.

Deviled Carrots

Yield: 12 portions

Prep time: 20 min
Cook time: 20 min

Equipment
French knife, cutting board, sauté pan, kitchen spoon

Ingredients
carrots, large, quartered lengthwise; 12
butter; 1 cup (230 g)
brown sugar; 4 tbsp
dry mustard; 4 tsp
tabasco; 4 drops
salt; to taste
black pepper; to taste
parsley, fresh, chopped; as needed

Method
1) Sauté carrots in butter for 7 minutes.
2) Add brown sugar, mustard, tabasco, salt, and pepper and cook for 10 minutes more or until tender.

Service
1) Garnish with parsley.

Potato Voisin

Yield: 12 portions

Prep time: 15 min
Cook time: 45 min

Equipment
French knife, cutting board, grater, electric slicer if available, muffin tin, small saucepan, pastry brush, pastry spatula

Ingredients
Idaho potatoes (do not substitute), peeled, sliced ⅛ in. (3 mm) thick; 12
Parmesan cheese, grated; 6 oz (170 g)
butter, melted, clarified; 8 oz (230 g)
salt; as needed
white pepper; as needed

Method
1) Dry the potatoes very well with clean kitchen towels.
2) Butter muffin tins.
3) In each muffin mold, place two slices of potato. Brush with melted butter and sprinkle with cheese. Repeat the process, two slices at a time, until the molds are full to the top. After each set of potatoes is inserted, compress into the mold with thumb. Repeat at the end, so that the potatoes are well compressed and the molds are full to the top.
4) Bake for 45 minutes in preheated 375°F oven. (Use 350°F for convection oven.)
5) Cool slightly, but while still hot, remove from molds to prevent breaking the finished potatoes.*

(See color plate 8)

---

*Potatoes can be held at room temperature, but serve quite hot.

Coulis of Fresh Tomato

Yield: 12 portions   Prep time: 10 min
                                            Cook time: 10 min

Equipment
French knife, cutting board, saucepan, sauté pan, blender or food mill, kitchen spoon

Ingredients
shallots, chopped fine; 6
garlic cloves, diced fine; 6
olive oil; 3 tbsp (60 ml)
tomatoes, fresh, peeled, seeded, diced; 2.2 lb (1 kg)
tomato paste; 3 tbsp (60 ml)
Chicken Stock; 1½ pt (750 ml)
bouquet garni
   bay leaf; 2
   thyme; 1 tsp
   parsley stems, chopped; ½ bunch
salt; to taste
black pepper; to taste

Method
1) Sauté garlic and shallots in oil until tender.
2) Add tomatoes, tomato paste, stock, bouquet garni, salt, and pepper and simmer for 10 minutes.
3) Discard bouquet garni.
4) Blend or process through food mill.

Potato Duchess

Yield: 10 portions   Prep & cook time: I hr

Equipment
saucepan, food mill, mixing bowl, kitchen spoon

Ingredients
potatoes, boiled, peeled; I lb (500 g)   nutmeg; to taste
butter; I¾ oz (50 g)   egg, whole; I
salt; to taste   egg yolks; 2
black pepper; to taste   heavy cream; 4 tbsp

Method
1) Grind potatoes in food mill.
2) Add remaining ingredients and mix well.

Variations of Potato Duchess

Potato Dauphine
Combine two parts of Potato Duchess with one part *Pâte à chou*.* Bake in hot oven to obtain "puff potato" effect.

Potato Lorette
Combine one part of finely grated Swiss cheese with eighteen parts of Potato Duchess. Use in same way as Potato Duchess.

Potato Vincent
Roll balls or cylinders of Potato Duchess in slivered almonds and bake or deep fry.

Potato Croquettes
Dip Potato Lorette in flour. Eggwash dip in breadcrumbs and deep fry at 375°F until golden.

*See page 308.

Gratin Dauphinois

Yield: 24 portions

Prep time: 20 min
Cook time: 45 min

Equipment
French knife, cutting board, peeler, large saucepan, large casserole, kitchen spoon

Ingredients
garlic cloves, split; 15
butter; 8 tbsp (160 ml)
milk; 8 cup (2 liter)
potatoes, peeled, sliced ¼ in. (6 mm) thick; 20
whipping cream; 8 cup (2 liter)
salt; to taste
black pepper; to taste
nutmeg; 1 pinch
Swiss cheese, grated; 3 cup (500 g)

Method
1) Rub the large casserole dish with garlic, then butter generously.
2) Boil milk in large saucepan.
3) Add potatoes and reduce to simmer. Simmer 15 minutes or until partly tender. Drain. (Milk can be discarded or saved for soup.)
4) Return potatoes to saucepan. Add cream, salt, pepper, and nutmeg and simmer for 15 more minutes or until potatoes are tender, but not falling apart.
5) Adjust seasoning, if required, with salt and pepper. Spoon potatoes, which should be quite moist, into casserole.
6) Bake in 375°F oven until golden brown on top.
7) Sprinkle with cheese during last 10 minutes of baking.

Crique Ardéchoise

Yield: 10 portions

Prep time: 20 min
Cook time: 10 min

Equipment
food mill, kitchen spoon, bowl, sauté pan, spatula

Ingredients
eggs, whole; 8
heavy cream; 1½ qt (1½ liter)
Idaho potatoes, peeled, mashed, cooked, squeezed dry; 2 lb (900 g)
chervil, chopped; 1 tbsp
Italian parsley, chopped; 1 tbsp
scallions, chopped; 1 tbsp
butter; as needed
vegetable oil; as needed

Method
1) Using a whip, combine eggs and cream. Add potatoes and herbs.
2) Sauté in the same shape as little crepes.

Ratatouille

Yield: 20 portions

Prep time: 45 min
Cook time: 25 min

Equipment
French knife, cutting board, sauté pans, hotel pan, kitchen spoon

Ingredients
eggplants, peeled, diced medium; 4
olive oil; as needed
zucchini, diced medium; 4
green pepper, diced medium; 2
onions, sliced thin; 2
tomatoes, fresh, peeled, seeded,
  diced; 4
Parmesan cheese, grated; 3½ oz
  (100 g)

garlic cloves; chopped fine; 6
thyme; 1 tbsp
basil, fresh; 10 leaves
salt; to taste
black pepper; to taste
lemon juice; of 1 lemon
cayenne pepper; to taste
parsley, chopped; 1 bunch

Method
1) Sauté eggplant in oil until tender.
2) Sauté zucchini until tender.
3) Sauté green peppers until tender.
4) Sauté onions until transparent.
5) Sauté tomatoes until tender.
6) While vegetables are still very hot, mix them together.
7) Add cheese, garlic, thyme, basil, salt, pepper, lemon juice, and cayenne. Hold in covered hotel pan on steam table.*

Service
1) Garnish with parsley.

*Vegetables will continue to cook while being held on a steam table.

Tian of Zucchini

Yield: 24 portions   Prep time: 20 min
                                      Cook time: 50 min

Equipment
French knife, cutting board, brazier, kitchen spoon, oven casserole dish

Ingredients
olive oil; ½ cup (125 ml)
butter; 3½ oz (100 g)
zucchini, washed, peeled, sliced very
  thin; about 11 lb (5 kg)
garlic cloves, crushed, diced fine; 8
onions, diced fine; 3
basil, fresh; 6–8 leaves (substitute 1
  tsp dry basil)

rice, long grain converted; 14 oz
  (400 g)
salt; to taste
black pepper; to taste
eggs, whole; 12
crème fraîche; 2 tbsp (40 ml)
milk; 6 cup (1½ liter)
Parmesan cheese, grated; 11 oz
  (300 g)

Method
1) Preheat oil and butter in brazier. Add zucchini, garlic, onions, and basil and sauté, mixing well, about 5 minutes.
2) Reduce heat. Add rice, salt, and pepper and sweat slowly, covered, for 30 minutes.
3) Adjust seasoning with salt and pepper if required.
4) Arrange the rice and sautéed zucchini on a well-buttered oven casserole dish.
5) Mix together eggs, cream, milk, and cheese. Pour on top of rice and zucchini.
6) Bake 20 minutes at 300°F.

*If unavailable, substitute a combination of 2 tablespoons buttermilk with 1 quart (1 liter) whipping cream.

Stuffed Cabbage

Yield: 40 portions   Prep time: 30 min
                                      Cook time: 30 min

Equipment
French knife, cutting board, large saucepan, brazier, kitchen spoon, sheet pan

Ingredients
butter; 18 oz (500 g)
salt pork, diced small; 18 oz (500 g)
onions, diced small; 8
tomatoes, peeled, seeded, diced; 15
spinach, frozen, thawed, chopped; 36 oz (1 kg)
rice, cooked, well drained; 3 lb, 12 oz (1½ kg)
salt; to taste
black pepper; to taste
cabbage, large leaves; 80 leaves
*Coulis of Fresh Tomato; 1½ lb (675 g)
Vegetable Stock; 1 qt (1 liter)

Method
1) Melt butter in brazier. When hot, add salt pork and onions and sweat slowly for 5 minutes.
2) Add tomatoes and spinach and mix very well. Sweat the mixture for 10 minutes more.
3) Add rice, salt, and pepper and combine well.
4) Blanch cabbage leaves carefully in boiling salted water, about 3 minutes. Remove from water, drain, and pat dry the leaves.
5) Stuff and roll cabbage leaves.
6) Arrange the cabbage rolls on a greased sheet pan with the loose end of the leaf on the bottom.
7) Cover with a mixture of Coulis of Fresh Tomato and stock.
8) Bake in 350°F oven for 30 minutes.

*See page 291.

Service

1) Serve with fish, meat, or poultry.

Jam of Onions Nouvelle Cuisine

Yield: 50 portions

Prep time: 20 min
Cook time: 60 min

Equipment
French knife, cutting board, brazier, kitchen spoon

Ingredients
onions, sliced thin; 22 lb (10 kg)
margarine; 18 oz (500 g)
salt; to taste
black pepper; to taste
sugar; 11 oz (300 g)
red wine vinegar; 1 pt (½ liter)
Burgundy wine; 3 cup (75 cl)
grenadine; 1 cup (25 cl)
raisins; 1½ cup (175 g)
orange zest, fine julienne; 1½ cup

Method
1) Sauté onions in margarine until transparent.
2) Add salt, pepper, and sugar and sweat covered for 30 minutes. Stir often.
3) Add vinegar, wine, grenadine, raisins, and orange zest and cook uncovered for 30 minutes more. Heat should be reduced to slow simmer.
4) When finished, consistency of jam of onions will be like a thick marmalade.

Uses
Use either as a vegetable or as a garnish. It is great with liver, for example, but it is also good with hot *foie gras* or fillet of fish.

(See color plate 6)

Summary

Today, unlike in years past when produce availability was strictly seasonal, an almost unlimited variety of fresh produce is available, all year. It is flown in, when out of season, from all points of the globe.

In addition, a great variety of frozen fruits and vegetables is always available. Freeze-dried and dehydrated produce are also an excellent source that is convenient and reasonably priced.

Of course, fresh produce tastes best and looks best. The customers perceive fresh produce to be better for their health. Thus, whenever possible, the fresh produce should be used.

Even though customers want vegetables because they perceive them as being healthful, they are bored with the routine methods of preparing them. But there are many delicious and novel ways of preparing memorable vegetable dishes. Wise chefs use these methods and recipes to get away from the "routine," and their profits reflect this wisdom.

Discussion Questions*

1) Why is now the best time in history to be a chef?
2) What is the difference in fresh produce availability between now and 30 years ago?
3) Why are frozen French fries usually better than those made fresh from scratch?
4) How do modern customers perceive fresh produce?
5) Why is it important to understand the seasonal pricing of produce?

Test Questions

1) To what degree of tenderness should Brussel Sprouts St. Malo be cooked, if they are to be served to American customers?
2) What cheese is used for Potato Croquettes Carême?
3) Describe the assembly of each portion of Eggplant Fulton.
4) What type of mustard is used in Deviled Carrots?
5) What are the ingredients in Potato Voisin?
6) List the ingredients for Potato Duchess.
7) List two variations of Potato Duchess.

*Some discussion questions require culinary deductive reasoning. They may not be answered *directly* in the text, but enough information is given to deduce the answer logically.

8) Describe the method of preparing *Gratin Dauphinois*.
9) What are the ingredients of Ratatouille?
10) Describe the ingredients in Jam of Onions Nouvelle Cuisine.

Chapter 12

✤ # The Desserts

A mericans, perhaps more than any other people in the world, love desserts. They eat them in vast quantities, invent new ones, read about them in newspapers and magazines, and worry constantly about growing fat as they consume them.

For that reason, desserts mean profits. Properly planned, your dessert menu is a very profitable part of your food sales. Depending upon the produce, profits can go as high as 200%.

Preparing the Menu

But for that kind of profit, you must choose your desserts wisely. You must know the tastes of your customers and what the big selling items are in your area. Cheesecake may sell well in Manhattan but flop in Dayton, Ohio. In America chefs are well advised to determine the desserts that sell well. These are usually old standards. They must then insure that they are procured or made in-house under the very highest standards of freshness and quality. These money-makers include the routine cakes, pies, and ice cream products. Once these items are determined, then chefs must find a few more special desserts to punctuate the pastry cart. These must not be just good; they must be great.

Do not be afraid to present high-calorie desserts. Although Americans are becoming more calorie conscious and aware of good eating practices than ever before in history, they still spend an incredible amount of money on fattening desserts. Pastry is sold in much higher volume in America than in any country in the world. Caterers who specialize in pastry indicate that sales are up. One little bit of psychology is very effective if your customers are calorie counters. If you make chocolate eclairs, for example, don't make large ones. Make them half size and serve two per order. Nothing has changed, but your customers will feel chic and virtuous.

Presenting Desserts

Your waiters must be trained to encourage dessert sales. Depending on your operation, a refrigerated dessert display or pastry cart is a valuable sales tool.

Above all, your products must look fabulous and taste even better.

The Recipes

The desserts we present in this chapter are unusual, delicious, and beautiful, although none is difficult to make. They will tempt even the most jaded palate and cause customers to talk about them. They are best suited for a top-of-the-line white-tablecloth operation.

Use your own judgment and taste as you introduce them to your customers, and see how they sell. If you find an item is not selling, take it off the list. Eventually you will end up with a dessert line that sells well. Stick with it!

Because of the high labor costs in the restaurant business today, many owners make a few very fancy, unusual desserts as house specialties and buy the rest in frozen form. This is sometimes far more cost effective than preparing everything in-house.

Chocolate Mousse *Hotel du Parc*

Yield: 36 portions

Prep time: 5 min
Cook time: 20 min
Chill time: 3 hr

Equipment
kitchen spoon, double boiler, whip, mixing bowl, individual serving bowls

Ingredients
semi-sweet chocolate; 24 oz (680 g)
instant coffee; 1 tsp (5 ml)
Crème of Cacao; ½ cup (125 ml)
Triple Sec; ½ cup (125 ml)
egg yolks; 6
egg whites; 8
whipping cream; 2 cup (½ liter)
sugar; ½ cup (100 g)

Method
1) Melt chocolate, using double boiler.
2) When chocolate is completely melted, dissolve instant coffee into a mixture of Crème of Cacao and Triple Sec. Add to the melted chocolate.
3) Remove mixture from heat and allow to cool slightly. Add the egg yolks one at a time, mixing well.
4) Beat egg whites into a stiff meringue and then fold into the chocolate.
5) Put chocolate mixture in refrigerator to chill to just below room temperature.
6) Whip cream with sugar and fold into chocolate.
7) Fill individual serving dishes and chill until service.

Suggested Wines
Coteaux de Layon or California Sauterne

Chef Chaton's Cheesecake

Yield: 12 portions

Prep time: 15 min
Cook time: 45 min

Equipment

mixing bowls, kitchen spoon, 10-in. springform pan, sieve, whip, spatula

Ingredients

Crust
- graham crackers, rolled into fine meal; 18 (or 1½ cup meal)
- butter; 3 tbsp (60 ml)
- sugar; 1 tbsp

Cake
- cream cheese, good quality; 24 oz (675 g)
- eggs; 5
- sugar; 1 cup (200 g)
- vanilla; 1½ tsp (8 ml)

Topping
- sour cream; 1 pt (½ liter)
- sugar; 4 tbsp
- vanilla; 1 tbsp (20 ml)

Method

1) To prepare crust, mix graham crackers, butter, and sugar well.
2) Press into sides and bottom of springform pan to form a crust. Do not make crust too thick.
3) Warm cream cheese to room temperature. Break up until smooth and easy to work with.
4) Add eggs, one at a time until all are well combined with cream cheese.
5) Add sugar and vanilla and mix very well. Force through strainer or sieve to insure that there are no lumps.
6) Pour into crust.
7) Bake at 325°F for 45 minutes. Cake should be well set, a bit stiffer than custard, when finished.
8) For topping, combine sour cream, sugar, and vanilla and mix well.
9) Remove cake from oven and add topping.
10) Return to oven and bake for 3 minutes at 475°F.
11) Remove from oven and cool completely at room temperature. Refrigerate.

Suggested Wines

Any sweet white wine or champagne

Bananas Foster*

Yield: 4 portions

Prep time: 10 min
Cook time: 5 min

Equipment
sauté pan, kitchen spoon, French knife, cutting board, slotted spoon, spatula

Ingredients
butter or margarine; ¼ cup (60 ml)
light brown sugar, packed firm; ½ cup
bananas, ripe, peeled, split lengthwise; 4
cinnamon, ground; ⅛ tsp
white rum; ½ cup (125 ml)
banana liqueur (Crème of Bananas); ¼ cup (60 ml)
vanilla ice cream; 1 pt (½ liter)

Method
1) Melt butter and sugar.
2) Add bananas in single layer and sauté until tender, about 2½ minutes on each side, turning only once.
3) When tender, sprinkle with cinnamon and pour in rum and banana liqueur, ignite with a lighted match.
4) Remove from heat and baste bananas until flame goes out.
5) Plate and add ice cream.

Suggested Wines
Iced water with touch of banana liqueur

*This is a most dramatic dessert when prepared at tableside.

Pâte à Choux "Oncle Louis"

Yield: 48 medium *choux*   Prep time: 10 min
                                        Cook time: 5 min

Equipment
saucepan, flour sifter, mixing bowl, rubber spatula

Ingredients
water; 1 qt (1 liter)
butter; 14 oz (400 g)
bread flour, sifted; 28½ oz (800 g)
sugar; 1½ oz (40 g)
salt; ½ oz (15 g)
eggs, whole; 24

Method
1) Bring water to boil.
2) While water is boiling, add butter. When butter is melted, add flour, sugar, and salt all at once. Remove immediately from heat and mix well.
3) Return to heat and mix well, constantly and vigorously, with rubber spatula until mixture does not adhere to sides and bottom of pan and tends to stick together in one mass.
4) Remove from heat and transfer the mixture to a large bowl. Use the rubber spatula to fold in the eggs, one at a time, mixing each egg completely into the dough before adding another, until all eggs are combined with the dough.
5) Chill until ready to use or use warm.

Uses
This dough is used to make eclair shells and Paris-Brest.

❉

Patissière Sauce

Yield: 2 dozen eclairs

Prep time: 5 min
Cook time: 15 min

Equipment
mixing bowl, whip, double boiler, saucepan

Ingredients
egg yolks; 12
sugar; 18 oz (500 g)
flour; 4½ oz (125 g)
milk, scalded; 1 qt (1 liter)
vanilla; ½ tsp (3 ml)

Method
1) Combine yolks and sugar and mix well.
2) Add flour a little at a time and mix.
3) Transfer ingredients to top of double boiler, over simmering water.
4) Add milk and stir with whip until thickened. When finished, sauce should be the consistency of a thick pudding.*
5) Chill immediately.†

---

*If ingredients are not measured correctly and the mixture will not thicken properly, add a little cornstarch or arrowroot.
†Products made with this sauce must always remain refrigerated; it is very perishable.

Tia Maria Mousse

Yield: 16 portions   Prep time: 10 min
                                   Cook time: 15 min
                                   Chill time: 3 hr

Equipment
mixing bowl, whip, double boiler, cup, electric mixer, 16 serving dishes

Ingredients
sugar, granulated; 2 cup (400 g)
egg yolks; 12
flour; 2 cup (220 g)
milk, scalded; 1 qt (1 liter)
instant coffee; 1 tsp (5 ml)
Tia Maria; ⅓ cup (85 ml)
whipped cream; 1 qt (1 liter)

Method
1) Combine sugar and egg yolks and mix well.
2) Add flour and mix.
3) Transfer ingredients to top of double boiler, over simmering water.
4) Add milk and cook until mixture thickens. It should be the same consistency as a finished Patissière Sauce.*
5) Add the instant coffee to Tia Maria in a cup and mix until the coffee is dissolved.
6) Add coffee mixture to whipped cream, whipping it in a little at a time.
7) Combine the whipped cream mixture and the egg yolk and milk mixture.
8) Spoon into serving dishes and chill at least 3 hours.

Service
1) Serve cold with or without additional whipped cream as garnish.

Suggested Wines
Vin de Paille or California Sauterne

*See page 309.

Raspberry Soufflé

Yield: 8 portions   Prep time: 15 min
                                      Cook time: 15 min

Equipment
mixing bowls, whip, 8 soufflé dishes, electric mixer

Ingredients
*raspberries; 13 oz (360 g)   salt; ¼ tsp
sugar, confectioners'; 5 oz (150 g)   butter, melted; 2 tbsp (40 ml)
lemon juice; ¼ cup (60 ml)   sugar, powdered; as needed
egg yolks; 4   †Coulis of Raspberry (fresh if avail-
egg whites; 12   able); as needed

Method
1) Blend raspberries and 3 ounces of confectioners' sugar.
2) Add lemon juice and egg yolks and blend well. Set aside.
3) Butter soufflé dishes and dust with confectioners' sugar.
4) Whip egg whites with a touch of salt until firm, but not quite as firm as ordinary meringue.
5) Add 2 ounces of confectioners' sugar and whip 30 seconds more.
6) Add a quarter of the meringue to the raspberry mixture and mix well.
7) Carefully fold the remaining meringue into the raspberry mixture.
8) Pour into soufflé dishes; fill to the top. Clean the top edge of the dish with thumb. (This helps the souffle to rise perfectly; a bit of sugar or dried meringue is enough to cause the souffle to rise unevenly.)
9) Bake at 350°F for 15 minutes.

Service
1) Garnish with Coulis of Raspberry.
2) Serve at once.

*If raspberries are frozen, thaw prior to use.
†See page 218.

Chocolate Zucchini Cake

Yield: 12 portions

Prep time: 20 min
Cook time: 1 hr

Equipment
mixing bowls, electric mixer, whip, kitchen spoon, French knife or grater, bundt pan or tube pan, cake rack

Ingredients
Cake
   butter; 12 tbsp (240 ml)
   sugar; 2 cup (420 g)
   eggs, whole; 3
   vanilla extract; 2 tsp (10 ml)
   orange zest, grated; 2 tsp
   milk; ½ cup (⅛ liter)
   all-purpose flour; 2½ cup (315 g)
   cocoa powder, unsweetened; ½ cup (50 g)
   baking powder; 2½ tsp

baking soda; 1½ tsp
salt; 1 tsp
cinnamon, ground; 1 tsp
zucchini, shredded, medium; 2
walnuts or pecans, chopped; 1 cup
Frosting
   sugar, confectioners'; 2 cup (265 g)
   milk; 2 tbsp (40 ml)
   vanilla extract; 1 tsp (20 ml)

Method
1) Cream butter and sugar together.
2) Add the eggs one at a time, beating well after each addition.
3) Add the vanilla, orange zest, milk, flour, cocoa, baking powder, baking soda, salt, and cinnamon and mix well.
4) Fold in the zucchini and nuts.
5) Pour batter into a greased and floured pan and bake in a preheated oven at 350°F for 1 hour or until a toothpick inserted in the center comes out clean.
6) Cool on cake rack. Insure that cake is cool before attempting to frost.
7) To make frosting, combine sugar, milk, and vanilla and stir until well mixed.
8) Pour over the completely cool cake.

Suggested Wines
Anjou (cold) or California Muscatel

Carrot Cake

Yield: 18 portions

Prep time: 20 min
Cook time: 50 min

Equipment
mixing bowl, kitchen spoon, grater, whip, 9 × 13 in. baking pan

Ingredients

Cake
- sugar, granulated; 2 cup (420 g)
- vegetable oil; 1½ cup (375 ml)
- eggs, whole; 3
- vanilla extract; 2 tsp (10 ml)
- all-purpose flour; 2¼ cup (315 g)
- ground cinnamon; 2 tsp
- baking soda; 2 tsp
- salt; 1 tsp
- carrots, shredded; 2 cup
- coconut, flaked; 2 cup
- pineapple, canned, crushed, drained; 8 oz (225 g)
- walnuts, unsalted, chopped; 1 cup

Frosting
- cream cheese, room temperature; 6 oz (170 g)
- butter, melted; ½ cup (125 g)
- milk; ¼ cup
- vanilla; 2 tsp
- salt; ¼ tsp
- sugar, powdered; 3½ cup (465 g)

Method
1) Combine sugar, oil, eggs, and vanilla in large bowl and blend well.
2) Stir in flour, cinnamon, soda, and salt and mix well.
3) Fold in carrots, coconut, pineapple, and walnuts. Insure that all ingredients are well combined.
4) Spoon into greased and floured pan and bake in a preheated oven at 350°F for about 50 minutes. Cake is done when tester inserted in center comes out clean and cake has begun to separate from sides of pan.
5) Cool in pan about 5 minutes. Then invert onto cake rack and allow to cool. Do not attempt to ice while hot.
6) For frosting use electric mixer to combine cream cheese, butter, milk, vanilla, and salt. Insure that all ingredients are well mixed.
7) Whip in enough powdered sugar to make mixture spreadable.
8) Frost top and sides of cooled cake.

The Incredible Lemon Cake

Yield: 1 cake   Prep time: 20 min
                                       Cook time: 1¼ hr

Equipment
mixing bowls, sifter, saucepan, French knife, cutting board, electric mixer,
whip, 8½ × 4½ × 2¾ in. loaf pan*

Ingredients
Cake
  all-purpose flour, sifted; 1½ cup
   (210 g)
  baking powder; 1 tsp
  salt; ¾ tsp
  butter, unsalted; ¼ lb (112 g)
  sugar, granulated; 1 cup (210 g)
  eggs, large; 2
  milk, whole; ½ cup (125 ml)

  lemon extract; 1 oz (30 ml)
  lemon juice; of 2 large lemons
  lemon zest; of 2 large lemons
  almonds, blanched, chopped very
   fine; ½ cup
Glaze
  sugar, granulated; ⅓ cup + 2 tbsp
  lemon juice, fresh; ⅓ cup

Method
1) Sift together flour, baking powder, and salt. Set aside.
2) Melt butter.
3) In bowl of electric mixer, combine melted butter and sugar and mix slowly.
4) Using mixer on slow speed, add eggs one at a time.
5) Add dry ingredients as follows: a third of the dry ingredients, half of the
   milk, a third of the dry ingredients, the last half of the milk, and finally the
   rest of the dry ingredients.
6) Add lemon extract and lemon juice.
7) Stir in lemon zest and almonds.
8) Pour into buttered and floured pan and bake in a preheated oven at 350°F
   for 65 to 75 minutes. When done, a skewer inserted to the bottom of the
   cake will come out clean. Also, a large crack on top of cake and separation
   from the sides of pan are indications that cake is done.
9) For glaze, combine sugar and lemon juice and heat until sugar is dissolved.
   Do not let boil.

*Do not use Teflon, black metal, or glass pan for this cake. Heavy gauge aluminum is best.
Recipe will fail if ingredients are increased or if baking is done in a larger pan. For
commercial use, simply bake cakes, batch by batch, using this recipe.

10) Apply glaze slowly over very warm but not hot cake and let cool before removing cake from pan.

Suggested Wines
French or California sweet white wines

Chocolate Chestnut Torte

Yield: 10 portions

Prep time: 20 min
Cook time: 1¼ hr

Equipment
whip, mixing bowls, saucepan, double boiler, kitchen spoon, sifter, 9-in. cake pan, spreader, electric mixer (optional)

Ingredients
Torte
  chestnut puree; 15 oz (425 g)
  cognac; ½ cup (125 ml)
  heavy cream; ⅓ cup (83 ml)
  sugar, granulated; ¾ cup (150 g)
  butter, unsalted, melted; 6 tbsp
  (120 ml)
  semi-sweet chocolate, broken into
    small pieces; 1 lb (450 g)

eggs, whole, room temperature; 5
egg yolks, room temperature; 2
cornstarch; 2 tbsp
Chocolate icing
  semi-sweet chocolate; 4 oz (115 g)
  butter, unsalted; 2 tbsp (40 ml)
  strong coffee; 1 tbsp (20 ml)
  cognac; 1 tbsp (20 ml)

Method
1) Using whip, combine chestnut puree, cognac, and cream in large bowl just until smooth. Do not overmix or cream will curdle.
2) Whisk in sugar and butter.
3) Melt chocolate over simmering water in top of double boiler. Stir occasionally.
4) When chocolate is melted and smooth, stir into chestnut mixture.
5) Add eggs and yolks to chestnut mixture, one at a time, beating well after each addition.
6) Sift cornstarch over batter and fold in.
7) Pour batter into buttered and floured pan.
8) Place pan in unheated oven and turn on oven to 300°F. Bake about 1 hour, until wooden toothpick inserted in center of cake is almost but not quite clean when withdrawn.
9) Remove from oven and cool on wire rack for 15 minutes.
10) Invert pan on serving plate and remove cake.
11) Wrap in plastic film and let stand at room temperature overnight.
12) To make icing, melt chocolate and butter in top of double boiler over simmering water. Stir constantly until smooth.

13) Stir in coffee and cognac.
14) Cool to room temperature before using.
15) Spread top and sides of cake evenly with icing.

Service
1) Because this cake is very rich, cut into small slices to serve.

Suggested Wines
Any respectable semi-sweet champagne

Crème Brûlée

Yield: 20 portions

Prep time: 15 min
Cook time: 1 hr
Chill time: 3 hr

Equipment
saucepan, mixing bowl, whip, electric mixer (optional), kitchen spoon, 20 heatproof soup or custard cups, hotel pan

Ingredients
half & half or light cream; 2 qt (2 liter)
eggs, whole; 6
sugar, granulated; 1 ¼ cup (260 g)
vanilla extract; 2 tbsp (40 ml)
brown sugar; 3 tbsp or as needed

Method
1) Heat cream almost to boiling.
2) Combine eggs and sugar and mix well.
3) Add the hot cream to egg and sugar mixture.
4) Add vanilla and mix well.
5) Fill individual cups with the mixture. Sprinkle brown sugar on top of each.
6) Using hotel pan about half full of boiling water, bake in water bath at 350°F for about 1 hour. The *brûlée* is done when it "jiggles" just a little when moved and stays together when spooned.
7) Chill 3 hours.*

Suggested Wines
Vin de Bergerac or California Tokay

*This dessert can be served in the cups or demolded. Demolding is accomplished by dipping cold cup in hot water and then inverting. If this presentation is planned, coat the bottom of the cups with caramel before cooking.

Lime Mousse

Yield: 17 portions

Prep time: 10 min
Chill time: 3 hr

Equipment
double boiler, bowl, whip, kitchen spoon, grater, juicer, 17 4-oz parfait dishes

Ingredients
butter, sweet; ½ lb (225 g)
eggs, whole, room temperature; 10
sugar, granulated; 2 cup (400 g)
lime juice; 1½ cup (375 ml) or of 10 limes
lime zest, grated; of 10 limes
whipped cream; 1 qt (1 liter)

Method
1) Melt butter in top of double boiler.
2) Combine eggs and sugar in bowl and beat until light and foamy. Add to the melted butter in top of double boiler and stir constantly until the custard forms, about 8 minutes.
3) Remove from heat and stir in lime juice and lime zest.*
4) Cool to room temperature.
5) Whip cream almost to the point where it turns to butter.
6) Stir whipped cream gently into cooled custard, just enough to combine.
7) Fill parfait dishes and chill for 3 hours.

Suggested Wines
Any sweet champagne or Asti Spumanti

*Add 1 tablespoon of gelatin to the custard if a lighter mousse is desired.

Crème Caramel au Rhum

Yield: 16 portions   Prep time: 5 min
                                            Cook time: 50 min

Equipment
small saucepan, whip, candy thermometer, kitchen spoon, 16 heatproof
soup cups, mixing bowl, hotel pan, boning knife

Ingredients
sugar, granulated; 1 cup (200 g)   egg yolks; 10
water; ½ cup (125 ml)   eggs, whole; 2
sugar, confectioners'; 1½ cup   milk; 3 cup (¾ liter)
  (220 g)   dark rum; 12 tbsp (240 ml)

Method
1) Combine granulated sugar and water in saucepan and heat over medium
   heat to boiling, just until sugar dissolves.
2) Heat without stirring until golden brown (300°F on candy thermometer).
   This is caramel. Work quickly, because it will harden as it cools. Put 1 tablespoon into each cup.
3) Gently whisk confectioners' sugar, egg yolks, and eggs in medium bowl and
   combine well.
4) Stir in milk and 4 tablespoons of rum. Skim off any foam. Divide milk mixture evenly among cups.
5) Place cups in hotel pan. Pour enough boiling water into pan to come halfway up sides of cups. Bake in a preheated oven at 350°F until custard is set
   around edges but still soft in center, about 50 minutes.
6) Remove cups from water. Cool completely at room temperature. Do not
   refrigerate.
7) Dip cups briefly in hot water and loosen edges of custard with knife if necessary. Unmold onto individual serving plates.
8) Heat remaining rum in saucepan. Ignite and pour over custards. (It may also
   be ignited with a lighted match at tableside, if desired.)

Suggested Wines
Crème of Vanilla liqueur

Coffee Soufflé Nouvelle Cuisine

Yield: 8 portions

Prep time: 10 min
Cook time: 25 min

Equipment
saucepan, whip, small electric mixer, mixing bowl, 8 soufflé molds, small sheet pan

Ingredients
instant coffee powder; 2 tsp
water; 2 tsp (20 ml)
sugar, powdered; 2 oz (60 g)
egg yolks; 4
egg whites; 7

Method
1) Mix together coffee, water, and sugar and heat to boiling. Cool.
2) Add egg yolks and combine well.
3) In a separate bowl, beat egg whites until very stiff.
4) Mix a quarter of the egg whites into yolk-coffee-sugar mixture.
5) Fold in the rest of the beaten egg whites.
6) Butter molds and dust with powdered sugar.
7) Fill molds evenly, to about ½ inch from rim. Using thumb, wipe inside rim of mold (this insures even rising of soufflé) and bake in a preheated oven at 325°F for 8 to 10 minutes.

Suggested Wines
Coffee liqueur or Irish coffee

Pineapples with Black Pepper*
(Ananas au Poivre)

Yield: 4 portions   Prep time: 10 min
                                     Cook time: 10 min

Equipment
French knife, cutting board, sauté pan, kitchen spoon

Ingredients
pineapple, whole, skinned, cored,   orange juice; 2 oz (60 ml)
  sliced ¼ in. (1 cm) thick, about 11   lemon juice; 1 oz (30 ml)
  oz (310 g); 1   *Crème de Cacao*; 2 oz (60 ml)
black pepper, freshly ground; ½ tsp   †brown butter; 1 oz (28 g)
butter; 1½ oz (40 g)   ice cream, vanilla, sliced from brick;
Crème de Cacao; 1 oz (30 ml)   4 portions
Sauce   orange zest, blanched; of 1 orange
  sugar, granulated; 4 oz (112 g)

Method
1) Sprinkle the pineapple with pepper.
2) Heat the butter, add pineapple and *Crème de Cacao*, and ignite with a
   lighted match. Set aside.
3) To make sauce, melt sugar until it is slightly brown (caramelized).
4) Add orange juice, lemon juice, and *Crème de Cacao* and reduce.
5) Add brown butter.
6) Combine ingredients and heat gently.

Service
1) Put the pineapple on a plate and arrange the ice cream on the middle of
   each slice. Pour hot sauce over pineapple slice and ice cream.
2) Garnish with orange zest.

Suggested Wines
Champagne Brut

(See color plate 17)

*Created by the Brothers Troisgros, Master Chefs in Roanne near Lyon.
†Butter that has been heated until slightly brown.

Champagne Custard (Sabayon au Champagne)

Yield: 12 portions

Prep time: 10 min
Cook time: 20 min

Equipment
mixing bowl, wooden spoon, whip, double boiler, 12 dessert dishes, extra bowls

Ingredients
egg yolks; 12
sugar; 2½ cup (525 g)
champagne; 2½ cup (625 ml)
cognac, Grand Marnier, or rum; 4 tbsp (80 ml)
fresh pears or sliced bananas; as needed

Method
1) Combine yolks with sugar and beat with wooden spoon until mixture forms a ribbon when dropped from spoon. This will take 7 to 10 minues.
2) Stir in champagne, blending well.
3) Transfer to top of double boiler and cook over medium high heat. Stir constantly until mixture thickens to custard consistency (like Patissière Sauce*).
4) Remove from heat and stir in liquor of choice.
5) Pour over fruit in dessert dishes and serve immediately.

Suggested Wines
Marsala Florio sweet

*See page 309.

Zabaione au Marsala

Yield: 8 portions

Prep time: 10 min
Cook time: 20 min
Chill time: 2 hr

Equipment
whip, double boiler, kitchen spoon, 8 serving cups, hotel pan, crushed ice

Ingredients
egg yolks; 7
sugar; confectioners'; ¾ cup (100 g)
lemon zest, grated; of ½ lemon
cinnamon, ground; pinch
vanilla extract; ½ tsp (3 ml)
sweet Marsala wine; 1 cup (250 ml)
heavy cream; whipped; 1 cup (250 ml)

Method
1) Prepare in the same manner as Hollandaise Sauce.* The egg yolks are beaten while heating in a double boiler over simmering water.
2) When nearly done, add lemon zest, cinnamon, vanilla, and wine.
3) When finished, ladle into serving cups and place in ice in hotel pan. Refrigerate at least 2 hours.

Service
1) Garnish with whipped cream.

Suggested Wines
Sweet Marsala wine

*See page 99.

Crepe Batter

Yield: 60 crepes

Prep time: 10 min
Rest time: 2 hr
Cook time: 1 hr

Equipment
mixing bowl, whip, crepe pans, ladle, spatula

Ingredients
bread flour; 18 oz (500 g)
eggs; 12
butter or vegetable oil; 4 tbsp (80 ml)
milk; 1½ qt (1½ liter)
salt; to taste
sugar; to taste
cognac; to taste (optional)

Method
1) Combine all ingredients and mix well.
2) Rest at room temperature for 2 hours.
3) Mix again and prepare in a manner similar to pancakes, except that they will be only light brown on each side.
4) Chill and use as needed.

Uses
Crepes are used for desserts, filled and rolled with jam or sweetened fruit; for appetizers, filled with seafood, chicken, or meat; or for entrées. They can even be used to line soup bowls for a novel presentation.

(See color plate 5)

Strawberry Soufflé Nouvelle Cuisine

Yield: 16 portions   Prep time: 5 min
                             Cook time: 12 min

Equipment
mixing bowl, electric mixer, whip, kitchen spoon, 16 soufflé molds, sheet pan

Ingredients
strawberries, fresh; 1 lb (450 g)
sugar, confectioners'; 4 oz (112 g)
lemon juice; of 1 lemon
*Coulis of Strawberry; 1 tbsp (20 ml)
egg yolks; 4
kirsch; 1 tbsp (20 ml)
egg whites; 14

Method
1) Mix strawberries, sugar, lemon juice, and coulis.
2) Add egg yolks.
3) Beat egg whites until firm but not stiff.
4) Fold in a quarter of the egg whites into the strawberry mixture. Rest 3 minutes and then fold in the remainder of the whites.
5) Butter molds and dust with confectioners' sugar and fill molds to the top. Using thumb, clean the top of mold.
6) Bake at 325°F for 8 minutes if individual molds are used. (For molds that serve two people, double cooking time.)
7) Serve at once; do not hold!

Suggested Wines
Strawberry liqueur

*See page 218.

Pie Dough

Yield: dough for 2 pies   Prep time: 20 min

Equipment
mixing bowl, scale, baker's table or dough board

Ingredients
bread flour; 2.2 lb (1000 g)
sugar; 1½ oz (40 g)
salt; 1 oz (20 g)
butter; 1 lb (450 g)
eggs, medium; 2
*water, cream, milk, or wine; as needed

Method
1) Combine flour, sugar, and salt.
2) Using both hands, knead in butter. Continue until dough looks like coarse cornmeal.
3) Add eggs and liquid as needed.
4) Rest 2 hours in cool place. †Fraiser.
5) Roll out dough to about ⅛ to ¼ inch thickness.

---

*Use water, cream, or milk for desserts. Use wine for quiche.
†See page 340.

French Bread

Yield: 28 10-oz (280-g) loaves   Prep & cook time: 2½ hr

Equipment
mixing bowl, whisk, sifter, mixer with dough hook, work table, baker's proof box or warm (about 90°F) area, dough cutter, scale, sheet pans

Ingredients
yeast, fresh; 8 oz (227 g) *or* yeast, dry; 4 oz (112 g)
water, warm; 8 lb (3.6 kg)
vegetable oil; 12 oz (350 ml)
bread flour; 14 lb (6.3 kg)
sugar; 4 oz (112 g)
salt; 4 oz (112 g)
corn meal; as needed
egg whites; 8 oz (250 ml)

Method
1) Using whip, mix yeast and water. Allow to work about 10 minutes until bubbles indicate the yeast is starting to work.
2) Add oil and mix.
3) Sift together flour, sugar, and salt.
4) Add the yeast-water-oil mixture to dry ingredients in mixing bowl.
5) Knead on #2 speed for about 20 minutes. Dough is finished when a small piece can be pulled (like taffy) to paper thin without breaking.
6) Bench rest for 20 minutes. Dough will rise.
7) Punch and allow to rise 10 minutes more.
8) Scale out and round. Allow to rest 5 to 10 minutes more.
9) Punch and roll dough into loaves, being careful to seal properly.
10) Place loaves, seal down, on sheet pans spread with corn meal. Allow to rest 10 minutes more.
11) Brush with egg whites and bake at 360°F until golden brown. Test for doneness by tapping with fingernail. If hollow sound is produced, bread is done.*

*Bread can be brown and undercooked. The average cooking time is approximately 35 to 40 minutes.

Summary

Even though Americans are becoming more and more health conscious, desserts are still a big seller and a high-profit item.

All of the desserts in this chapter are proven sellers. Special attention should be paid to *Pâte à Choux "Oncle Louis"* and to Patissière Sauce. Although these are classic recipes that are adaptable to myriad variations, their use has become rare in modern America. Probably this is due to three factors: the shortage of trained kitchen help; the availability of cheap artificial substitutes; and the fact that compared with the artificial substitutes, they are relatively expensive. But the taste is extraordinary. Using them is well worth the cost. Even if it raises the dessert prices, the customers will be happy.

As with the entrées, chefs should try a wide variety of desserts to determine which sell the best.

Discussion Questions*

1) What do we mean by the statement that the *Pâte à Choux "Oncle Louis"* and Patissière Sauce recipes are classics?
2) Why are the classic versions of *Pâte à Choux "Oncle Louis"* and Patissière Sauce used only in the best restaurants?
3) How is a pastry cart best used for dessert sales?
4) What are the advantages and disadvantages of using commercial frozen ready-to-serve desserts?
5) Why is it important that front-of-the-house staff sell desserts to customers?

Test Questions

1) List the ingredients and describe the method of making *Pâte à Choux "Oncle Louis."*
2) List the ingredients and describe the method of making Patissière Sauce.
3) List the ingredients for Chocolate Chestnut Torte.
4) List the ingredients and describe the method of making *Crème Brûlée.*
5) List the ingredients required for French Bread.
6) List the ingredients in New York Cheesecake.
7) How is the method of making *Zabaione au Marsala* similar to the method of making Hollandaise Sauce?

*Some discussion questions require culinary deductive reasoning. They may not be answered *directly* in the text, but enough information is given to deduce the answer logically.

8) Compare a finished crepe to a pancake. What are the differences?
9) Name three possible crepe fillings.
10) What is unusual about The Incredible Lemon Cake recipe?

Appendix: General Review Questions for Discussion*

1) Why is Chef Chaton uniquely qualified to write this textbook?
2) You have learned many new techniques, some of which are known only to the best chefs in the top restaurants in the world. List some examples of how this knowledge will put you a step ahead of your competition when you begin your first job.
3) Why is it necessary to use standardized, kitchen-tested recipes, regardless of the skill level of your kitchen staff?
4) What are some problems in recipe conversion?
5) Why would a new hotel manager benefit by reading this textbook?
6) Why is cooking considered to be both an art and a science?
7) Why is it that a recipe, which may be perfect in New York, will not work so well in Rome?
8) Why, in the "Method" portion of many recipes, are you instructed to "adjust taste" at the end of the cooking process?
9) In converting cake recipes to larger or smaller quantities, what are the problems with leavening agents like yeast or baking powder?
10) Why is it important for students to have hands-on experience?
11) As our civilization becomes more and more "high-tech," are basic cooking techniques likely to change significantly?
12) Is spit roasting ever used in commercial cooking today?
13) Is there any real reason to sear meat before roasting?
14) How many orders at one time could a very good sauté cook be expected to handle?
15) What are the main advantages to pressure frying chicken?
16) Are there any advantages to boiling food rather than simmering it?
17) How important is the microwave in the daily operations of a three-star kitchen?
18) What type of meat is usually cooked by braising?
19) In making French fries from scratch, why is it necessary to blanch them before cooking?
20) How were the basic cooking techniques developed?

*Some discussion questions require culinary deductive reasoning. They may not be answered *directly* in the text, but enough information is given to deduce the answer logically.

21) Why are American customers usually very impressed by exceptional hors d'oeuvres?
22) Why is Puff Pastry so important in the preparation of a wide variety of hors d'oeuvres?
23) What is the function and purpose of the hors d'oeuvre?
24) What are the disadvantages of using the commercial frozen "heat and serve" type of hors d'oeuvres?
25) Can you list twenty variations of hors d'oeuvres?
26) Why do so few restaurants make Puff Pastry from scratch?
27) Is there anything wrong with the practice of buying frozen sheets of puff pastry dough?
28) The Russian style of hors d'oeuvre service is now very popular in France. Explain this variation.
29) What is the basic rule of hors d'oeuvre preparation and service?
30) Why is it important that the chef know how to make a wide variety of hors d'oeuvres?
31) Why are good stocks so important in food production?
32) What are the ingredients for classic White Stock?
33) What is the cooking time for White Stock?
34) What are the ingredients for Brown Stock?
35) What is the method and cooking time for Brown Stock?
36) What happens to Brown Stock if it is cooked too long? Not cooked enough?
37) What are the ingredients of Fish Stock?
38) What is the cooking time for Fish Stock?
39) Name the ingredients for Vegetable Stock.
40) What is the normal cooking time for Vegetable Stock?
41) Describe five different ways aspic could be used in a buffet presentation.
42) Is chopped lean beef one of the ingredients used in the clarification of beef aspic?
43) Name some other ingredients that would be used in the clarification of beef aspic.
44) Chopped into small cubes, how would aspic be used?
45) Should aspic be strongly or lightly flavored?
46) Why is Court Bouillon used for poaching fish and some meats?
47) Is gelatin used in classic aspic?
48) What flavor aspic would be used for eggs?
49) What flavor aspic is used for fish?
50) What flavor aspic is used for tongue?
51) Why are sauces called the "soul of cuisine"?
52) What is the function of a sauce?

53) List the mother sauces. Why are they called "mother sauces"?
54) Explain the difference between roux and beurre manié.
55) What is the standard technique used to avoid curdling or "breaking" a sauce when cream is added to a hot sauce to finish it?
56) List the ingredients in Italian Mint Sauce.
57) Describe the method, list the ingredients, and specify the uses of Provençale Sauce #1.
58) List the ingredients and describe the method of making Lobster Thermidor Sauce.
59) Describe the correct consistency for service of *Marchand de Vin Butter*.
60) List the ingredients and describe the method of making Shrimp Sauce Chef Chaton?
61) In your opinion, how important is the soup in a "white tablecloth" operation?
62) How often should fresh soups be made? How long can they be held without risk of spoilage or taste deterioration?
63) What would be the appropriate season for the service of Mint Cucumber Soup?
64) Describe the method of preparing, list the ingredients used in, and name the country of origin of Guadeloupean Red Bean Soup.
65) What are the basic categories of soups?
66) What must be done to prepare the conch for Carribean Conch Chowder?
67) What is the garnish for French Riviera Soup (*Aïgo Saou*)?
68) Must the stock be clarified in the preparation of Tomato Consommé with Fennel?
69) Is Andalusian Gazpacho a cold or hot soup?
70) List the ingredients and method for preparing Potage St. Thibery.
71) Why is it important that an entrée look beautiful (as well as taste good) when it is placed in front of a customer?
72) In what ways, and why, must color be considered when choosing the sauce and vegetable to accompany an entrée?
73) What type of pepper is used in the preparation of Steak Diane?
74) Describe the presentation of *Côte d'Agneau à la Nelson*.
75) Describe the method of preparing and cooking the grouper in Grouper Renée Flament.
76) What is the total time needed to prepare and cook Classic Couscous Tunisian with Lamb and Two Sauces?
77) If Sole, Salmon, and Scallop Mousse is prepared correctly, what will the three colors be when the sliced product is presented (excluding the sauce)?
78) If crepes are filled with Seafood Stuffing, what would be two possible appropriate sauces?

79) What is the cooking method for Ramekins of Shrimp and Scallops?
80) In preparing Filet of Beef Wellington, describe the size differences between the top and bottom pieces of puff pastry.
81) Why is customer perception a factor in selecting produce for your menu?
82) Describe the ingredients and method of preparing Spinach Flan with Fresh Tomato.
83) List five entrées with which it would be appropriate to serve Jam of Onions Nouvelle Cuisine?
84) What is Coulis of Fresh Tomato?
85) Can hollowed out cooked potatoes be stuffed with Potato Duchess?
86) Why is a good, cooperative, well-informed vegetable vendor an asset to any busy chef?
87) What is Potato Voisin?
88) Describe the ingredients and method in preparing *Crique Ardéchoise?*
89) List the ingredients of Eggplant Fulton.
90) List the ingredients and method used in preparing Tomatoes Florentine.
91) Why is it important for waiters to use a dessert cart or other techniques to sell desserts?
92) How many separate times is the dough required to rise in the preparation of French Bread?
93) Describe the technique of preparing Bananas Foster.
94) What type of pan is used to bake Chef Chaton's Cheesecake?
95) Describe the method and ingredients used in the preparation of Raspberry Soufflé?
96) What are the three different liquids that may be used in the preparation of pie dough, depending upon its intended use?
97) List the ingredients and describe the method of making Coffee Soufflé Nouvelle Cuisine?
98) Which are most fashionable today, large individual pastries or small ones?
99) What is meant by "water bath" in the baking of *Crème Brûlée?*
100) List the ingredients and describe the method of making *Crème Caramel au Rhum.*

Glossary of Advanced Cuisine

This glossary is composed of technical cooking terms that are mostly French in origin. The terms are used internationally in advanced cuisine because, in many cases, there is no translation. "Sauté," for example, is a kitchen term used as often in London, Rome, or Paris as in New York or Peoria. The definitions given are basic and classic; nevertheless, some variations in meaning will be found in local usage.

aiguillette: A long, thin slice of meat, fish, poultry, or game. Fish fillets are often cut in this way and then breaded and deep fried for "fish fingers."

al dente: Pasta or vegetables that have been cooked to the point where they are done but still slightly firm, rather than soft or mushy.

appareil: Various ingredients combined together, usually in advance, for the final preparation of a food product when needed. The flavoring and rising ingredients of a soufflé and the breading ingredients of a fried product are good examples of this.

aromates: Natural herbs, spices, or vegetables that are used to season foods that impart taste and aroma. Examples are thyme, garlic, and mirepoix.

arrowroot: A digestible starch, used as a thickening agent in sauces and soups. It is made from the roots of the maranta plant [*Marania arundinacea*] and is used in a powder form, like cornstarch.

aspic: A jelly made from the concentrated stock of meat, fish, or poultry. It is used for glazing and enhancing the appearance of a large variety of cold dishes. Made from scratch, the gel effect is obtained from the natural gelatin extracted from the bones used in the process of making the stock.

au blanc: "With a *blanc*," which is a thin paste made of flour and water. Vegetables are often cooked in this mixture to maintain whiteness.

au bleu: This term refers particularly to trout when they are poached in a court bouillon immediately after killing. Trout fresh-killed and cooked in this manner is usually served with the skin on. The skin becomes bluish in color when cooked.

bain marie: A pan of hot water into which another vessel containing food is placed. Food is either cooked or kept hot in this manner. Examples are a double boiler and a steam table.

ballottine: A piece of meat, game, or poultry that is boned, stuffed, and braised. This dish is usually served hot. Do not confuse this term with *galantine.*

bard: The use of pork fat or bacon in the process of cooking meat or poultry. The fat, which is sometimes placed on top of the meat and sometimes inserted in the meat, prevents scorching and adds moisture.

barquette: A pastry shell shaped like a boat, used both in dessert and entrée preparation. In desserts, the shells are often baked blind (empty) and then filled with fruit mixtures, butter cream, etc.

baton: A thin strip of meat or vegetable, about the same size as a wooden kitchen match; like small julienne, except longer.

beurre manié: A cold roux consisting of sixteen parts butter combined with eighteen parts flour. The ingredients are combined until the result looks like pie dough. It is added to boiling soups and sauces as a thickening agent. It is superior to cooked roux in that the thickness of the product can be more carefully controlled. It is very stable, and products thickened with it will not break even under storage and reheat conditions.

bisque: A thick, rich soup of pureed fish or shellfish, which is often highly seasoned.

blanch: To cook slightly. For example, vegetables are blanched by adding them to boiling water and then quickly cooling with cold water. French fries are blanched by dipping them in hot fat before final cooking. Some meats (including very salty bacon and salt fish) are blanched by putting them in cold water and bringing the water to a boil; this removes the blood and impurities.

bouchée: 1) A small pastry shell, usually of puff pastry, that is baked blind (empty). It can be filled with various ingredients and used in both appetizers and desserts. 2) A certain type of petits fours.

bouillon: Stock, usually strong and clear, that is made from meat, fish, poultry, game, or vegetables.

broil: To cook (usually meat) directly over or under the fire. *Grill* means the same thing.

bouquet garni: Parsley, thyme, and bay leaf, usually inside a pouch of cheese-cloth, that is tied to the pot with string. The pouch is used to flavor stews, sauces, or soups and removed either after cooking or when the desired taste is attained.

brunoise: 1) A method of shredding or chopping vegetables into small pieces and then sweating the vegetables in butter; 2) Small diced vegetables or a mixture of vegetables that are cooked in butter and then added to liquid to make soup; 3) Small diced aromatic vegetables like carrots, celery, and onions that are added as flavorings to crayfish and other dishes.

buisson: The arrangement of foods (shrimp or oranges, for example) in a cluster or pyramid that is pleasing to the eye.

canapé: Small pieces of fancy-cut bread, toast, crackers, or pastry used as a base for a variety of ingredients such as meat, cheese, *pâté*, fish, etc., and used for hors d'oeuvres.

caramel: Burnt sugar used for coloring or as a flavoring in candy.

casserole: A fairly shallow covered ovenproof vessel, which is made of a variety of materials such as glass, steel, and earthenware.

cassolette: A sort of mini-casserole used for individual service.

chaudfroiter: The process of coating meat, fish, poultry, or game with an appropriate sauce and then with aspic.

chemiser: The process of creating the outside covering of a molded dish. It is accomplished by coating the inside of molds with jelly or whatever ingredient desired and then filling the mold with the main ingredient. Thus, when the product is removed from the mold, the thin coating in the mold is the exterior coating in the final result (the same principle used in Pineapple Upside-Down Cake).

chiffonade: All vegetables or herbs that are cut into strips or shredded, like lettuce or spinach. Specifically, a combination of lettuce and sorrel cooked in butter. Many chiffonades are used to garnish soups.

chinois: Any strainer or sieve, especially the china cap.

ciseler: 1) To make shallow cuts or slashes in the backs of fish to reduce the cooking time. 2) To cut any leafy vegetable into julienne strips; to make a chiffonade.

clarify: When referring to stocks, the process of clearing the liquid. Ground meat, crushed eggshells, and slightly beaten egg whites are added to the stock, which is brought to a slow boil. When a raft of impurities forms on the top, it is carefully skimmed off. The resultant liquid is then strained through cheesecloth until a perfectly clear stock results.

concasser: To chop vegetables coarsely. The term is most often used to describe a method of cutting tomatoes.

crème: Whipped cream, butter cream, and the various custard creams used in pastry.

croustades: Any of a variety of deep pastry shells, hollowed-out bread rolls, or shaped or molded pastry shells filled with various meats, seafoods, etc. (as in the case of dough baked on scallop shells to produce shell-shaped croustades).

croûte: Broiled, fried, or toasted thick-sliced bread. Meat, fish, or poultry entrées are served on the croûtes.

croutons: Small bread cubes fried, broiled, or baked in butter until golden brown. Used as a garnish for soups, salads, and some entrées.

cuisson: 1) Stock or broth that results from cooking a food—like mushrooms, veal bones, or calf's head. 2) The cooking of any kind of food. 3) Cooking time.

dariole: Individual small molds in any of a variety of shapes.

deglaze: The process in which the cooked bits of food, juices, etc., that remain in a pan after sautéing or roasting are diluted with wine, stock, or water. The resulting liquid is used for sauce or flavoring.

dégorger: The soaking of certain foods in cold water. Depending upon the food, this is done to remove strong flavors, improve color, or to remove blood. Calves heads and veal sweetbreads, for example, are soaked in water to make them intensely white.

dépouiller: To skim fat off the top.

détendre: The process of diluting a liquid, such as a sauce or a glaze, to a thinner consistency.

détrempe: 1) A paste made of water and flour to be used in the preparation of pastries, as in the first step of preparing Puff Pastry. 2) The paste used to seal casseroles.

dry duxelles: A mushroom hash seasoned with salt and pepper and sometimes nutmeg. The mixture is used for garnishing as well as flavoring, especially poached fish and Beef Wellington. Basic recipe: sweat 2 ounces of finely chopped shallots in butter. Add 1 pound of finely chopped mushrooms and sweat until nearly all the moisture has evaporated.

étuver: Cooking slowly without much liquid (just a little butter or oil) in a tightly lidded pot. The liquid that vaporizes from the food condenses on the lid and drips back on the food in a constant slow basting action. This method can be used for virtually all foods, including meat, fish, poultry, game, vegetables, and fruit. This is a variation of *poêler*.

farce: All forcemeats and stuffings used in many different applications. It should not be confused with *farci*, which is a dish made with forcemeat common to the South of France.

flambé: To add a flammable spirit (such as brandy, rum, or kirsch) to food and ignite it. It should be noted that this technique is used in cuisine for two reasons. The most important is for taste, as when a sauce requires the taste of a certain burnt liquor. The other reason is for pure showmanship as when foods are flambéed at tableside simply to impress and please the customer.

foncer: The process of lining pans, rings, molds, etc. For example, lining of roasting or braising pans with mirepoix prior to cooking or lining baking tins with pastry.

faire la fontaine: To "make a fountain," which refers to the first step in making dough, when flour is heaped on the pastry board and a hole or well is made in the pile of flour. Water is added into the well and combined with the flour, little by little, until the dough is made. This technique prevents the water from running off the board and at the same time allows the baker to control the final consistency of his dough.

forcemeat (*farce*): Finely chopped seasoned fish or meat used as a stuffing, a garnish, or an ingredient in any number of dishes.

fraiser: A technique of blending or kneading ingredients together in various types of dough. It is especially applicable when pie dough is made by hand. The dough is stretched, rubbed, and pressed forcefully (all at the same time) against a flat surface with the palm of the hand.

fricassee: A white stew of poultry, usually chicken. The meat is sautéed lightly and then finished in sauce.

fumet: A concentrated stock made from meat, fish, poultry, or vegetables, which are used to flavor a variety of dishes. For example, reduced Chicken Stock becomes chicken fumet; reduced Truffle Stock becomes truffle fumet.

galantine: A piece of meat or poultry that is boned, stuffed, shaped symmetrically, rolled, and cooked in gelatinous stock. Do not confuse with a *ballottine*.

glaze: This is a technical cooking term with many applications. 1) To give a golden color to foods sauced with buttery sauces by putting them briefly under a hot broiler. 2) To give meat a shiny appearance by brushing it with stock reduced almost to paste. 3) In baking, to dust a pastry heavily with powdered sugar and then briefly put it in a hot oven until the sugar melts into a shiny coat. Also, to coat with fondant icing or to dip the product in hot melted sugar.

gratin: A style of cooking that is characterized by a thin brown crust covering the finished product, as in potatoes au gratin. The formation of the crust, usually achieved under the broiler or in a very hot oven, is often assisted by sprinkling the top of the product with bread crumbs or cheese or both. Many entrées and vegetables are prepared in this manner.

julienne: Rectangular-shaped strips of meat, vegetable, poultry, or fish of various sizes. There is small julienne, medium julienne, etc. When cutting food in this manner, it is important to strive to make all pieces precisely the same size, both to please the eye and also to insure that each piece is cooked to the same degree.

lardon (lardoon): 1) Various size strips of pork fat and sometimes bacon that is used for larding—the insertion of the fat into large cuts of meat prior to cooking by using special needles. This process keeps the meat moist and reduces shrinkage during cooking and also insures that it is juicy when finished. 2) Diced salt pork or bacon used to flavor various dishes like stews. The use of larding needles is rare in modern cookery, but the same technique is still used. For example, the standard number 109 beef cut (prime rib) is always packed with a thick slab of beef fat held on top of the roast by a string net.

liaison: The thickening agent used to give body and consistency to food products like sauces, soups, and stews. The agent used may be roux, beurre manié, egg yolk, cornstarch, arrowroot, etc. The type of liaison used depends upon the type of food product to be thickened. Roux or beurre manié, for example, is appropriate for meat sauces but not for fruit sauces; cornstarch is excellent for fruit sauces and fillings but not for meat sauces.

lustrer: To coat with aspic, resulting in a shiny appearance that brings out food colors and textures.

macerate: To soak in flavored liquors such as rum, cognac, and bourbon.

marinate: To soak pieces of meat for a specified period of time in a specially prepared liquid—a combination of water, wine, fruit juice, or milk and spices, herbs, flavorings, or other aromates, often with oil added. The purpose of the process is both to flavor and to tenderize.

matignon: A puree of vegetables that is used as a garnish on a large number of dishes. The typical matignon consists of carrots, celery, onion, ham, thyme, bay leaf, salt, and pepper and is normally stewed in butter and finished with Madeira wine.

médaillon: A round slice of meat, fish, shellfish, poultry, or game. The word means the same as *tournedos* (used for beef) and *collops* (used for veal and poultry).

mijoter: To stew a food slowly in liquid for a long time (for example, a ragout of venison set on a very low fire to simmer for many hours).

mirepoix: A basic flavoring consisting of aromatic vegetables (carrots, celery, and onions), sometimes with ham added. They are usually diced and sautéed before being added to soups, sauces, stews, etc. Many cooks use it as a sort of raft underneath roasting meat both for flavor and to allow hot air to circulate under the meat and avoid stewing it in fat.

monter: To make frothy by beating, as when egg whites or cream are whipped. Literally, the term means to aerate. A very precise saucier might say "Monter au beurre," which means to finish a sauce by beating small bits of butter into it.

mousse: A light dish that, depending upon the ingredients, can be either an entrée or a dessert. The dish usually contains eggs and cream. A mousse served as an entrée may be made with meat, fish, poultry, or game. Chicken Mousse, Salmon Mousse, Mousse of *Foie Gras*, and Mousse of Quail are good examples. Dessert mousses can be made with fruit or in any flavor (for example, Chocolate Mousse, Apricot Mousse, and Strawberry Mousse). Many mousses are served hot with sauce, and others are served cold, with and without sauce. The texture and firmness of mousses will vary with the ingredients. Some are as delicate as whipped cream, and others must be sliced carefully with a sharp knife.

napper: To glaze lightly or cover a food product with liquids like sauce, custard, and aspic.

noisette butter: Butter heated until temperature-induced chemical change causes it to become brown and emit a slight aroma of nuts. Because of consumer perception that it is unhealthful, this type of butter has lost popularity in modern cookery.

panade (panada): A binding agent made of liquid, butter, and starch. Depending upon the intended use, it is made either in a soupy consistency or in a paste-like consistency. There are five basic types: *Flour Panade* is made with flour, water, salt, and butter and cooked. This is used for quenelles. *Frangipane Panade* is made with flour, egg yolks, butter, milk, salt, pepper, and nutmeg and cooked. This is used for fish and chicken forcemeat. *Bread Panade* is made from white bread and milk and is uncooked. This is used for fish forcemeat. *Potato Panade*, is made from potato puree, milk, butter, salt, pepper, and nutmeg and cooked. This is used for white meat quenelles. *Rice Panade* is made with rice, White Stock, and butter and cooked. This is used for many different forcemeats.

paner: Using eggs beaten with milk (egg wash) or simply beaten eggs to moisten the product and cause the coating to stick, to coat with bread crumbs, cracker meal, cake crumbs, nuts, etc. When meats are coated, they are usually lightly dusted with flour before dipping in the egg wash. Fried chicken is a good example.

papillote: The paper cases in which food is often cooked and/or served. In Grouper *en Papillote*, for example, the fish is sealed in parchment paper and baked. This has the advantage of steaming the fish in its own juices and avoids the drying effect of the oven. To serve the food in the paper enhances the presentation, especially when the paper is opened at tableside, instantly releasing a small cloud of fragrant steam.

pâte: A general term for dough, which includes all the vast variety of doughs in use, including pastry dough, sweet pastes, batters, and bread dough.

pâté: Originally, a dish made of meat or fish that was completely enclosed in pastry and eaten either hot or cold. Today, it includes terrines and, in fact, even vegetable preparations that have been ground (like forcemeat) and baked without pastry. Thus, a pork *pâté*, without pastry, which can be eaten only cold (actually a terrine), is called by the same name as a pork pie which is filled with forcemeat.

paupiette: A thin slice of meat (usually beef but also lamb, veal, and fish—especially sole) that is stuffed with forcemeat, often wrapped with a slice of bacon, braised, and served with a sauce and vegetable garnish.

poach: To cook gently in hot water, just at or below the simmering point. All manner of foods can be poached with good results—meat, fish, poultry, game, eggs, and many dishes made from these foods.

poêler: A method of pot roasting foods (especially meats) usually on a bed of root vegetables in a tightly fitted roasting pan. Except for a little butter or oil, no liquid is used. This is a variation of *étuver*.

quenelles: A dish that consists of forcemeat that has been seasoned and shaped (usually in cylinders or ovals) and cooked by poaching in liquid. They are made from veal, chicken, fish, game, etc., and are nearly always served with sauce.

refresh: Cooling and rinsing meat, vegetables, or fruit in cold water just after blanching. It stops the cooking process and restores color.

réchauffé: A dish consisting of food that has been previously cooked and reheated.

reduction: The process of increasing the strength and/or the thickness of a liquid food by evaporation. For example, a stock is simmered uncovered until the required strength is reached; a sauce is simmered in the same manner until the required consistency is attained.

revenir: To brown quickly in hot fat. This is done not to cook, but to seal the juices in the food or to provide a final color before adding stock or sauce to complete the cooking.

roux: A thickening agent for soups and sauces that is prepared by cooking fat and flour together. Butter or margarine are most commonly used. The three kinds of roux are white, blond, and brown.

royale: 1) Molded custard used as a garnish, especially for consommés. 2) A number of poached poultry dishes coated with velouté and finished with truffles and other garnishes.

saisir: To sear meat under very high heat to seal in the juices as well as to enhance taste and appearance.

saupoudrer: To sprinkle food with condiments, seasonings, or other dried foods (including salt, cheese, bread crumbs, sugar, and minced nuts).

sauté: To fry a food item quickly, in hot fat, in a pan.

sauteuse: A saucepan that is shallow and usually slope sided.

singer: The first step in braising meats. The meat is sprinkled with flour and browned rapidly in fat before the stock is added.

soubise: A seasoned puree of onions enriched with cream. It is used both as a garnish and as a sauce for meats, especially grilled meats. Sometimes it is made with rice and sometimes with Béchamel Sauce depending upon the consistency desired.

suprêmes: 1) Usually, the boneless breast of chicken. There are about fifteen classic recipes using the term in this way, including Suprêmes of Chicken Ambassadrice, Suprêmes of Chicken Carême, and Suprêmes of Chicken à l'Impériale. Some purists insist that the real suprême is the little strip of breast muscle found on the inside of both sides of the chicken breast. This idea is not without merit but would be neither cost effective nor practical for most commercial applications. 2) Sometimes, the boneless breasts of game birds and fillet of fish.

sweat: A low-key version of *sauté*. The food is stewed gently in butter and its own juice. It is never allowed to become hot enough to brown.

timbale: In its widest meaning, any kind of food served in a pie crust. In modern usage, it usually means any kind of food that has been prepared in a drum-shaped mold. It may also refer to the shape of the serving dish.

tomatoes concassées: Tomatoes that have been peeled, seeded, and chopped.

tomatoes fondues: Concasséed tomatoes that have been cooked in butter with salt, pepper, and garlic until soft. They are used as a garnish with various dishes and to fill croustades.

travailler: "To work"; this term usually applies to foods that must be mixed together for a long time, like doughs.

truss: To tie together poultry with string prior to cooking. It is done in different ways, depending on how the bird is to be cooked. In the case of lobster, it means to insert the claws inside the body for decorative presentation.

vanner: Stirring sauces to prevent the formation of skin on the top, to prevent scorching, and to encourage even cooking and combining of ingredients.

velouté: a basic white sauce made from meat, fish, poultry, and game. In essence, it is the stock with cream added. Thickeners and seasonings are also added, depending upon the intended function. Soup of the same name is made in a similar fashion.

zest: The outer skin or rind of any citrus fruit. When using zest, the white pith, which has a bitter taste, must always be removed. It is used for flavoring and for garnish in a multitude of different applications.

Bibliography: Must Reading for Working Chefs

Pellaprat, H.-P. *Modern French Culinary Art*. London and Coulsdon: Virtue and Company Ltd., 1978.
This is an encyclopedic reference work that covers the entire spectrum of French cuisine. It consists of detailed recipes, detailed explanations of technique, and much more. It is somewhat difficult to use because most of the kitchen terminology is written in British usage. It is, however, a critical reference work to have on hand for any serious chef or teacher.

Wenzel, G., *Wenzel's Menu Maker*. Boston: Cahner's Books, 1979.
This book provides a wide range of standard American recipes. More importantly, it provides detailed data on food specifications, costs, labor-reducing techniques, etc. It is invaluable to new chefs, operations managers, and teachers.

Montagné, P., *Larousse Gastronomique*. New York: Crown Publishers Inc., 1961.
This is a genuine encyclopedia of French food, wine, cooking, and culinary history. Probably most useful for teachers, it should still be on the executive chef's reference shelf.

Saulnier, L., *Le Répertoire de la Cuisine*. Woodbury, N.Y.: Barron's Educational Series, Inc., 1976.
This book is a must for all chefs and teachers. It contains 6,000 dishes variously classified as hors d'oeuvres, soups, eggs, fish, entrées, salads, pastas, vegetables, and pastries. All recipes are "memory joggers"—one or two line recipes with no quantities and only the slimmest hint of method. It assumes that the chef is already knowledgeable. It is very useful for new ideas.

Gisslen, W., *Professional Cooking*. New York: John Wiley and Sons, 1983.
This is an excellent text for basic culinary arts students. It is useful for chefs to have on file for those times when they must train inexperienced staff.

It is useful for the advanced culinary arts teachers who find it necessary to fill the gaps in their student's basic culinary training.

Wolfe, K.C., *Cooking for the Professional Chef: A Structured Approach*. Albany, N.Y.: Delmar Publishers, Inc., 1976.
This is a useful basic culinary arts textbook. It is written for untrained personnel and new students.

D'Ermo, D., *The Chef's Dessert Cookbook*. New York: Atheneum, 1976.
This book is probably more useful to the chef than to the teacher. It covers pies, cookies, breads, European favorites, frozen desserts, puddings, frostings, fruit desserts, and low-calorie gourmet desserts. D'Ermo is the proprietor of Dominique's Restaurant in Washington, D.C. All the recipes are suitable for any "top-of-the-line" white-tablecloth operation.

Page, E.B., and Kingsford, P.W., *The Master Chefs*. New York: St. Martin's Press, 1971.
This book is an excellent, well-illustrated history of cuisine. It covers the development of cuisine from the ancient Egyptians and Greeks to Escoffier and the death of César Ritz in 1918. It not only provides chefs and students with a sense of perspective, a sense of where they are, and the historical origins of what they are doing; it also provides a glimpse into the past. It provides us with insight into a class and style of cuisine that the world will never see again.

Index